BOUNDARIES AND CATEGORIES

BOUNDARIES AND CATEGORIES

Rising Inequality in Post-Socialist Urban China

Wang Feng

STANFORD UNIVERSITY PRESS

STANFORD, CALIFORNIA

2008

Stanford University Press
Stanford, California
©2008 by the Board of Trustees of the Leland Stanford
Junior University. All rights reserved.

Printed in the United States of America on acid-free,
archival-quality paper

Typeset by Newgen in 10/14 Sabon

Library of Congress Cataloging-in-Publication Data
Wang, Feng.
Boundaries and categories : rising inequality in post-socialist
urban China / Wang Feng.
       p. cm.—(Studies in social inequality)
   Includes bibliographical references and index.
   ISBN 978-0-8047-5794-2 (cloth : alk. paper)
   1. Equality—China. 2. China—Social conditions. 3.
China—Economic conditions. 4. Socialism—China. I. Title.
   HN740.Z9S64655 2008
   305.0951—dc22
                                                    2007012400

CONTENTS

CHAPTER SIX

Varieties of Inequality   169

Tables

Figures

The time spent on researching and writing this book is almost as long as the time span covered by the book itself, about one and a half decades. The research ideas emerged in June 1989, when I was finishing a postdoctoral fellowship at the East-West Population Institute (EWPI) in Honolulu, Hawaii. My wife Yang Haiou had just completed her Ph.D. degree in sociology at the University of Hawaii. From that beautiful paradise island in the middle of the Pacific Ocean, we were half way on our return to China.

By that time, profound social and economic upheavals had already engulfed the Chinese landmass, reversing three decades of the socialist rule. People's Communes in rural China were dismantled in the early 1980s. Chinese farmers had already begun farming under the household organization, just as they had prior to the days of the collectivization. Rural nonagricultural activities were on the upsurge, and some rural Chinese had started migrating into cities. For Chinese living in the cities, price reforms in the preceding years resulted in double-digit inflation not seen by Chinese citizens for decades.

Meanwhile, loopholes created by the same reforms allowed those who had access to political power to reap substantial benefit. The emerging economic inequality was thus perceived by the population as being a result of political corruption. Popular appeals for political reform, complicated by internal power struggles within the Chinese Communist Party, led to massive demonstrations in Beijing and elsewhere during spring, and ended with a bloody crackdown, on June 4, 1989, that shocked the world. Our planned return to Beijing, on June 17, had to be postponed. In our company were many other Chinese visitors who were attending meetings and workshops at the East-West Center.

One of these visitors was a statistician from China's National Bureau of Statistics (then the State Statistical Bureau), Mr. Li Xuezhen. In the days following the Tiananmen crackdown, we talked at length about the underlying social forces that provoked such a massive movement. Rising inequality was one of the subjects. Shortly before his return to Beijing, Li Xuezhen offered to help me establish ties with his colleagues, in order to obtain household survey data to study the trends and patterns of urban income inequality. Between 1990 and 1996, I organized a number of workshops at the East-West Center, attended by staff members of China's National Bureau of Statistics and colleagues in Chinese universities. These workshops led to the establishment of computerized data files and codebooks for the data and to identifying collaborative research questions. In the summer of 1995, I undertook my first extensive field visit to Liaoning province, one of the provinces studied in this book. By the time I moved to the University of California at Irvine in 1996, the initial preparations for this study were largely complete.

In the fall of 1998, after finishing a collaborative book project on Chinese demography and society, I returned to this project in full gear. A grant from the American Council of Learned Societies allowed me to carry out more fieldwork in the summer of 1999 in Chongqing and in the following year in Sichuan and Guangdong, and a visiting professorship position in the spring of 2000 at Peking University served as an excellent opportunity for me to learn in depth from my colleagues about their research.

Two events in 1999 were critical in setting the direction of this research project and this book. The first was a field trip I took with colleague and friend Wang Tianfu, then a Ph.D. student in sociology at the University of Chicago. We set out to observe rising inequality among urban residents in different cities in Chongqing, which was formerly a part of Sichuan province. To our surprise, the most common remarks and sometimes complaints from our respondents were not about rising inequality but about persisting equality. Discussions during the field trip with Wang Tianfu, and at various times at Peking University with professors Yang Shanhua and Wang Hansheng, led me to broaden the scope of investigation from merely focusing on the trends to the patterns of inequality, which also encompasses the enduring equality.

The second event was a visit from Wang Youjuan at Peking University. Wang Youjuan was a participant of a 1995 East-West Center workshop.

By 1999, he was the Division Chief of the Urban Socio-economic Survey Organization within the National Bureau of Statistics, in charge of urban household surveys. Wang Youjuan kindly encouraged me to reestablish working ties with his organization and to continue the collaboration that was interrupted by my move to California in 1996. That collaboration allowed the extension of empirical survey data used in this study to the year 2000.

The writing of this book took place in Irvine, California; Beijing and Hong Kong, China; and Tokyo, Japan. Whereas most data analyses were carried out in Beijing and in Irvine, most writing was completed with the benefit of three visits to Keio University, Tokyo, and a sabbatical quarter as a visiting professor at Hong Kong Baptist University between December 2002 and April 2003. The first Tokyo visit, in July 2001 at Keio's Center of Excellence, helped draft several chapters. A second visit, between February and March 2002, led to the completion of the first draft. A third visit, in June and July 2006, allowed revision of the whole manuscript. For all three visits, I am deeply grateful to Keio University, and in particular, to Noriko Tsuya, who invited me for these trips. I am also grateful to Jessica Tang, who provided editorial assistance in Tokyo in 2006. Between the latter two Tokyo visits, the visit in Hong Kong was spent revising the book manuscript and completing the Appendix of the book. I would like to thank Ruan Danqing for making that visit possible.

Many colleagues read earlier drafts of the manuscript and offered extremely valuable criticisms, suggestions, and encouragements. Among them, I am especially grateful to Cai Yong, Chen Jieming, Philip Cohen, Deborah Davis, Matt Huffman, William Lavely, James Lee, Albert Park, Dorothy Solinger, Su Yang, Andrew Walder, Wang Tianfu, Martin Whyte, and Xueguang Zhou, who not only read the manuscript but also posed hard questions and provided extremely valuable suggestions and help.

Whereas it is obvious that any failures and shortcomings are entirely my own, the book would not be nearly where it is without the critical input from the colleagues listed here, especially Xueguang Zhou and Andrew Walder, whose advice and suggestions helped focus and sharpen the arguments of the book. Su Yang and Dorothy Solinger, two colleagues at UC-Irvine, provided both intellectual and spiritual support. A number of individuals who assisted in my field research include Chen Xiaojie, who went with me to Shenyang and Fushun in Liaoning province in 1995; Li

Dongshan, who accompanied me to Chengdu and to Zigong in Sichuan and helped arrange many interviews in 2000; and Ren Ping, who helped with arranging several interviews in the same year in Guangdong. Chen Shengli, a long time friend, provided crucial help in setting up visits in Sichuan and Guangdong. Qiu Lixia, Lingnam Hung, and Pearl Li provided assistance in data file construction and data cleaning. To all these colleagues and friends, I am deeply indebted.

The research related to the content of this book also benefited from the financial support of many organizations over the years: the East-West Center, University of Hawaii, American Council of Learned Societies, Peking University, Keio University, Center for the Study of Democracy and Center for Asian Studies at the University of California at Irvine, the Ford Foundation, and the Pacific Rim Research Program of the University of California.

Above all, throughout the long process of research and writing of this book, my wife Haiou and son Max have been constant sources of unconditional support and love. To them a thank you is simply not enough.

INTRODUCTION

CHAPTER ONE

From Equality to Inequality

Among all the sweeping social changes that defined the twentieth century, none compares in scope and depth with the socialist experiment that prevailed in a large number of the world's countries. On the eve of the worldwide collapse of the socialist system near the century's end, over one-third of the world's population lived under one or another version of this system (Kornai 1992; Lane 1996).[1] Beginning with the Bolshevik revolution in 1917 and ending with the collapse of the Berlin Wall in 1989 and the dissolution of the Soviet Union in 1991, the twentieth century witnessed a full circle of the rise and fall of the state socialist system.[2]

A major attraction of socialism in these countries was its promise of a greater degree of equality. In the backdrop of the pervasive inequality and poverty that accompanied the rise of capitalism and of global colonialism in the eighteenth and nineteenth centuries, the promise of greater equality appeared immensely attractive. The impact of the "socialist camp" formed by the end of World War II reached far beyond its own geographic boundaries. The Cold War not only provided a rationale for countries in the "capitalist camp" to expand a dangerous arsenal to fight communism but also kept these countries on their toes in carrying out social reforms, which may well have served to extend the longevity of capitalism itself. In the wake of the rise of capitalism, no other social system could compare with the twentieth-century socialist experiment in terms of its promise, just as few could compare with it in terms of the enormous social costs it entailed (Ashton et al. 1984; Milanovic 1998; Gerber and Hout 1998; Courtois et al. 1999).[3]

With nearly a quarter of the world's population, China was a central player in these worldwide transformations into, and then away from, socialism. During the second half of the twentieth century, China struggled through two transformations simultaneously. As China strived to move from an agrarian to an industrial society, it also carried out a socialist experiment as the basis for its economic, political, and social organizations. During this dual transition, China experienced accordingly two distinctive stages of economic and social inequality. It became, in the process of the socialist industrialization from the 1950s to the 1970s, one of the most egalitarian societies in the world. Then, in the two decades following the early 1980s, China became by some measures one of the more unequal societies in the world, with the fastest growing inequality recorded among major regions in the late twentieth century. Moreover, with its significant proportion of the world's population, what happens in China has a profound impact on any assessment of the worldwide picture of income inequality. Whether or not China is included in studies of world income inequality often changes the fundamental conclusions reached. When China is excluded, for instance, studies generally find a trend of rising world inequality in recent decades; whereas, when data are weighted by each country's population size and when China is included, studies generally reveal no clear pattern of worldwide divergence of income inequality among countries (Firebaugh 1999; Goesling 2001).[4]

In examining urban China's rising inequality during its post-socialist transformation, this book intends to serve three purposes. First, by tracing and discussing the trend of inequality—mostly income inequality—in urban China, it serves as a recent historical account of China's transformation away from socialism (see Chapters 2 and 3). Second and more important, it uses the recent Chinese experience to illustrate how economic and social inequality is created and maintained. Specifically, it focuses on the important roles of institutions and social categories, hence the title of the book, *Boundaries and Categories*. I document and argue in this book that both the equality created under socialism and the inequality that emerged after socialism have their categorical sources (Chapter 2). Rapid increase in inequality in post-reform urban China was not just an outcome of differential individual rewards but also a prominent result of rising inequality between groups (Chapter 4). Beneath the facade of an overall increased inequality level, therefore, there exists a layer of persistent equality within categories. The post-socialist urban Chinese society is thus increasingly segmented, following the boundaries of one's group membership. Rising inequality in post-socialist urban China therefore contains two contradictory scenes: increasing inequality *between* categories and a certain level of persistent equality *within* categories. The prominent roles of the inequality-generating categories have their contemporary foundations in China's evolving system of political economy and historical roots in the collectivist nature of the Chinese social and cultural tradition (Chapter 5). Finally, using the Chinese case an as example, I hope to advance the general understanding of inequality creation and maintenance by raising the question of inequality distribution, namely why the same overall level of inequality is distributed differently in different societies across individuals and social groups. I discuss the implications of inequality distribution, that between versus within categories for a society and for its members (Chapter 6). In this sense, then, rising inequality in post-socialist urban China is treated as a case study of social inequality in general.

FROM EQUALITY TO INEQUALITY

China, once considered a model of achieving equality under socialism, has become in the decades since the early 1980s one of the world's more unequal societies. The table on page 7, published by the World Bank in 1997, summarizes the Chinese experience and provides a comparison between China as a whole (with urban and rural parts combined) and other parts of the world.

In the early 1980s, around the time when China began to abandon its socialist planned economy in urban areas, China's overall inequality ranked near the bottom of the inequality distribution among major regions of the world. China, together with Eastern European socialist societies, was among the least unequal societies; its Gini index, a commonly used measure of inequality (with 1 meaning highest inequality and 0 total equality), was less than 0.3. China's inequality level was lower than developing countries in other parts of the world and also lower than an average of developed capitalist countries.

Urban income inequality was even lower, as concluded in another study by the World Bank in the early 1980s. Using 1980 data from China, that analysis reported a remarkably low level of income inequality: the poorest 40 percent of urban households had an estimated 30 percent of total urban household income, whereas the richest 20 percent received only 28 percent of total urban income. Elsewhere in Asia, the corresponding numbers were only 11 to 19 percent for the poorest 40 percent of the population, and 44 to 56 percent for the richest 20 percent. The Gini index of income inequality for urban China was only 0.16, less than half of that in other large, Asian developing countries at the time (World Bank 1983, 86).

It should be noted at the outset, however, that such a low level of income inequality also conceals the true level of economic inequality under the socialist system. As observed by numerous scholars who examined the socialist system, welfare provision under socialism (such as housing, schools, medical care, and supplies of consumption goods) disproportionately benefited officials who controlled such redistribution. Welfare allocation was thus an important feature of the redistributive economy, and income was not the most important measure of economic well-being. The low-income inequality figures, therefore, underrepresent the true extent of economic inequality in socialist societies, such as those in housing and in access to benefits (Lane 1982; Szelényi 1978; 1983, Bian 1994).

By the late 1990s, after nearly two decades of economic and social reforms, China by several authoritative estimates had reached a level of income inequality that was largely comparable to market industrialized societies. Diversification of the economy and the reform of publicly owned economic sectors led not only to rapid growth of income and living standards, but also drastically increased inequalities. The estimates by the World Bank in Table 1.1 show that China ranked third, after only Latin America/the Caribbean and Sub-Saharan Africa, in the worldwide ranking of income inequality. Also, China had ascended in the ranking of growing inequality with the *fastest* rate. Its change in the Gini index is several times that of other regions of the world. The percentage change in the Gini index for China is more than twice that of Eastern Europe and more than four times that of Sub-Saharan Africa (see Table 1.1).

China's Gini index of income inequality at the end of the twentieth century was higher than almost all transitional countries, with the exception of the Russian Federation, Georgia, and Tajikistan.[5] But unlike in the former Soviet republics, China had not experienced an absolute decline in living standard or in life expectancy, and its increase in poverty was also much below the tenfold increase in Russia between 1987 and 1996 (Gerber and Hout 1998). In urban China, the setting of this study, income inequality among all residents also increased rapidly, nearly doubling within about a

TABLE 1.1
China's ranking in income inequality in the world (Gini index)

Region or country	1980s	Ranking	1990s	Ranking	Percentage change (Gini index)
Eastern Europe	0.25	8	0.29	8	15.6
High-income countries	0.33	6	0.34	6	1.8
South Asia	0.35	5	0.32	7	−9.1
East Asia and Pacific	0.39	4	0.38	4	−1.6
Middle East and North Africa	0.41	3	0.38	5	−6.2
Sub-Saharan Africa	0.44	2	0.47	2	8.0
Latin America and the Caribbean	0.50	1	0.49	1	−1.0
China	0.29	7	0.39	3	34.5
Urban China	0.16	—	0.30	—	87.5

sources: Adapted from the World Bank 1997, 2. Urban China 1980s: The World Bank 1983, 86. Urban China 1990s (for 1994): China's National Bureau of Statistics 2000 report. Gini index for per capita income.

decade (see Table 1.1). The level of inequality for urban China, however, is lower than that of China as a whole.

Other sources have reported an even higher degree of economic inequality. A national survey conducted in 1995 by a team of American and Chinese economists, for example, revealed that the degree of income inequality in China was significantly higher than what the World Bank reported (cited in Table 1.1). By adopting an income definition that was broader than the one used by the World Bank study, that survey produced a Gini index of per capita income for China that was as high as 0.45 (Khan and Riskin 1998; Riskin, Zhao, and Li 2001).[6] This number would propel China's level of income inequality to one "higher than those for India, Pakistan and Indonesia and perhaps about the same as that for the Philippines" (Khan and Riskin 1998, 247). This higher estimate of the degree of inequality was also confirmed by other studies.[7] In fact, this level of inequality put China on par with the United States, which had a Gini index of 0.45 in 1996 (Ryscavage 1999, 71). By the 1990s, by these accounts, only in Sub-Saharan Africa and Latin American countries could one find greater inequality.

Such a drastic increase in inequality was almost unprecedented in China. Rapid increase in inequality in a society that was long prepared ideologically and structurally for equality seems to be a ready fuse for unrest, if not revolution. Large income differentials can also serve as walls separating groups and individuals, and therefore result in a China that is divided economically as well as socially. Concerns over increasing inequalities have consequently become common not only in Chinese and overseas media reports and academic discourse, but also among the Chinese public (e.g., He Q. 1998; Yang et al. 1997). Public opinion surveys in recent years show an increasing concern over inequality at both extremes of the social spectrum. "Income inequality" topped the list of the most serious social problems in a survey of 133 high-level officials attending the Central Communist Party School in 2002 (21.8 percent chose this answer among 14 choices). At the same time, survey respondents also ranked rising inequality as the area that had the least improvement in 2002 (46.6 percent ranked measures taken as "extremely ineffective" and 48.1 percent as "ineffective"; Qing 2003:126, 128). In a 2002 national survey of over 3,000 respondents conducted by the Institute of Sociology of the Chinese Academy of Social Sciences, respondents ranked corruption and disparity between the rich and the poor as the only two areas (out of 13 choices) where the situation had changed for the worse or much worse (Xu 2003, 122).

Yet, aside from the mass demonstrations in Beijing in 1989 and protests of laid-off workers in the 1990s, heightened inequality has attracted much attention but has not led to any clear signs of a revolution or social unrest in Chinese cities. This seeming acceptance of a much more unequal society can be understood only by examining the political and ideological forces at work, and more important, by examining the underlying patterns of the rising inequality, both of which are the subjects of this book.

What have emerged, as the study covered in this text shows, are two countervailing trends. On one hand, a polarization in income and wealth unknown to the Chinese for decades has emerged. Opportunities brought about by economic reforms, along with loopholes in the political and transitional economic systems, have produced an increasing number of the newly rich. Their level of wealth, and especially their rate of wealth accumulation, not only startles their fellow Chinese but also their capitalist counterparts elsewhere in the world. The same economic reforms, characterized by the state's withdrawal from providing basic employment and welfare guarantees, have also thrown millions of workers out of jobs and into the streets. A division between the rich and the poor is therefore more than evident.

On the other hand, although overall levels of inequality increased rapidly, a certain degree of equality has been maintained within various groups or categories. What has divided China is not just across-the-board inequality among all individuals but also inequalities among different groups or categories, including industries, local regions, work organizations, and ownership type. Of particular importance are the increasing roles of locales and work organizations. Sociologists in China were among the first to anticipate the emergence of such a pattern in the rising inequality (Yan et al. 1990; Li et al. 1992; Wang et al. 1992). The contradiction of increasing inequality and persisting equality has caught the attention of many Chinese scholars (one of the earliest articles to make such an observation was Yan et al. 1990; also see Li 1998 and Zhao and Li 1997). Between 1986 and 2000, the time period of the current study, the rise of intergroup inequality has surpassed that of intragroup by several methods of grouping. Such an increase in intergroup inequality accompanied an effort to distribute income and benefits somewhat equally within each economic and social group. China, in other words, is not only divided by an emerging polarization of the rich versus the poor in general, but also by a differentiation that is based on group membership of individuals. Global inequality across China and local equality within one's group, in other words, exist side by side.

EXPLAINING RISING INEQUALITY

Rising economic inequality following China's transformation away from socialism is by no means unexpected. It was in the design of the reform programs, expressed as "allowing some people to get rich first." One of the chief criticisms of the socialist redistributive economic system was its lack of material incentives and associated economic injustice. Income inequality reported as low during China's socialist era, while concealing true economic inequality due to its omission of differential welfare provision, reflected a level of inequality that was artificially compressed by the socialist egalitarian distributional policies. Socialism in this sense did not follow the socialist distributional principle of "to each according to his contribution." A market-based economy, on the contrary, implies a reward system that differentiates individuals by their attributes, thus leading to higher inequality among individuals but also a greater degree of economic justice.

Inequality is expected to be higher in a post-socialist economy, because in a market system that lives on efficiency and profitability, regional differences in resources inevitably result in higher regional disparity once governmental invention is decreased. Indeed, China's reforms targeted different regions with different policies, beginning with the establishment of Special

Economic Zones. Such differential policies exacerbated previously existing regional differences in standards of living and in income and consequently resulted in a greater degree of overall inequality. Rising inequality, in other words, has been explained and understood mostly as an economic outcome of the post-socialist market-oriented reforms.

Economic Change and Inequality

Economic interpretations of rising inequality are further articulated at both the macro and the micro levels. At the macro or the societal level, there is a widely held belief, almost a doctrine, that economic growth at least in its initial stage inevitably results in an increased level of income inequality. The articulation of the relationship between economic growth and inequality follows the highly influential Kuznets' inverted-U-curve hypothesis, which predicts an initial rise and then a fall in income inequality following economic growth (Kuznets 1955; Lindert and Williamson 1985; Lindert 1991). China's recent spectacular economic growth has involved all three factors that are believed to serve as underlying forces shaping the inverted-U pattern: labor force growth, skills deepening in the labor force, and sectoral technological imbalance. A second macro level economic interpretation, more closely related to the arguments in this book, is that rising inequality simply reflects uneven regional economic development, which is an inevitable component of economic growth. In the Chinese case, it is also in part an outcome of deliberate state policies.

Commonly seen economic interpretations of rising income inequality also focus on the micro or individual level factors, especially on individual earning capabilities and rewards. Under the socialist planned economic system, economic efficiency was sacrificed for the political purpose of maintaining equality. Individuals under such a system actually suffered economic injustice precisely because of the lack of differential rewards. China's move to a market economy was intended to change the unjust distribution system that characterized the socialist days, by rewarding individuals according to their abilities and contributions to the market economy. As individuals are rewarded differently, inequality rises. Increased income inequality is therefore not only natural but also a positive outcome of market development, because it increases efficiency.

Most studies of rising inequality in recent China have followed these and other standard economic interpretations. These studies have produced ample empirical evidence to support some of the economic arguments, depicting rising regional disparities on the one hand and the increasing importance of human capital in income determination on the other (e.g., Knight and Song 1991; Griffin and Zhao 1993; Zhao, Li, and Riskin 1999; Li et al. 2000; Khan and Riskin 2001). These and other studies have laid out a rich empirical background for studying inequality in China. The economic interpretations of rising inequality used in these studies will be considered and examined together with the social process of inequality creation, which is the focus of this study.

Inequality as a Social Process

What this study intends to show and to emphasize is that China's rising inequality is also fundamentally a social process, by which individuals are socially restratified. Rising inequality is seen as a social process that involves proactive human agencies. At the micro or individual level, such agencies are individuals possessing different traits and abilities, all seeking to advance their personal interests. At the macro or the societal and structural level, the inequality level changes because, regardless of individual preferences and actions, it is the newly formed social and economic structure that allows some individuals to achieve their goals while denying the wishes of others. The agencies at this level are the various social groups or categories that create and maintain inequalities and that make certain individuals enjoy higher incomes than others regardless of their individual traits.

Results of this study show that even when the individual-level characteristics are taken into account, categorical differences in income persist. Moreover, these categorical differences are not simply functions of their economic attributes, such as firm profitability or regional level of economic development. Instead, they are outcomes of differential positions of social categories that originate from China's post-socialist political economy and from a deep-rooted social and cultural tendency that privileges group membership and within-group egalitarianism. Such a sociological approach to inequality, in other words, does not dismiss or dispute the important roles of economic factors in shaping inequalities. Rather, it brings in the proactive roles of human agencies, social structures, and cultural and cognitive orientations. It reveals the social process of inequality creation and maintenance.

For nearly two decades since the start of China's reforms and the onset of rising inequality, sociological explanations for an emerging social stratification order have been framed largely under a paradigm known as the "market transition theory." Initial formulations of this theory predicted a shift of economic power and returns from state bureaucrats, who were power holders under the planned or redistributive economic system, to entrepreneurs and individuals directly participating in economic activities in the market economy (Nee 1989).

Such a formulation stimulated much debate and often served as a reference for subsequent studies. At the same time, it also contributed to a research tradition that largely dominated sociological studies of restratification orders in transitional economies. Empirically based research on income inequality in China and other formerly socialist countries focused largely on changing economic returns to individual attributes. Research within this body of literature revolves around the questions of which *individual* characteristics get rewarded more during the transition period than under the socialist redistributive regime and focuses on the identities of the winners and losers in the process of social reconfiguration and restratification (Nee 1989, 1991, 1996; Bian and Logan 1996; Róna-Tas 1994; Gerber and Hout 1998; Xie and Hannum 1996; Cao and Nee 2000; Zhou 2000; Wu 2002).

More often than not, the arbitration comes down to the comparison of regression coefficients for two variables included in analyses: party membership (labeled as political capital) and educational attainment (labeled as human capital). Without specifying the institutional contexts and processes, however, such individual-level analytical results are incapable of directly revealing the institutional changes in these societies, as has been noted by more than a few (e.g., Parish and Michelson 1996; Walder 1996; Heyns 2005).[8] Moreover, such studies are unable to explain directly and satisfactorily the overall sharp increases in income inequality in societies such as China or to account for the sources of the increased inequality.

Not all studies of post-reform Chinese society followed the market transition paradigm of analyzing only individual-level data. Throughout much of the 1990s, two other important lines of research focused more directly on the *institutional changes* that defined the emerging new political economy. One line of research centered on property rights arrangement and reform (Nee 1992; Walder 1992a; Nee and Su 1996; Oi and Walder 1999). The other focused on the changing behaviors of local governments

(Oi 1992, 1995; Lin 1995; Walder 1994, 1995). In addition, the role of work organizations in urban China has also received prominent attention and explicit modeling in empirical studies of inequality (Wu 2002). By and large, however, these two different investigative traditions, one focusing on individualistic attributes of income determination and the other on institutional changes, have not been integrated into studies to explain changes in inequality. With a few exceptions (Xie and Hannum 1996; Wang 1998; Wu 2002; Wang and Wang 2007), institutional factors are not used as explicit inequality-driving forces, but as individual attributes in the form of their institutional affiliations.

This study brings these two lines of research together, using institutional changes at the societal level to explain changing patterns of inequality among individuals. The Chinese experiences documented and analyzed in this book show that it is not just the individual characteristics that have resulted in the drastically increased inequality; at least equally important is the fact that rising inequality is a process driven by groups or categories that have been realigned or created in China's post-socialist transformations. These group membership characteristics, or categories, include a broad range of levels and dimensions, including ownership type, industrial sector, geographic location, and the work organization. They also include other social categories not confined within geographic or physical boundaries, such as gender, seniority, and occupation.

BOUNDARIES AND CATEGORIES:
SOURCES OF INEQUALITY

The study of social inequality, including its prevalence, structures, and consequences, is at the very core of the work of sociologists (Grusky 2001). Influenced by the egalitarian ideologies that accompanied the rise of capitalism, and especially under the heavy shadows of Karl Marx and Max Weber, generations of scholars have placed the study of social inequality as their primary mission. One can characterize the difference between two disciplines in the social sciences, economics and sociology, in such a way: while economists devote most of their efforts toward determining the best way to make the biggest pie within given resource constraints, sociologists spend their lifetimes trying to understand how and why the pie is divided in a particular way.[9] Not all those who study social inequality, however, share the same perspective. Consequently, approaches to understanding social inequality oscillate between those that privilege the individual and those that focus on the society.

From Individual to Structure

Scholarly work on social stratification and social inequality to date has almost without exception used Western industrialized or non-Western industrializing societies as the referential social settings, with the belief that industrialization fundamentally redefined the institutional basis of social organization (Lipset and Benedix 1959). In contrast to the earlier Marxist approach that attributed inequalities to structural, especially economic, forces embedded in the capitalist mode of production, much contemporary empirical research on stratification and inequality uses the individual as the unit of analysis. Such an individualistic preference is congruent with the ideological underpinnings of Western capitalist societies and facilitated by technical advances in social sciences research methods in the past half century. Ideologically, a more open society and increased social and economic mobility in the West have reinforced the belief that individuals are more capable of changing their fate than ever before and that they are free from the various group boundaries that defined patterns of inequality in the pre-industrial era.[10] Methodologically, collecting individual-level data via sample surveys and application of multivariate statistical methods have also made the individualistic approach both convenient and attractive. With Western industrial societies oriented toward the individual as the general social setting, an approach focusing on individual attributes and outcomes was almost the default model in examining economic and social inequalities and in understanding human behavior in general. The elegant formulation of human capital theory made it the standard reference in both economics and sociology (e.g., Blau and Duncan 1967; Featherman and Hauser 1978). At the same time, the status achievement model based on individual and parental traits was emulated by generations of sociologists (e.g., Sewell and Hauser 1975).

Such an individualistic approach to examining social inequality, however, has also been challenged as inadequate and narrow-minded. In the early 1980s, a structuralistic approach to stratification research emerged when scholars revived their interests in the structure of positional inequality, or "empty places," in the economy—that is, places "both more important and logically prior to individual attainment" (Baron and Bielby 1980, 737). Pioneers in this research tradition suggested the following list of structural aspects for studying inequality: class, authority, organization size, and labor market sector. In studying different levels of social organization and corresponding units of analysis, the list might include societal/economy, institutional/sector (market, industry), organization/firm, role/job, and individual/worker (Baron and Bielby 1980, 743). Prominently, they added the firm to this list, for its role in linking "the 'macro' and 'micro' dimensions of work organization and inequality" (738).

Increasingly, sociologists, following colleagues in institutional economic analysis, have shown that the roles of individual traits in social mobility are not uniform across different sectors of the society (e.g., Diprete et al. 1997; Treiman and Ganzeboom 2000). Rather, the roles of individual characteristics are dependent upon which economic sector an individual is located in. A modern market economy, far from being the ideal free market, is now generally accepted as segmented. It is differentiated into core and periphery, primary and secondary, or formal and informal sectors. Some see this division as an inevitable stage of market capitalism, as it moves from entrepreneurial to corporate capitalism (Gordon, Edwards, and Reich 1982). Others attribute the existence of such divisions to a firm's ability and willingness to compensate its workers, which in turn are often based on profit margins, the workers' power to demand higher pay, or both.

These new approaches, especially the segmentation approach, have already enlightened the work on social inequality in socialist societies. In the case of urban China, Yanjie Bian's study represents a systematic and focused examination of the impact of ownership types and work organizations on the social stratification of urban workers in socialist China. Driven by system-oriented goals and strategies, Bian argues, the socialist planned economy systematically rewarded certain sectors and work organizations more than others. These goals were determined according to the ideological interests of the Communist Party, the national interests of the state planners, and the control interests of the government administration. According to Bian, "workplace segmentation in socialist planned economies is an institutional expression of government interests" (Bian 1994, 207). In contrast to a market economy where resource allocation is driven by profit margins, in a socialist planned economy, where "allocation of labor and incentives is associated primarily with workplaces and secondarily with occupations, work-unit status is a more important status criterion for social mobility than is one's occupation" (Bian 1994, 210). Such a reward system in turn resulted in a segmented socialist planned economy. As Bian concludes, "the organizational structures created and maintained by the socialist government are a generic source of political, economic, and residential inequalities" (1994, 211).

Categories as Explicit Units of Stratification

In contrast to earlier attempts at modifying the unsatisfactory individualistic approach by bringing the structural factors back in, there has been a recent call for a return to recognition of social categories as explicit units of social stratification. This call has emerged similarly as a response to the individualistic approach that still heavily influences research on social inequality. The most succinct summary of criticism for the individualistic approach comes from Charles Tilly:

> . . . individualistic analyses of inequality have all the attractions of neoclassical economics: nicely simplified geometric analogies, reassuring references to individual decision-making, insistence on efficiency, avoidance of inconvenient complications such as beliefs, passions, culture, and history. They lend themselves nicely to retroactive rationalization; confronted with unequal outcomes, their user searches the past for individual differences in skill, knowledge, determination, or moral worth that must explain differences in rewards. These analyses fail, however, to the extent that essential causal business takes place not inside individual heads but within the social relations among persons and sets of persons. (1998, 33)

In his 1998 book, *Durable Inequality*, Tilly offers a systematic construction of a macro-social structural approach to revisiting inequality. Tilly's work maps out the agents and the mechanisms of social inequality. The agents in his framework are social categories or groups, not individuals. Durable inequalities that persist over lifetimes and organizational histories and carry over from one social interaction to another, according to Tilly, are outcomes of collective efforts by group members aimed at maintaining or enhancing advantages these members possess, not outcomes of personal attributes, propensities, or performances (1998, 7).

What are categories? While Tilly does not in his book provide a formal definition and classification for the term *category*, his description of the term *organization* serves the same purpose: an organization in the broad sense "encompasses all sorts of well-bounded clusters of social relations in which occupants of at least one position have the right to commit collective resources to activities reaching across the boundary." The examples he uses include "corporate kin groups, households, religious sects, bands of mercenaries, and many local communities" (1998, 9–10). Social categories, in other words, are formed by individuals who are related to each other by a certain type of social relation and who have a similar claim to common collective resources. Social categories are social groups with "unequal access to and unequal distribution of resources and social opportunities" (Lamont and Molnár 2002).

For social categories to exist and to function, boundaries need to be drawn to define membership and to separate insiders and outsiders. Boundary-drawing is a routine exercise in our daily life. To facilitate the boundary-drawing process, members of the society often resort to or employ existing markers. Such markers can be either geographic, such as a common residence area, workplace, or country of origin; or biological, such as kinship, gender, skin color, or age. Boundaries as such are simply products of social construction, as noted by the sociologist Harrison C. White: "Boundaries in social action are not given facts and they are not manipulatable. Boundaries are, instead, subtle and complex products of action" (White 1992, 127). It is through the process of social construction that these and other markers are used to serve a social function of collective identity and of closure and exclusion (Parkin 1979).

Boundaries exist because social categories are not only social constructs themselves but also constructs that must be perceived by the human mind in order to be meaningful. As pointed out by social psychologists who have studied categories in social cognition, "the term *category* is commonly used to describe the totality of information that perceivers have in mind about particular classes of individuals (e.g., Germans, plumbers, pastry chefs), and this knowledge can take many forms (e.g., visual, declarative, procedural)" (Macrae and Bodenhausen 2000, 96). Boundaries, in other words, are also symbolic, with their origins derived not only from material but also cognitive and communicative dimensions (Lamont and Fournier 1992).

Socially constructed and cognitively resident, boundaries exist in two forms. Certain boundaries form and exist to coincide with easily identifiable physical boundaries where members of a social category share a common physical space, such as households, local communities, and workplaces.

There are also boundaries that transcend local physical space and permeate to the larger society. Members in such social categories share a characteristic that allows them to have access to resources and opportunities without being confined to a common, local physical space. Examples of the latter include gender, ethnicity, citizenship, religion, geographical origin of ancestors, occupation, education, and age.

Opportunity Hoarding and Rent Seeking: Mechanisms of Inequality

How do social categories, or "empty places," engender and sustain inequalities? There are two broad types of mechanisms that generate inequalities in society: one based on coercive power, or physical or political forces, in the forms of open extraction and oppression, and the other relying on the use of one's advantageous position in society to reap benefits, or "rents," without necessarily resorting to explicit oppression or exploitation. Tilly (1998) classifies these two causal mechanisms of inequality as exploitation and opportunity hoarding. Some examples of the former are forced labor under different social systems or class relations, such as that of an unfair employer/employee relationship under capitalism. Examples of the latter include relations among ethnic groups, between citizens and immigrants, as well as those among different locales and work organizations in this study.

Rising inequality in post-socialist China results clearly in part from exploitation of all forms. When urban factory workers were forced to leave their jobs with little or no compensation, so their factories could be sold inexpensively to foreign capitalist investors, it was clearly exploitation by the joint hands of the state and capitalists, not opportunity hoarding. Similarly, when farmers were evicted from or forced to give up their property with little compensation so their land could be used for development to benefit developers and local government officials, and when rural migrant workers were subject to low wages and harsh working conditions in cities, the inequality created clearly involves exploitation, not just opportunity hoarding. The mechanisms this study focuses on, however, are not the different forms of exploitation that have emerged in post-socialist urban China, but opportunity hoarding, which I believe accounts for a significant share of the rising inequality.

Opportunity hoarding is an organized effort by which members of a group or network utilize their shared advantageous positions, monopolist or otherwise, to benefit economically or socially. According to Tilly: "If members of a network acquire access to a resource that is valuable, renewable, subject to monopoly, supportive of network activities, and enhanced by the network's modus operandi, network members regularly hoard access to the resource, creating beliefs and practices that sustain their control" (1998, 91). An example given by Tilly is the inequality among different ethnic groups: "Opportunity hoarding often rests on ethnic categories, members of which reinforce their control over hoarded resources by means of their power to include or exclude other members with respect to language, kinship, courtship, marriage, housing, sociability, religion, ceremonial life, credit, and political patronage" (1998, 154). In this sense, opportunity hoarding is not different from what is known as rent seeking, by which incumbents of social groups or positions reap benefits based on their membership.

In order to hoard opportunities, groups or categories need to be formed and their membership delineated. Boundaries, in other words, need to be drawn and protected. These boundaries, while clear, are by no means rigid, as pointed out by Tilly: "None of these mechanisms requires categories with closed perimeters, equally well-defined from every angle of approach. All they entail is a boundary separating two zones of unequal reward and their occupants, plus stable definitions of ties across the boundary" (1998, 99). Once formed, these categories become important players or agents in producing and reproducing what Tilly labels as "durable inequalities" (1998, 154).

In addition to the two main inequality-generating mechanisms described, inequalities are also created and maintained by two other mechanisms: emulation and adaptation. In emulation, inequalities arise when social relations and models of inequality are copied or transplanted from one setting to the other. Moreover, inequalities spread and persist because we allow ourselves to adapt our daily routines according to categorically unequal structures. To use Tilly's words: "Exploitation and opportunity hoarding favor the installation of categorical inequality, while emulation and adaptation generalize its influence" (1998, 10).

The idea of opportunity hoarding relates closely with another concept used in both economics and sociology. This is the concept of rent. Aage Sørensen, a sociologist who has introduced the economic concept of rent and related rent-seeking behavior into sociology, explained how such a concept can be used in understanding social inequality. According to Sørensen, property rights and associated rent-seeking behavior are the very sources of social inequality: "Rent is any advantage or surplus created by nature or social structure over a certain period of time . . . Because rents can be obtained without active participation by individuals in production, they allow for the transparent separation of benefit and use rights and therefore create distribution processes that are independent of the efforts and abilities of individuals and tied to aspects of social structure" (Sørensen 1996, 1344–45). Rent can be created by nature—for example, land of varying fertility—or by monopoly. Rent can be based on a single resource or a combination of resources (composite rents). Rent and rent-generating behaviors have far-reaching implications for the understanding of social inequality: "Rent-generating resources have properties that mean the benefit of rent can be obtained without any effort or sacrifice by the recipients. These resources or assets therefore have the property that they can become organized in social structure in such a manner that they provide advantages for incumbents of social positions that are independent of the characteristics of the incumbents. Inequalities created by rents may become inequalities created by social structure" (Sørensen 1996, 1361).

Opportunity hoarding and rent seeking are indeed among the most important inequality-generating mechanisms in post-socialist urban China. These are also mechanisms that rely on categories, not individuals, to operate. This study shows that much of what we observe in China during the time under examination fits quite well under the scheme of opportunity hoarding or rent seeking. Chinese localities and work units were created and then evolved into organizations of opportunity hoarding. Opportunity hoarding was no stranger to Chinese work organizations. Enterprise hoarding was a defining characteristic endemic under the socialist economic system and the major culprit responsible for the system's label of shortage economy (Kornai 1980). Just as the Italian-Americans in Mamaroneck, New York, illustrated by Tilly, who formed a bounded network based on common origin (a rural Italian village), Chinese urban workers formed their networks by common employment history and a shared public means of production. Similar to the Italian-Americans who relied on their group to gain access to resources, including a set of employers, clients, and jobs in shopkeeping and landscape gardening, these Chinese economic organizations engaged in a full range of economic activities, from production to distribution.

Reforms of the socialist planned economy, by allowing the birth of non-public economic sectors and by giving publicly owned institutions more rights, have magnified the salient legacy of the socialist segmented property ownership. The de facto "minor public," or the workplace endowed with ownership of the means of production, has gained a new and more vibrant life. Instead of breaking up the segmented economy under socialism, post-socialist reforms have contributed to further segmentation. Relying on their resource endowments and market positions, work organizations have become more important categories in generating income.

New group-based inequalities have been created as government policies granted more freedom to certain areas and sectors than to others. Decentralization policies have also encouraged local areas to set up their own protections. Within such a context, the Chinese cultural tradition of group membership identification and limited egalitarianism within groups has further facilitated a trend of between-group inequality, coupled with within-group equality. Group membership, either geographic or occupational, has joined a person's other traits at birth, such as ethnicity, gender, race, parental wealth, or nationality, as a new and more important ascriptive criterion determining welfare and standing in the society.

STUDY SETTING, DATA SOURCES, AND ORGANIZATION

To understand rising inequality in post-socialist China from an institutional or categorical perspective, I focus on the experiences of urban Chinese and utilize both household survey data and information collected by personal interviews. In the following, I briefly outline the scope of this study in terms of its setting, data sources, and overall organization.

Urban China: The Study Setting

Urban China is the setting of the current study. Confining the study to only the urban sector of China has a strong substantive rationale. During China's socialist experiment, two separate economic systems were created within the same country: an urban sector where a socialist planned economy was genuinely pursued and practiced, and a rural sector where the majority of the Chinese population resided and where a collective responsibility system prevailed (see Chapter 2 for a more detailed discussion of this differentiation). Whereas urban residents' incomes are mostly in the forms of wages and salaries, the rural population derived their incomes mostly from selling their agricultural products. Given the dichotomized nature of Chinese society, urban and rural parts of China need to be treated separately. The urban population covered in this study, moreover, includes only residents who had permanent non-agricultural household registration status in Chinese cities. The study population, therefore, does not include rural-to-urban migrants, who since the mid-1980s have represented an increasingly large proportion of all residents in urban China. Exclusion of this segment of the urban population has implications for interpreting the results of this study (see Appendix for discussion on such implications).

Detailed analytical results of quantitative data are mostly for urban populations in three provinces: Liaoning in northeast, Sichuan in southwest, and Guangdong in south China. These three provinces were chosen partly due to data availability and partly due to the different characteristics they possess. While these three provinces cannot be said to represent all of urban China, they are nevertheless appropriate cases representing different parts of China that have undergone different kinds of changes in the wake of economic reforms. Guangdong province was the first province to enjoy a policy relaxation from the central government, granting them more freedom to carry out economic reforms from the early 1980s.[11] It therefore had, until the mid-1990s, the fastest pace of economic change and the most rapid increase in income.

Liaoning province, having served as an important industrial base under the socialist planned economy, has suffered the most from this legacy. Its heavy concentration of large state-owned enterprises has made the economic transition much harder. Sichuan, the largest Chinese province until the mid-1990s, is located economically somewhere in between the other two provinces.[12] It contains a mixture of different economic components and has had a rise in income inequality similar to that of Liaoning but without the heavy industrial legacy that characterizes Liaoning. Focusing on three contrasting provinces allows the examination of the impact of differential economic reforms processes on trajectories and patterns of inequality.

Main Data Sources

This study draws upon two types of data: household and individual-level income and expenditure data collected by the Urban Social and Economic Survey Organization of China's National Bureau of Statistics and data from field interviews that I conducted between 1995 and 2000. The survey data, covering three provinces, about 30 cities of various sizes, and over 2,000 households annually over a 15-year period (totaling approximately 35,000 household and 120,000 individual records), provide the basic data sources for constructing indices of the trends in inequality in Chapter 3, as well as for conducting statistical analyses of income-determining patterns in urban China in Chapter 4. Household income survey data, while the only available longitudinal data source for such a study, are subject to a number of deficiencies common to household income surveys. Chief among them are sample coverage, definition of income, and income reporting. The limitations of the survey data, which bear implications for the results as well as the interpretations, are discussed in the Appendix.

Field interviews and other survey data supply important sources of information in addition to the household surveys. These additional data, mostly analyzed and reported in Chapter 5, provide information on income distribution within various types of urban work organizations, a major group of interest in this study. They also supply information on how individual urban residents have experienced changes in employment and in income and how they perceive the level and pattern of inequality. Combined with the quantitative data from the surveys, these interview materials provide fresh and in-depth knowledge for an understanding of China's changing pattern of inequality.

Organization

The main thrust of the book lies in its documentation, examination, and interpretation of the structural sources of the rising inequality in urban China. Given the primacy of categories in defining inequality, and given that the current pattern of inequality cannot be divorced from the political economy foundations prior to China's recent reforms, in Chapter 2 I highlight the importance of using categories as explicit analytical units in studying inequality and introduce the important categories for the urban Chinese case. Categorical inequality was an inseparable feature of the socialist system that strove to create equality. Therefore, Chapter 2 also reviews the structural basis that defined the pattern of inequality during the later years of China's socialism and discusses briefly how such inequality-generating categories have changed over the course of China's reforms.

Chapters 3 through 5 focus on post-reform changes. Chapter 3 examines changes in the urban Chinese household, documents the process of rising income and standards of living, and provides a summary of rising inequality between 1986 and 2000. Chapters 4 and 5 are devoted to examination of group-based inequalities among cities, sectors, industries, and work organizations. Specifically, Chapter 4 shows the significant roles of categories in producing and reproducing inequality and reports how such categorical inequalities persist after taking into consideration factors of economic change and individual characteristics of income determination. In Chapter 5, I trace changes in the Chinese political economy in the context of income inequality and explain how boundaries are maintained to form and to reinforce categories.

The last chapter, Chapter 6, places the Chinese case under a comparative lens. The Chinese experiences examined in this volume are discussed in a historically comparative perspective, in reference to the debate over development versus inequality, and in the context of other transitional societies. By comparing the Chinese pattern of income inequality with two other societies, Japan and the United States, I raise the issue of distributions of inequality and suggest how the findings in this book may have implications for studying transitional socialism and for comparative studies of social inequality. Through a comparative perspective, I come to the conclusion that while inequalities in different societies all share the basic feature of being categorically structured, diverse political economies, histories, and cultures result in different categories. A society's political economy, history, and culture also shape different patterns of inequality distribution, in terms of between and within categories.

CHAPTER TWO

Categorical Sources of Inequality

Of all the categories that define and maintain inequality, what are the most salient in post-socialist China? How did these categories emerge and how have they evolved? How are the boundaries drawn and protected? Among the categories that exist in China, four figure prominently in shaping inequality in both socialist and post-socialist urban China: ownership type, industry, locale, and work organization. Three of the four, industry, location, and work organization, are categories that exist in every society and that play to a varying degree a role in affecting inequality in almost all societies. The same categories that also exist elsewhere, however, do not necessarily have the same meaning as they do in the case of China. For China, these categories emerged largely as a product of China's planned economy. They served as the basis of economic organization, social control, and benefits distribution under socialism and, yet, have evolved into more permanent sources of economic inequality in post-socialist China. Understanding the origin and evolution of these categories is crucial for examining the underlying pattern of rising inequality in post-socialist urban China.

During no other period in its history did China pursue equality more rigorously than in the three decades between 1950 and 1980. With a socialist experiment, China transformed itself into one of the most egalitarian societies in the world in no more than a decade's time. The internal logic of the very same social system, however, also dictated the creation of new social categories as the basis of economic and social organization. If pre-socialist China can be characterized as a society stratified along clearly defined vertical hierarchical orders, the post-revolution society was differentiated by not only vertical but also horizontal social categories of unequal positions. China's post-socialist social transformation was similarly accompanied by realignment and repositioning of these categories.

SOCIALISM AND THE CREATION OF CATEGORIES

For more than two decades, until the death of Mao Zedong in 1976, China pursued a socialist developmental strategy of industrialization. Reacting to China's humiliating encounters with the West during the century prior to 1949, the new government under Mao's leadership set industrialization and a strong national economy as its top economic goals. A strong and independent national economy was deemed essential not only for sustaining China's newly gained independence but also for supplying empirical proof of the superiority of the socialist economic system and lending the political leadership its legitimacy. Industrialization was at once both a nationalistic and a socialist mandate.

This socialist approach to industrialization contained two basic elements. First, economically, socialist industrialization took place under public ownership of the means of production and was organized by a centralized planning system. Centralized economic planning and resource allocation were the shortcuts to rapid industrialization, an approach often adopted both in socialist economies and in capitalist market economies during wartime. Second, politically, socialist industrialization differentiated itself from industrialization under capitalism by adopting an egalitarian distribution of income and other benefits. This egalitarian orientation was congruent with the deeply rooted sentiment of equality within Chinese cultural tradition; it was also in accordance with the Marxist ideology that inspired and legitimized the Chinese socialist revolution. The sentiment of egalitarianism was especially intense in the wake of the socialist revolution. Decades of incessant international and domestic wars and associated rampant corruption, severe poverty, and massive inequality all prepared a population for a new form of economic and social organization.

In contrast to a market economy society where income and wealth redistribution relies heavily on taxation, the pursuit of equality in socialist planned economies does not start at distribution, but rather with employment and production. The government dictates what to produce and how much to produce and also directly creates jobs and allocates people to these jobs.

TABLE 2.1
Changes in types of employment, urban China, 1952–2000

	PERCENTAGE OF EMPLOYEES IN EACH OWNERSHIP TYPE		
Year	State-owned	Collective	Private/other
1952	63.56	0.93	35.51
1957	76.46	20.28	3.26
1962	72.93	22.31	4.76
1970	75.92	22.56	1.52
1980	76.19	23.04	0.77
1986	70.21	25.74	4.05
1987	70.04	25.31	4.65
1988	69.98	24.72	5.3
1989	70.24	24.34	5.42
1990	70.24	24.09	5.67
1991	69.85	23.76	6.39
1992	69.97	23.17	6.86
1993	68.40	21.25	10.35
1994	66.69	19.54	13.77
1995	64.92	18.14	16.94
1996	64.10	17.19	18.17
1997	62.44	16.30	21.26
1998	56.90	12.33	30.77
1999	55.03	10.99	33.98
2000	54.06	10.00	35.94

SOURCES: Up to 1995, calculated from NBS 1997, 96–97; for 1996–2000, calculated from NBS 2002, 121–122.

NOTE: Employment numbers by ownership type in the sources do not add up to the totals given in the sources after 1989. The totals on which the composition is calculated in this table are the sums of the separate categories, not the totals given in the sources.

The most effective means that allowed the pursuit of equality was no doubt the organization of individuals into groups under government control. Under socialism, the Chinese population was more collectivized than it had ever been before. In rural China, the form used was the commune system, which not only spread the economic risks but also equalized gains. In urban China, starting from the early 1950s until the mid-1980s, the planned economy gradually incorporated almost all laborers into the state-controlled employment system. The process of incorporation of individual workers into state-controlled work organizations can be seen from the numbers in Table 2.1, which reveal a rapid process of eliminating self-employment in the early 1950s. By 1957, at the end of China's first Five-Year Plan, an overwhelming majority of urban workers were employed in state or collectively owned enterprises or institutions. In 1980, less than 1 percent of urban employees worked outside of state- and collective-owned organizations.

It was not until the mid-1980s that non-public employment returned to the level of the 1950s, with about 5 percent of urban laborers working outside the state or the collective sectors. Such a trend continued along with Chinese reforms in the last two decades. By 1995, one out of every six urban laborers was employed by non-state and non-collective sectors, and by 2000, over a third of urban laborers worked outside of the state or the collective sectors.

The government's control over employment and production bestowed upon it the ability to stipulate wage and benefit provisions. Wage policies under socialism contained a strong egalitarian component. Although the state wage scales contained many types and steps, wage differences between top administrators, senior technical personnel, and ordinary workers were remarkably small (Korzec and Whyte 1981; Riskin 1987, Chapter 10).

The inner logic of that very same centrally planned economic system, however, also required the creation of new social and economic categories. In addition to categories such as gender and political affiliation, new categories based on employment were needed to implement the socialist developmental goals. Employment replaced kinship as the basis, and the state replaced the family as the agency in the process of creating new categories. The new groups thus created served as the basis for organizing economic production and political mobilization and as the basis of distributing economic and social welfare as well (Walder 1986; 1992; Bian 1994).

The centrally planned economic system relied on the creation of new categories for its existence. First, economic activities under the planned economy system needed to be organized by economic sectors, such as the production of food, steel, coal, machinery, textiles, and so forth. In contrast to industrial sectors in market economies, the sectors formed under the socialist planned system were organized bureaucratically to facilitate planning and control. Mirroring the Soviet planned economy system, each industrial sector in China had its corresponding ministry during the planned economy days. These sectors were also further politically arranged into systems.[1] Second, workers were organized into units with suitable sizes for carrying out productive activities. This led to the creation of the new work organizations, or *danwei*, in urban China. Third, given the size of the Chinese economy, individual work organizations could not be directly supervised by the central state power. Economic power and responsibilities were therefore shared between the central government and various lower-level governments. Work organizations were accordingly classified into different ranks: some were under the direct jurisdiction of a central government ministry, while others were under provincial or municipal governments. Fourth, with China's history of nationalization, of industrial production, and of state investment, work organizations were also differentiated by ownership type, mostly between state-owned and collective-owned.

Not all categories enjoyed an equal status. Though achieving equality was no doubt a fundamental goal of the socialist experiment in China, it was not the only goal. Achieving equality also had to be coordinated with rapid industrialization. In order to achieve the goal of rapid industrialization, equality had to be compromised. Inequality across categories was tolerated because some categories were deemed more important than others to the state economy. Those sectors or work organizations considered more essential to the goal of industrialization received more state investment. Employees in the favored sectors or work organizations also worked in better environments and lived in better apartments. To the extent that equality needed to be maintained, it was best and most easily maintained within the boundaries of each category.

EVOLVING CATEGORIES FROM SOCIALISM
TO POST-SOCIALISM

Urban versus Rural China

Though the study setting of this book is urban China, it is nevertheless instructive to bear in mind the two most important social and economic categories created under socialism in China: urban and rural sectors. The separation between urban and rural China is one of the most glaring legacies of Chinese socialism. In the process of China's industrialization under socialism, the urban sector was privileged over the rural sector, though the latter accounted for up to 80 percent of China's population. Not only did China's industrialization rely heavily on an extraction of resources from the countryside and an exploitation of peasants, but in addition, urban Chinese who were more centrally involved in industrial development received much better rewards.[2] In order to accumulate capital quickly for China's industrialization, the government arbitrarily set low prices for agricultural products and high prices for industrial goods. Such a biased policy provided a basis for cheap raw materials and low costs for the urban laborer and for a high profit rate for industrial goods. When the government realized that it could not provide the same benefits to the whole population, it enacted strict regulations to prevent migration from rural to urban areas. China's socialist industrialization, contrary to its goals of equality, effectively created two societies and resulted in two different systems within the same country.[3]

Urban and rural China differed in several fundamental ways: ownership structure, working conditions, income and benefits, and ultimately, life chances. Unlike the state-controlled urban economy where government ownership of the means of production provided the basis for national economic planning, the rural economy was based on a localized, de facto collective ownership. The basic decision-making and accounting body was at the local level, either a cluster of households within a village, or a village. Whereas urban employees received guaranteed wages and benefits, such as housing, pension, and medical care, the rural population depended on annually fluctuating harvests for their living. Whereas the state-appointed leaders for urban enterprises and government organizations, leaders of the basic production units in rural China were elected or selected through negotiation between local peasants and the government.

As a result of segregation between urban and rural China, the income gap between these two categories widened substantially under socialism. The estimated urban-rural income gap ranged between a factor of 2.1 to 6.1 by the late 1970s (Riskin 1987). A large-scale survey conducted in 1988 revealed a gap of 2.4 to 1 in that year (Griffith and Zhao 1993). Moreover, such an income gap did not take into consideration the massive benefits received by urban residents. Even the 2.4 to 1 income gap did not place China favorably in an international comparison with other developing countries. In Indonesia, for instance, the gap was 1.66 to 1 in 1987, and in Bangladesh—the highest gap observed in the 1980s—it was only 1.85 to 1, both significantly lower than China. It was this large urban-rural gap that made China one of the most unequal societies in terms of urban and rural equality, even as China's overall Gini index remained low by international standards (Riskin 1987; Griffith and Zhao 1993).

The income gap captures only part of the broad inequality between urban and rural China. Urban and rural Chinese were segregated by at least 14 kinds of institutional arrangements (Guo and Liu 1990; Knight and Song 1999; Wang 2005). Fundamentally, the Chinese population was differentiated by their household registration status, as non-agricultural and agricultural. On the basis of that differentiation, urban and rural Chinese were separated in terms of grain supply, supply of non-staple food and fuel, housing, supply of production materials, education, employment, medical care, old-age support, labor insurance and protection, personnel policy, military conscription, marriage, and childbearing. In summary, urban and rural Chinese faced totally different life chances based on their identities. The dichotomy between urban and rural therefore went far beyond geographical or residential divisions; it was economic, social, and political (Walder 1989; Porter and Porter 1990; Whyte 1996a; Wang 2005).[4]

Ownership Type

Within urban China, the study setting of this book, new groups were also created. The first division was based on a definition of ownership. Until 1997, the classification of ownership in urban China was mainly along the lines of the state-owned, the collective-owned, and individually owned (private economy) sectors. The former two, state- and collective-owned, formed what was considered the public ownership sector. Since the late 1980s, the rise of the private economy has been accompanied by the formation of a variety of ownership types beyond the state and the collective sectors. These include joint-ventures between Chinese and foreign capital, various kinds of privately owned units, and individuals who are self-employed. Official statistical sources now add several new forms of ownership, such as cooperative, joint ownership, limited liability, and shareholding.

Important differences existed not only between the public and the private sectors but also between the state- and the collective-owned sectors. The state-owned sector under socialism was the most privileged sector under the planned economy system. This sector was perceived as the backbone of the state-controlled planned economy. The state invested heavily in this sector, controlled capital and labor allocation, production, and distribution of profits, and provided better benefits for employees in this sector in comparison to other sectors. In the early 1950s, this sector employed about 64 percent of all urban employees, and by 1970, it employed 75 percent of all urban employees (see Table 2.1). The state sector produced 41.5 percent of the gross industrial output in 1952, and this share rose to 53.7 percent in 1957, and to 87.6 in 1970 (NBS 1997, 413). The share of state-owned industries in terms of total gross industrial output did not decline until

the mid-1970s, when a larger share was produced by collective-owned enterprises. It further declined after the mid-1980s, when privately owned
enterprises and enterprises of other ownership types began to produce a
larger and larger share of the industrial output. By 1995, each of the three
components (state, collective, and other) produced about an equal share of
the total gross industrial output.

The collective sector never enjoyed the same status as the state-owned
sector during the days of the planned economy. It was always the step-
child when compared with the state-owned sector in the family of the
planned economy. This sector traces its origin to the mid-1950s when the
socialist transformation in urban China merged many individually owned
handicraft, commercial, and service businesses into collective-owned
cooperatives. Some enterprises established later on by local urban street
committees and by state-owned organizations to solve local unemployment problems also joined the ranks of the collective organizations. These
collective-owned units, though nominally owned by all their employees,
functioned more or less like the state-owned institutions in the absence of
a market economy. They also relied on the dominance of the state-owned
sector for their production and followed state regulations in production and
wage and benefit scales. Due to the fact that many enterprises in this sector were not as capital-intensive and were in the service and light industry
sectors, they also received much less state investment and fewer benefits
during the planned economy period. In 1980, for instance, investment of
fixed assets averaged 2,469 yuan per employee in the state-owned sector,
whereas it was only 190 yuan for the collective-owned, a ratio of 13 to 1.
This investment advantage enjoyed by the state-owned sector lasted until
1990.[5] Less favored by the state's developmental strategy and investments,
wages and benefits in this sector in general also lagged behind those in the
state sector before the economic reforms of the 1980s.

Private and other types of ownership virtually disappeared during the
planned economy period in urban China. These types accounted for less
than 1 percent of all urban employees in 1970. Economic reforms in the
1980s were accompanied by a steady rise in the number of employees in
the non-public sector. This sector, however, is highly heterogeneous, composed of self-employed individuals, individuals working in small businesses
owned by private individuals, and individuals working in joint-venture or
foreign-owned enterprises. The percentage of urban employees in this sec-

TABLE 2.2

*Wage differences among staff and workers of different ownership types,
urban China, 1978–2000*

| Year | AVERAGE YEARLY WAGE (RMB YUAN) | | | | |
	State-owned	Collective	Percentage of state	Other	Percentage of state
1978	644	506	79		
1980	803	623	78		
1985	1213	967	80	1436	118
1986	1414	1092	77	1629	115
1987	1546	1207	78	1879	122
1988	1853	1426	77	2382	129
1989	2055	1557	76	2707	132
1990	2284	1681	74	2987	131
1991	2477	1866	75	3468	140
1992	2878	2109	73	3966	138
1993	3532	2592	73	4966	141
1994	4797	3245	68	6303	131
1995	5635	3931	70	7463	132
1996	6820	4302	63	8261	121
1997	6747	4512	67	8789	120
1998	7668	5331	70	8972	117
1999	8543	5774	68	9829	115
2000	9552	6262	66	10984	115
1996					
Liaoning	5894	3462	59	6648	113
Sichuan	5476	3644	67	6338	116
Guangdong	9494	6799	72	10569	111

SOURCES: NBS 1997, 123; NBS 2002, Table 5-20; survey data.

tor rose to above 5 percent of the workforce in 1988, 10 percent in 1993, over 15 percent in 1995, and over a third in 2000 (Table 2.1).

Employees in the state-owned sector on average enjoyed higher wages until the mid-1990s. As shown in Table 2.2, the average wage in collective-owned units was never higher than 80 percent of that in state-owned units in urban China. The wage disadvantage of the collective sector worsened in the early 1990s, dropping to below 70 percent of the average wage in the state-owned sector. In 1996, for instance, the average yearly wage for employees in collective-owned work organizations was just 63 percent of those in state-owned organizations. In the three provinces that are the focus of this study, this percentage varied between 59 percent in Liaoning and 72 percent in Guangdong province.

Since its reemergence in the mid-1980s, in the highly mixed "other" sector, the average wage was higher than in the state sector. Such a higher wage partly reflects the higher productivity and higher profit in this sector and partly represents compensation for the fact that many employees in this sector did not receive a broad range of benefits, especially housing. In the early 1990s, wage advantage for non-state and non-collective employees was as high as 40 percent compared with those working in state-owned organizations. Such an advantage quickly diminished during the second half of the 1990s as average income levels among state employees increased at a faster pace than those in the non-state sectors: between 1995 and 2000, the average yearly wage rose 69.5 percent in the state sector, compared with 59.3 percent in the collective sector, and 47.2 in the "other" sector. In the three provinces, the non-public sector wage advantage in the mid-1990s ranged from 11 to 16 percent.

The difference in benefits provision among different ownership types is even greater than that in wages. For instance, in 1996, in addition to the wage advantage, employees in state-owned units officially received on average 1,462 yuan in subsidies and allowances (NBS 1997, 122). Such a number is nevertheless a severe undercount of the real level of benefits, as housing, medical care, and pension are not accounted for. But even so, the amount received by those in state-owned units was equivalent to an over 20 percent boost to their already higher-wage income. This amount was more than twice the average amount received by employees in collective-owned units (664 yuan) and close to 1.5 times that paid to individuals working in units of other types of ownership (982 yuan). This difference in benefits is by no means a recent phenomenon. In 1985, employees in state-owned units received on average a benefit of 224 yuan, roughly equivalent to 20 percent of their wage. In the same year, those in collective-owned units received only 129 yuan in benefits (NBS 1997, 122).

In terms of income distribution, economic reform in the past decades has given new significance to the role of ownership type. The changes are both political and economic. Politically, an ideological shift has allowed the rapid growth of economic sectors outside of state ownership and control. Economically, the picture is more complex. On one hand, newly emerged private sectors are not subject to the same income distribution stipulations as those in the state-owned sectors. Unable or unwilling to match the welfare benefits provided with employment in the publicly owned sectors, firms in the private sectors also used higher pay to compensate for the lack of benefits, especially housing. On the other hand, in comparison to collective-owned and privately owned enterprises, employees in the state-owned sector also consistently received the most state backing. Until the late 1990s, state-controlled banks provided a huge amount of loans and subsidies to keep nonprofitable enterprises afloat, a privilege not enjoyed by those outside of the state-owned sector. Whereas some firms have prospered with the backing of the state, others have declined due to a loss of state support. After structural reforms, many state-owned or state-controlled enterprises quickly assumed monopoly positions in the new market economy, such as in utilities, communications, and banking.

Industrial Sector

In contrast to market-based economies where industrial sectors are formed over time in response to changing production needs and technological specificities, under state socialism, industries were created with the heavy hand of the state. Industrial sectors were created in accordance with the needs of the socialist planned economy. With the forced industrialization developmental strategy, industries that were deemed more central to this strategy, such as geological surveys and heavy industries, received more state investment, which often meant higher wages as well. In 1956, when the last major wage policy before the mid-1980s was formulated, wages were deliberately set higher for heavy industries and other sectors deemed more important, as well as for jobs requiring higher technical skills or performed under harsh working conditions (Zhu 2001, 20). More important, due to their relative abundance of resources, work units in the favored industries were also able to provide better benefits for their employees.

Relative wage advantage across industries reflects changing economic rewards under different developmental models and strategies. Shown by industry in Table 2.3 are the average wages of staff and workers in state-owned units for selected years between 1986 and 2000. In 1986, near the end of the socialist planned economic era, those industries with the highest average wages were mining, construction, geological surveys, and transportation/communications. These were all industries that occupied a critical position in the planned economy and thus received explicit favors in wages from the state. Prior to the post-socialist reforms, Chinese employees in industries such as banking and real estate received compensations no higher than the national average.

TABLE 2.3

Wage differences among staff and workers of different industries, urban China, selected years

Industrial sector	YEAR							
	1986	1988	1990	1992	1995	1998	1999	2000
Average (yuan)	1414	1853	2284	2878	5625	7479	8346	9371
Industrial sector	Percentage relative to average							
Farming, forestry, animal husbandry and fishery	75	70	68	64	63	61	58	55
Mining and quarrying	116	110	121	113	106	97	90	89
Manufacturing	98	101	100	100	95	94	93	93
Electricity, gas, and water production and supply	107	108	116	117	137	140	138	137
Construction	122	118	117	118	116	100	96	93
Geological prospecting and water conservancy	114	109	108	112	106	106	106	103
Transportation, storage, post and telecommunications	114	115	118	120	135	131	132	131
Wholesale and retail trade and catering services	90	94	89	86	81	78	77	77
Banking and insurance	101	99	96	103	135	142	144	144
Real estate	96	94	98	107	122	138	138	135
Social services	100	99	101	105	106	111	111	110
Health care, sports, and social welfare	97	97	99	100	107	114	116	117
Education; culture and arts; radio, film, and TV	95	95	93	95	97	100	102	101
Scientific research and polytechnical services	106	104	106	109	122	137	139	145
Government agencies, Party agencies, and social organizations	96	92	93	96	98	104	108	107
Other					122	113	121	118
Coefficient of variation	0.116	0.117	0.134	0.139	0.184	0.209	0.221	0.230

SOURCES: NBS, 1997, 2005.

Dismantling the planned economy system in the last two decades has resulted in a reordering of industrial sectors. Industries deemed essential under the planned economy system, such as mining, geological survey, construction, and heavy industry, lost their old glory, as new sectors such as electricity, telecommunications, banking, and real estate rose to become new stars. As it did during the early days of the planned economy, the state has played a major role in shifting the perceived importance of industrial sectors. A priority investment program in the early 1980s, for instance, allocated 96 percent of total investment in three sectors: energy, transportation, and materials industries (Naughton 1997, 134). By the mid-1990s, market-oriented reforms had produced the new winners: banking, electricity, real estate, and transportation/telecommunications. By the end of the 1990s, as shown in Table 2.3, the average wages in mining and construction dropped from some 20 percent *above* the national average in 1986 to about 10 percent *below* the national average, while wages for those in the electricity sector stood at nearly 40 percent, transportation and communications at over 30 percent, banking at 44 percent, and real estate at over 30 percent above the national average. In a period of one and a half decades, the degree of variation in average wages among the major industries also rose sharply, with the coefficient of variation doubling from 0.116 in 1986 to 0.23 in 2000 (see Table 2.3). Rent seeking based on industrial and especially organizational monopoly of resources, sanctioned by the state, is clearly a primary reason underlying this rising income differential among sectors.

Benefits information by industry obtained from surveys reveals an even more telling picture of segregation by industrial sectors. According to China's 1985 Industrial Census of over 8,000 firms, those in heavy industries, favored by the state during the industrialization period, enjoyed a much higher level of collective benefits under the planned economy regime. Compared with those outside this industry, work units in heavy industry enjoyed 80 percent more housing space (18.6 versus 10.4 m^2 per 100 workers), more than twice the health-care resources (1.8 versus 0.84 personnel per 100 workers), four times the within-*danwei* schooling for children (16.2 versus 4.4 and 12.2 versus 2.8 elementary and secondary students per 100 workers), and almost twice the recreational space (0.45 versus 0.26 m^2 per 100 workers) (Naughton 1997, 180, Table 7.2). Based on an analysis of survey data collected in the city of Tianjin in 1986, Walder (1992a) also found that employees in work organizations in manufacturing, education, and government sectors received more benefits.

Geographic Location

Due to China's continental scope and its high degree of heterogeneity in natural environment and subregional history of economic development, sharp differences in economic output and in income had long existed across different regions in China, at a level far higher than most countries (Riskin 1987, 225). Socialist policies initially contributed to some degree toward reducing the differences in productivity and capital stock in different provinces and resulted in a relative convergence of provincial industrialization (Riskin 1987, Chapter 10). Most noticeably, by setting a national scale for wages for all state employees, income during the planned economy period was highly equalized (Zhu 2001). Along with the national wage scales, regional income difference was also part of the state-stipulated policy. China was classified into 11 "wage zones" according to cost of living in the 1956 wage policy and into seven zones in the 1985 wage policy reform. Each wage zone carried a wage differential allowance (Zhu 2001, 19–20, 26).

These equalizing efforts, while significant, were not able to eliminate all the regional differences. The same state-stipulated wage scales implemented in 1956 also allowed higher wages in "key areas of socialist construction and certain coastal areas" (Zhu 2001, 20). Some provinces, such as Liaoning, still had a level of per capita industrial output that was 2.6 times the national average by the end of the 1970s, whereas others, such as Guangdong and Sichuan, were below the national average.[6] Within each province, similar if not greater differences existed. In Sichuan, for instance, various cities had different industrial endowments. These differences in endowment led to sharply increased regional disparities following the reforms.

The same political power that was used to reduce regional differences has been used recently to generate greater disparity. Under the planned economy system, China's urbanization was a highly controlled and planned process, under the mandate of socialist industrialization. As a consequence, Chinese cities were built primarily as sites of industrial growth during the process of socialist industrialization. This approach meant that some of the largest factories were not located where they made the most economic sense, but rather close to political centers to facilitate control. In some cases, cities were created in anticipation of an economic devastation resulting from potential military conflict with China's perceived enemies at the time. Such cities include those created in the "Third Front" in inland provinces, including some in Sichuan province (included in this study). Whereas cities created as such made economic and political sense under the planned economy system, they also formed a major structural basis for post-socialist economic growth and income distribution.

With the demise of a centrally planned economic system, the role of cities in economic growth has increased sharply in recent decades, resulting in a much increased economic disparity among cities. This increased disparity is an outcome of the socialist legacy, which provided each city with a different endowment and placed it at a different starting point in the post-socialist economic boom. It is also an outcome of post-socialist government policies. Reform measures in the early 1980s deliberately targeted certain regions, for example, through the establishment of Special Economic Zones, allowances for a more open economic policy in coastal provinces of Guangdong and Fujian in 1980, a similar special policy for an expanded list of coastal cities in 1984, and the development of the Shanghai Pudong area in the early 1990s. More favorable fiscal arrangements between these cities and the central government, along with more flexible and favorable terms to attract foreign capital, have not only propelled economic growth in these special regions, but by their very design, they have also created unequal treatment toward different regions.

Danwei *and the Formation of the Minor Public*

At the very basic level of society, urban Chinese were organized into *danwei*, or "work units." Lü and Perry (1997) classify *danwei* into three types, according to their economic and political functions, as well as their location in the political hierarchy. These three types are *qiye*, "production," such as a firm; *shiye*, "non-production," such as a university; and *xingzheng*, "administrative or government organizations."[7] With the disappearance of the private economy in urban China by the late 1950s, almost all urban Chinese were incorporated into work units. *Danwei* served as the employer, social welfare benefits distributor, and an arena for political mobilization and control (Henderson and Cohen 1984; Walder 1986; Bian 1994; Lü and Perry 1997; Li 2004; Bray 2005). Even after more than two decades of reforms, as of 1999, only 15 percent of all urban laborers worked outside a *danwei* or organization as self-employed, and nearly three-quarters of all urban employees still worked in publicly owned organizations (NBS 2000, 118).

Such a form of organization was highly effective for a planned economy. For instance, as summarized by Naughton, the 1985 Industrial Census of China included 8,285 large firms, of which 7,946 were state-owned. These large organizations comprised less than 2 percent of all state-owned enterprises but accounted for 45 percent of state light industrial employment and 64 percent of state heavy industrial employment. They accounted for almost two-thirds (62.3%) of the total profit and tax generated by industrial enterprises with an independent accounting status (1997, 179).

Whereas both China and the former Soviet Union utilized work units to organize and control the urban population, there was an important difference between the two systems. The difference was in the allocation of public housing, the primary component of welfare provision. In the former Soviet Union, municipal governments provided urban employees with housing. In urban China, although funds for housing also came from the state, work units provided 90 percent of the housing during the Socialist era (Lü and Perry 1997, 10). At the same time, in the case of urban China, "More than 70 percent of state enterprises ran schools of some kind. About 40 percent of all general hospital beds were in the state-owned industrial system. State enterprises constructed most of the new housing in cities and owned a large share of the total housing stock" (Naughton 1997, 178).

Socialist industrialization was a direct force in creating the *danwei* system. Naughton (1997) traces the formation of the *danwei* system under the planned economy system to the 1960s. He points out that it was after the disastrous Great Leap Forward that both job allocation (of up to 95 percent of first jobs in urban areas) and migration control were regularized and, with that, the *danwei* system cemented. By comparison, in the former Soviet Union and Eastern European socialist countries, the state routinely assigned jobs only for graduating students, while ordinary workers changed jobs frequently. The *danwei* system was further cemented by a series of political measures, such as Third Front investment in China's inner areas during its conflict with the Soviets in the late 1960s, which created a large number of enterprises in previously undeveloped areas.

Though mostly associated with the Chinese planned economy system, the *danwei* system also has its historical and cultural roots in Chinese society. Some attribute the origin of the *danwei* system to the communist guerrilla war period, during which military and administrative units were required to engage in self-sufficient production activities and a "free supply system" prevailed (Lü 1997). Others go back farther, linking this new institution to more generic roots of the Chinese tradition. As remarked by Henderson and Cohen, "Overall, it appears that the structural characteristics of the unit system reinforce the traditional dependent modes of interaction"

(Henderson and Cohen 1984, 140). The similarities between the traditional Chinese family group and the contemporary Chinese work units are highly evident, as elucidated by Lü and Perry (1997, 8): "The functions of *danwei* can be divided into two main areas: political and social. These two functions may be characterized as 'paternalistic' and 'maternalistic' respectively. As in a traditional family, the *danwei* acts as a patriarch who disciplines and sanctions his children, while at the same time serving as a maternal provider of care and daily necessities." A vivid example of the historical roots of the *danwei* system is provided by Wen-hsin Yeh, who used a Shanghai bank before the socialist era to illustrate not only an impressive modernizing banking organization but also "a profound moralistic managing philosophy, which was in full accordance with the senior leadership's neo-Confucian outlook" (1997, 65). Yeh documents that "In the late 1920s, the bank, like many other Chinese owned modern enterprises at the time, began building housing compounds for its employees in city after city. . . . The bank believed that there were many advantages in having employees living next to one another: 'order,' 'convenience,' 'friendship,' 'unity as a group,' and 'uniformity in thinking'" (1997, 68). And she points out: "Shanghai's leading financial institutions built a communal style of corporate life containing features that call to mind the socialist *danwei* of the 1950s. This community was the expression of a patriarchal conception of authority. Membership in it was often described in kinship terms. The corporation was a large family" (1997, 81). Yeh concludes that "Issues surrounding a moralistic conception of authority . . . sometimes transcend divisions between a 'capitalist' and a 'socialist' system of economic life . . . Until the rise of cultural critiques directed specifically at these underlying assumptions in the organization of social relationships in the Chinese world, then, we may expect to see the basic demands of the *danwei* system reconstituting themselves in one fashion or another, permitting a broad range of dependency in a variety of economic forms" (1997, 83).

The significance of the *danwei* system goes far beyond its roles under the planned economy system. With it a segmented public property rights regime was created. The public ownership of the means of production, on which the socialist planned economy was based, was never public in its true meaning, because it was simply not feasible for the whole public to participate in decision making. While the state relied on a complex system of control to enforce its rights over public property, through planned allocation, appointment of managers, and various monitoring and evaluations, bargaining between producers and the state and resource hoarding by each producer were widely known practices under the planned economy system. Such hoarding was directly responsible for the creation of what has been known as the "shortage economy" (Kornai 1980, 1992).[8] What existed under the state, or the large-scale public ownership, was therefore at least a partial ownership of the means of production by the minor public, be it a local area or a work unit.

Such a property rights regime bears far-reaching ramifications for social inequality in the post-socialist era. When the state started to withdraw its feeding and controlling hand over each and every organization, and in the absence of a wholesale privatization as seen in the former Soviet Union and some other Eastern European societies, these urban Chinese work organizations assumed the role of the minor public, directly affecting the income and welfare of their members. The endowment that these different work organizations received in capital, technology, and the product market positioned them at different starting points in the race toward building the new economic order. In Chapters 4 and 5, I provide concrete examples and further analyses of the roles of the work organization in inequality generation.

MAINTAINING BOUNDARIES

The categories created under socialism, the urban-rural divide, the ownership sector, the industrial sector, locale, and work organization were maintained by a number of institutional arrangements during the socialist planned economy era. Chief among them were differential government investment and taxation policies that protected the status quo of different regions, industries, and work organizations; strict control over migration that separated rural-urban as well as urban-urban movements; and a labor and housing system that further curbed job mobility.

In the process of industrialization under socialism, the state not only created categories by differential investment according to the needs of the economic plan but also enforced the boundaries between different categories by continued preferential investment and taxation policies. As discussed earlier in this chapter, the state's investment varied by types of economic ownership, by economic sector, and by region. Once created, locales and work organizations that occupied more important positions in the planned economy used their position as leverage to bargain for continued support from the state.

For over two decades between the late 1950s and the early 1980s, the household registration system, backed up by employment assignments and the food rationing system, effectively erected an invisible wall between China's urban and rural sectors (Chan 1994; Lavely, Lee, and Wang 1990). Under the system of residential and employment control, a person was either designated with "agricultural" or "non-agricultural" status and a change of status from rural to urban was virtually impossible (Cheng and Selden 1994; Wang 1997; Wang 2005).

Chinese cities, in other words, were segregated from vast rural areas and protected by "invisible walls" (Chan 1994). Instead of avoiding all the social evils associated with rapid urbanization in the early development of capitalism and observed in many contemporary developing countries, a socialist dualistic society with Chinese characteristics was created. Within this dual society, urban residents became a collectively distinctive and privileged caste, an outcome largely unanticipated by the early scholars in urban developmental studies.[9] Coupled with an urban-biased developmental policy, such strict control over population movement only exacerbated rural underemployment and poverty, which in turn provided the strongest and earliest impetus for launching China's reforms in the late 1970s (Yang 1996; Solinger 1999; Taylor 1988).

Even within urban China, change of residence between different cities was also kept at a minimum. With the state's control over employment, housing, and provision of daily necessities, it was almost inconceivable for an individual to move to a different city, unless the move was state-sponsored. For instance, in Shanghai, China's largest metropolis and also the city with the most effective migration control during the planned economy era, the total migration rate (including both those moving out and moving in) dropped from 10 percent in the late 1950s to less than 3 percent in the 1960s and 1970s. In fact, state-imposed migration control reduced the city population by over a million during that time period (Wang, Zuo, and Ruan 2002).

Within urban China, the government-controlled labor system assigned jobs and discouraged labor movement. Job mobility, as a consequence, was extremely low (Davis 1990, 1992; Walder 1986; Zhou, Tuma, and

Moen 1997). As noted by Deborah Davis, "Inter-firm job turnover was deliberately restricted and moves were more often the result of transfers requested by superiors than individual strategies of advancement" (Davis 1992, 1063). Chinese urban job mobility was far lower than that of capitalist market economies and also much lower than other planned economies. As observed by Naughton, "Voluntary job turnover was about a hundred times more common in the Soviet Union than in China under the *danwei* system. Moreover, in the Soviet Union, two-thirds of all hiring was done directly by the enterprise (at the factory gate, in the case of industrial enterprises) and another 10 percent consisted of voluntary matches arranged by municipal labor bureaus" (1997, 173).

Even after the rise of the private economy, the bankruptcy of numerous state- and collective-owned enterprises, and the declining significance of household registration and migration control, urban job mobility was still quite low as late as the end of the 1980s.[10] Recent studies of urban labor markets reported a persistent low level of voluntary job mobility for urban employees at the end of the 1990s (Knight and Yueh 2004; Knight and Song 2005). Chinese urban employees at the end of the 1990s still had an average job duration or tenure of 19.9 years, in contrast to 17.5 years in Poland, 11.3 years in Japan, and 7.4 years in the United States (Knight and Song 2005, 135).[11] Moreover, as later chapters of this book will show, in some cases, boundaries created to separate categories, such as work organizational affiliation and employment status (whether a regular or a temporary employee), have been transplanted into reformed economic entities and utilized to separate insiders and outsiders within the same work organization.

In the process of China's pursuit of socialist industrialization, categories were created as the basis of economic organization and welfare distribution. Economic reforms in the wake of China's post-socialist transformation have weakened some boundaries but, at the same time, have fortified others and even created new ones. China's socialist legacy therefore occupies a prominent position in defining the structure of post-reform inequality. The divisions created under socialism paved the way for the emergence of a stratification and inequality pattern after the 1980s. In urban China, where the socialist planned economy had reached its full extent, not only did the overall degree of inequality increase following economic reforms, but the importance of the groups formed under socialism also rose to new heights in determining inequality. The apparent contradiction between measured high inequality and perceived high equality can be understood once one looks more closely at China, examining it group by group. At the same time that an increasingly larger number of urban Chinese employees were leaving the work groups created by the planned economy, the predominant majority (over 80 percent) were still working within a state- or collective-owned institution as of the mid-1990s. For this majority, geographic location, employment sector, and in particular, work organizations have all become more important than before the reforms in determining their livelihood and status in the society.

TRENDS AND PATTERNS

CHAPTER THREE

Prosperity and Inequality

Rising inequality in urban China unfolded during one of the greatest moments of economic prosperity in China's history. In the last two decades of the twentieth century, urban Chinese witnessed both an unprecedented increase in the standard of living and, accompanying it, an unprecedented increase in inequality at the societal level. Drastic improvement in material well-being set China apart from most other transitional state socialist societies, in which personal incomes of the average person suffered a great depression. In the last decade of the twentieth century, China's economic growth far exceeded any other transition economy, with a GDP increase of 246 percent between 1989 and 1999—in contrast to all Eastern European and Baltic countries where states GDP in 1999 barely recovered to its level in 1989 and to CIS states (Russia and Central Asia) where the GDP level in 1999 was only about half of what it was in 1989 (Cornia and Popov 2001, 4).[1]

For China, the decade following the start of urban economic reforms in the mid-1980s can indeed be labeled as the decade of returned prosperity (Ikels 1996).[2] Notwithstanding the ups and downs during the turbulent decade and a half, these years also brought the fastest rise ever in standards of living for urban Chinese in China's recent history. During the same time period, urban Chinese also experienced rampant inflation, witnessed the beginning of large-scale corruption by some government officials and those connected to them, and started to feel insecurity in employment and for some even in basic livelihood. All these came as a cost for achieving economic prosperity under a new economic and social system.

The return of prosperity, in other words, was also accompanied by a surge in inequality that was unprecedented in China's recent history.

Together with changes in the political system that drastically reduced the importance of political participation in daily life, the new economic system emerging during this time period led to a fundamental reconfiguration of the Chinese society, altering the roles of the central and local governments, work organizations, and the family organization in individuals' social and economic lives. The overall direction of change is unambiguous: the state gradually returned much of the economic decision-making power to lower-level economic organizations and, ultimately, to urban Chinese households and individuals. Later chapters in this book will focus on the increasing roles of these lower-level economic organizations, especially local governments and work organizations, as crucial categorical sources in defining the pattern of inequality in post-socialist urban China.

In this chapter, before delineating the contours of rising inequality, I first provide a few glimpses into the changes in the basic economic and social unit in urban China, the household. Changes among households, especially in employment of household members, reflect the broad demographic and economic changes at the societal level. Household strategies directly affect household members' income-generating capacities and ultimately their relative standing in the income distribution. Compared with the days of the planned economy system when the state assumed a paternalistic role in arranging individuals' lives from cradle to grave, urban Chinese families in this new environment enjoyed an unprecedented degree of empowerment and opportunity, at the same time as they faced a much elevated level of risk and uncertainty (for discussions of the impact of reforms on Chinese families, see Davis and Harrell 1993; Davis 1993; 2000a; Whyte 1996b). Following this brief survey of urban Chinese households, I turn to a summary of the impressive improvement in standards of living, as reflected in income level, changing sources of income, and housing and consumer goods. It is within such a context that income inequality, as well as poverty, increased rapidly for the first time in decades, which will be the subject of the last section in this chapter.

THE URBAN CHINESE HOUSEHOLD

Demographic Profiles

As the most basic social and economic organization that supplies labor and shares consumption, the average urban Chinese household itself underwent substantial changes during the one and half decades since the mid-1980s. Over this time period, urban Chinese households became smaller in size and less complex in composition. At the same time, the average age of the household head among these households also increased, while the number of households headed by women declined. In Table 3.1, I provide four basic characteristics of the urban households based on the urban population samples from three provinces: household size, composition, household head's age, and gender.

First, the mean household size shrank substantially, from close to four persons per household in 1986 to only three in 2000. The demographic source for this reduction in average household size is informed by the changes in household composition, a second characteristic of households shown in Table 3.1. In 1986, nearly half of all household members were children or parents of the household head. Less than three percent were in other categories, such as grandparents or grandchildren, other relatives, or non-family household members. By 2000, the percentage of household members who were either the head of the household or the spouse of the household head represented over 60 percent of all members, and the percentage of children declined from over 40 to 30. At the same time, household members who were parents of the household head also became a smaller share of the household composition.

What this means is that by the late 1990s, most urban Chinese households were truly nuclear households, composed of a married couple and one child. These two categories represented nearly 95 percent of all household members at the end of the 1990s. Given that the increase in single-parent households in urban China by the late 1990s was at best trivial, even following a notable increase in divorce from the previously very low level, the main sources of such a change were the low urban fertility that started in the late 1960s and a more recent shift in living arrangements. By the end of the 1990s, China's well-known birth control policy of one child per couple had been in place for two decades. Unlike in rural China where most cou-

TABLE 3.1

Characteristics of urban households, three provinces of China, selected years

| Year | SIZE | | HOUSEHOLD COMPOSITION (PERCENTAGE OF MEMBERSHIP AS) | | | | HEADSHIP | | | N |
	Mean	S.D.	Head and spouse	Children	Parent	Other	AGE Mean	AGE S.D.	GENDER Percentage female	Household
Three provinces combined										
1986	3.83	1.12	51.46	40.87	5.12	2.55	41.23	11.29	43.76	2066
1990	3.39	0.97	57.14	36.68	3.85	2.33	44.44	10.96	39.08	1950
1995	3.19	0.82	60.90	33.24	3.66	2.20	44.61	10.69	36.81	2749
2000	3.09	0.82	62.53	30.45	3.95	3.07	47.49	11.54	36.32	2698
Liaoning										
1986	3.97	1.17	50.27	44.02	3.75	1.96	41.03	10.92	34.85	705
1990	3.33	0.84	58.76	35.69	3.75	1.80	41.56	10.61	41.56	600
1995	3.23	0.78	60.70	33.86	3.23	2.21	44.57	10.89	30.70	1049
2000	3.10	0.81	62.77	31.06	2.77	3.40	49.01	11.88	26.80	1000
Sichuan										
1986	3.76	1.05	52.64	37.59	6.95	2.82	38.93	10.35	49.77	861
1990	3.27	0.99	59.09	33.96	4.40	2.55	45.99	11.25	38.47	800
1995	3.02	0.76	63.85	30.54	3.92	1.69	43.94	10.70	45.15	1100
2000	2.94	0.83	65.02	27.58	3.96	3.44	47.54	12.00	44.26	1098
Guangdong										
1986	3.77	1.16	51.23	41.74	4.08	2.95	45.44	12.17	46.00	500
1990	3.65	1.02	52.99	41.17	3.24	2.60	45.33	10.29	32.55	550
1995	3.46	0.89	56.51	36.57	3.97	2.95	45.93	10.19	32.17	600
2000	3.36	0.73	58.14	34.16	5.76	1.94	44.88	9.48	37.67	600

ples managed to stay out of such an unprecedented government population control policy, few urban Chinese had a second child during the two decades after 1980. As a result, whereas in 1986 some urban households still had more than one child in residence, due to children born prior to the one-child policy, this was no longer the case by 2000.

At the same time as the number of children living in urban households was uniformly reduced to only one or fewer (when the child left the household), there were also fewer three-generation households by the late 1990s compared with a decade earlier. The decline in the proportion of household heads' parents in these urban households is mostly due to the decline in co-residence with one's older parents. A major factor contributing to this change in residence pattern was the improved urban housing conditions that allowed younger couples to move into their own apartments (see more discussion later in this chapter on housing improvement).

A third characteristic of the urban Chinese household is the aging of household heads. Despite a reduction in average household size due to fewer children, the average age of the household head did not become younger. On the contrary, it became substantially older, from barely above 40 to over 47 years of age. Such an increase can well be the outcome of two countervailing forces: whereas the ages of some households became younger when young people established their households, others became older when old people lived by themselves and headed their own households.

The fourth and last characteristic of the urban households is the sex composition of those reported as household heads. Contrary to the perceived patriarchal characteristic of the Chinese family in general, in these urban Chinese households, a fairly large proportion of them were headed by women. The percentage of female household heads was well over 40 percent at the beginning of the study period, 1986, and dropped to 36 percent in 2000. In the three provinces under study here, in other words, between one in three and two in five of all households had a female as head of household.

There are also some noticeable differences among the three provinces. The average household size declined most substantially in Sichuan province, followed by Liaoning and Guangdong. Guangdong province has the largest average household size of all three provinces, partly a result of its higher fertility over the other two provinces. Compared with Liaoning and Guangdong, Sichuan province is by far much more gender-egalitarian, with as many as 45 to 49 percent of all households reporting a woman as the head.

Employment Diversification and Household Strategies

In contrast to the socialist planned economy era when employment was a guaranteed right for almost every urban Chinese, by the year 2000, a significant share of urban Chinese were unemployed. Changes in employment were more pronounced for women than for men and were most clearly seen for urban residents at older ages. These changes are shown in Figure 3.1, which compares employment rates by age and gender between 1990 and 2000 for urban residents in the three provinces. In 1990, though several years into reforms, employment was still essentially universal in urban China, especially for men of prime working ages. Virtually every urban male between ages 25 and 54 was employed, as were females aged 25 to 49 (shown by the darker lines). By 2000 (shown in the lighter lines), more than 10 percent of young urban Chinese were not working at ages 25 to 29. For women, even in the prime working ages of 30 to 44, nearly 10 percent were not working. Moreover, the percentage of unemployed women in these provinces reached 20 percent by ages 45 to 49, and more than 50 percent by ages 50 to 54. Nearly 40 percent of urban men also left their jobs before reaching age 60. Urban layoffs in the late 1990s, by making entry into the labor market more difficult for the young and by firing older employees first or forcing their early retirement, clearly resulted in these changes in employment patterns.

Faced with an increasingly uncertain employment prospect and a reduction in size and complexity, urban Chinese households in the two decades after reform became more vital for the well-being of their members, both in generating income and in managing an increased level of consumption. While some urban households became specialized in engaging economic activities outside of the formal employment within the state and the collective sectors, others diversified their members in different economic sectors to spread the risk and to maximize the gain. Because most housing remained under public ownership until the late 1990s, some urban Chinese households chose to let some of their members remain employed in state-owned work organizations for the housing and other benefits, while other members moved to non-state-owned firms to earn higher incomes. A diversified household like this was called "having two systems within one family," thereby getting the most from both systems.

One can detect some of these changes within urban households by com-

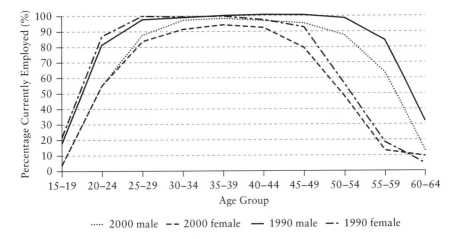

Figure 3.1   Changing patterns of employment, urban China, three provinces, 1990 and 2000

paring the characteristics of the household heads and their spouses. Table 3.2 presents a few key characteristics of the heads of the households and their spouses.[3] Bear in mind, however, that the term *household head* is often self-determined by the surveyed households, rather than following any pre-specified rules. Such a decision could be made on gender—in most cases the adult male is expected to be the head, but that apparently is not always the case in these urban households (see Table 3.1). It could also be based on housing allocation, in which the person through whom housing is obtained was considered the head. Moreover, it could also be based on the political or economic status of the individual, or even on inter-spousal power. It was not uncommon in an urban Chinese household to find the adult woman or the wife considered the head because that person was truly in charge.

Intra-household stratification mirrors increasingly social stratification outside of the household. At the beginning of the decade that coincided with the waning days of the socialist planned economy system, only small differences existed between household heads and their spouses in terms of their socioeconomic characteristics. As shown in Table 3.2, the heads were only slightly more represented in the state-owned employment sector and in the occupational categories of "cadre" and "staff" than were their spouses. Around the turn of the decade, with the rising importance of the household in participating in economic activities, a gap in the social

TABLE 3.2
*Selected characteristics of household heads and spouses,
urban China, three provinces*

	1986–1987		1988–1991		1992–1995	
	Head	Spouse	Head	Spouse	Head	Spouse
Education (%)						
University	10.92	11.67	16.04	12.24	21.27	16.07
Technical school	14.51	11.91	12.14	12.8	13.83	13.22
Senior high school	16.25	14.93	19.17	18.45	21.87	22.68
Junior high school	43.17	45.12	41.18	41.28	35.47	38.86
Primary school	14.88	14.75	11.19	14.37	7.38	8.8
Other	0.27	1.61	0.29	0.85	0.18	0.37
Employment sector						
State	76.45	74.23	77.45	70.25	77.01	68.69
Collective	22.76	23.58	21.05	27.51	17.52	24.39
Private	0.52	1.06	0.82	1.4	2.91	4.02
Other	0.27	1.13	0.68	0.85	2.57	2.9
Occupation						
Cadre	10.44	8.73	10.92	6.32	9.04	6.65
Professional	2.92	2.65	7.55	5.76	9.82	7.69
Technician	13.2	13.75	14.05	13.18	15.96	15.05
Staff	35.53	30.91	33.19	32.12	29.81	29.91
Workers	37.91	43.96	34.3	42.62	35.37	40.7
N	3287	3282	6584	6584	7941	7941

and economic status between household heads and spouses emerged. More household heads possessed university or college degrees than their spouses (16.04 versus 12.24 percent), a larger share stayed in the state-owned sector (77.45 versus 70.25 percent), and more held cadres' positions (10.92 versus 6.32 percent). By 1992 to 1995, whereas the gap in educational and occupational attainment between household heads and their spouses remained, a larger gap emerged in their employment sectors. Over the three periods under comparison in Table 3.2, the share of household heads who were employed in the state-owned sector remained unchanged, in contrast to those reported as "spouses," whose share in employment in the state sector dropped from 74.23 in 1986–87 to 68.69 percent in 1992–95. Whereas for both heads and spouses the share of employment in the non-public sector increased, more spouses were in the newly emerging non-state sectors.

Among what types of households were spouses more likely to be employed in non-public sectors? To gain some understanding of the underlying dynamics of both non-public employment and the roles of households in the economic transformation, I examine the characteristics of the spouses who

TABLE 3.3

Factors affecting employment in non-public sector, spouse of household head, urban China, selected periods

Variable	1986–1987 Odds ratio	P	1989–1991 Odds ratio	P	1992–1995 Odds ratio	P
Self characteristics						
Age	1.06	0.00	1.03	0.03	0.97	0.00
Female (Male = reference)	3.16	0.00	1.00	0.98	1.02	0.93
Education (University = reference)						
Technical school	—	—	0.44	0.34	0.56	0.10
Senior high school	3.24	0.15	2.64	0.09	2.33	0.00
Junior high school	3.38	0.11	5.67	0.00	1.85	0.01
Primary school	5.53	0.03	6.00	0.00	4.98	0.00
Other	10.58	0.01	20.46	0.00	1.30	0.83
Household head characteristics						
Female (Male = reference)	1.38	0.29	0.85	0.44	0.87	0.52
Education (University = reference)						
Technical school	1.57	0.57	0.69	0.44	0.55	0.02
Senior high school	2.51	0.24	1.60	0.23	0.63	0.03
Junior high school	2.26	0.28	1.39	0.39	0.56	0.01
Primary school	4.48	0.05	1.67	0.22	0.75	0.31
Other	—	—	—	—	0.84	0.88
Sector (State = reference)						
Collective	0.80	0.51	1.08	0.72	0.94	0.73
Private	25.04	0.00	6.98	0.00	18.26	0.00
Other	11.86	0.01	2.82	0.11	1.88	0.09
Occupation (Cadre = reference)						
Professional	1.45	0.77	0.98	0.98	2.01	0.03
Technician	1.32	0.66	0.81	0.63	1.61	0.12
Staff member	0.98	0.96	1.27	0.47	1.97	0.01
Production worker	1.22	0.70	1.11	0.76	1.72	0.06
Province (Liaoning = reference)						
Sichuan	1.29	0.43	5.80	0.00	1.05	0.80
Guangdong	1.26	0.52	6.80	0.00	3.41	0.00
N	2875		6574		7941	
Likelihood Ch-2	116.10		181.62		567.66	
Pseudo R^2	0.17		0.13		0.21	

were employed in non-public sectors.[4] I also include in the analysis the characteristics of the household heads with whom the spouses are associated. The results of the analyses are given in Table 3.3. The analytical method used is logistic regression, where the likelihood or odds of being employed in the non-public sector is assumed to be a function of the spouse's as well as the household head's characteristics.[5] The odds ratio represents the change in the likelihood of being in non-public sector employment associated with one unit change in the characteristics. In the case of categorical variables, such as education or occupation, it represents the relative likelihood compared with those in the reference category. Only those odds ratios with a P-value smaller than 0.05 are statistically meaningful and therefore worthy of attention.[6] So for example, for 1986–87 one additional year of age was associated with a 6 percent increased likelihood of being in the non-public sector and, compared with males, a female spouse was 3.16 times more likely to be in the non-public sector.

The gap in employees' social characteristics between public and non-public sectors have closed considerably in a decade and a half. In 1986–87, spouses who were older, female, and the least educated (in primary and "other" educational categories) were more likely to be in the non-public sector. In addition, these spouses were from households in which the household heads also had the least education and who were in non-public sectors themselves. In other words, at the beginning of the decade, the few who were in the non-public sectors were the least educated and from households with similarly low levels of education.

By the turn of the decade, 1989–91, some changes were evident in the characteristics of the spouses and their household heads in non-public employment. First, gender was no longer a factor, which means that it is no longer the female spouse who is more likely to get into the non-public sector. Second, though the most educated (with university education) were still somewhat less likely to be found in the non-public sector compared with the less schooled, there was some increase in education among those who were employed in the non-public sector. In contrast to the first period in which only the least educated were more likely to be found in the non-public sectors, spouses with higher educational attainment (junior high school) were also more likely to be in the non-public sector. Third, a regional difference emerged, with Sichuan and Guangdong provinces having significantly more non-public employment than Liaoning. At the same time, the "household effect" continued; with households in which the heads were in the private sector continuing to have a higher likelihood of the spouse being in the same sector.

The picture of non-public sector employment had changed considerably by the mid-1990s. First of all, younger people were more likely to get into the non-public sectors. An odds ratio smaller than 1 means that one year of age is associated with a 3 percent smaller likelihood of non-public employment, controlling for other factors in the analysis. Such a change reflected both changes in the broad economic system, where the state was no longer assigning jobs for school graduates and where the non-public sector employment had expanded, and more willingness among the young, who started to find the non-public sector an increasingly more attractive alternative to employment in the public sectors. Second, there was a further upgrading in educational attainment of the individuals who joined the non-public sectors. It is no longer only the primary or junior high school educated who were more likely to be in the non-public sectors, but also those with senior high school education. What's most interesting, however, are the changes in the characteristics of the household heads. By this time, non-public sector employment was no longer dominated by households with a low social status but embraced by the best-endowed households. Compared with households whose heads were university-educated, those households headed by someone with a technical school or senior and junior high school education were about 40 to 45 percent less likely to have spouses employed in the non-public sectors. Compared with households whose heads were in the cadre category, households with heads in the professional category were also found to be twice more likely to have a spouse in the non-public sector. At the same time when non-public employment in urban China was still clustered around certain households by way of specialization, households with high endowments in education and technical skills also began to diversify into different economic sectors, as a way to enhance their household incomes.

RISING INCOME AND CONSUMPTION

Changes in the urban Chinese households described in the preceding sections took place at the same time as income and consumption levels increased. Drastically increased income and consumption levels in urban China, as noted earlier, form the background of rising inequality to be summarized in the second half of this chapter. In this section, I document the trajectories of rising income, changing income sources, and rising consumption levels.

Rising Income Levels

In contrast to the socialist decades of the 1950s to the 1970s, during which a developmental strategy of high capital accumulation and low consumption resulted in only marginal increases in urban standards of living, urban

China has witnessed a tremendous income increase since the late 1970s. By the mid-1990s, an average urban employee's nominal income had risen severalfold compared with a decade before. In Guangdong, the province with the fastest growth, nominal income for urban employees rose by ten- fold in a decade's time. Other main indicators of household and personal economic well-being, such as housing and ownership of consumer durables, show similarly remarkable improvements.

The rapid increase in personal income following the initial reforms was something that most urban Chinese had long forgotten. The magnitude of the increase therefore far exceeded the imagination of most people at the outset of the reforms. Optimistic forecasts in the late 1970s projected a qua- drupling of China's per capita GNP in 20 years, by the year 2000. For ur- ban China, however, if measured by nominal average income, this goal was achieved within a single decade. In 1980, the average annual income for urban employees was 762 yuan. It rose to 1,148 yuan by 1985, 2,140 yuan in 1990, and 5,500 in 1995 (NBS 1997, 30–31, not adjusted for inflation). The last major wage increases before the reforms were in the mid-1950s and the early 1960s, following a major readjustment in industries. On average, for over a quarter of a century, between 1952 and 1978, the mean wage of employees in state-owned enterprises and organizations increased only 15 percent. This is a truly dismal increment, if measured in terms of annual increase, as it amounted to an average annual rate of increase of only 0.0054 percent during this time period. By comparison, following the reform mea- sures of the late 1970s, in two years the real mean wages rose by 14 percent, close to the gains for the previous 26 years combined.[7] Following years of income stagnation, this rise in wages was more than welcome and it gener- ated widespread support for the reform agenda.

Rising income in urban China during the decade under study did not follow a smooth upward trajectory. Rather, it resembled the path of a roller coaster, mirroring the different phases of reforms, as shown in Table 3.4 for the three provinces under close examination. In the two provinces that more or less resembled the overall level in China, Liaoning and Sichuan, urban employees' average yearly monetary income rose about fourfold in one decade. In the fast growing province of Guangdong, average nominal income rose tenfold. In other words, in the mid-1980s, the average urban employee in all three provinces made about 100 RBM yuan a month. By the mid-1990s, monthly income had risen to more than 400 yuan in Liaoning

TABLE 3.4

Rising income: Changes in mean yearly income among urban employees

Year	UNADJUSTED (RMB YUAN)			ADJUSTED FOR INFLATION (IN 1986 RMB YUAN)		
	Liaoning	Sichuan	Guangdong	Liaoning	Sichuan	Guangdong
1986	1303	1428	1334	1303	1428	1334
1987	1342	1476	1490	1259	1185	1064
1988	1894	1822	2880	1486	1190	1589
1989	2130	2000	3629	1413	1090	1639
1990	2430	2191	3834	1561	1151	1776
1991	2507	2425	4608	1519	1221	2087
1992	2835	2827	6249	1610	1325	2638
1993	3353	3480	8397	1632	1396	2905
1994	4631	4736	11720	1787	1485	3351
1995	5591	5631	13696	1859	1484	3463
1996	6157	6136	15664	1892	1472	3694
1997	6707	6831	16461	1985	1560	3802
1998	7073	7364	17767	2098	1685	4179
1999	7389	8053	19707	2220	1878	4711
2000	8889	8499	20288	2671	1988	4745
Ratio 1995/1986	4.29	3.94	10.27	1.43	1.25	2.60
Ratio 2000/1995	1.59	1.51	1.48	1.44	1.34	1.37

NOTE: Inflation indices used for adjustment for different provinces are from China's National Bureau of Statistics.

and Sichuan and to over 1,000 in Guangdong. While nominal (unadjusted) income, as shown in the left panel of Table 3.4, rose consistently from year to year, changes in real income, adjusted for inflation, reveal a highly different picture. In the process of converting the pricing system from an administratively set to a market-based one, all parties had an incentive to bid up their prices and no one was willing to lower prices voluntarily. The outcome was escalating price bidding at the society level.

Currency in circulation also rose sharply, resulting largely from deliberate government efforts to facilitate price reforms and to pay for subsidies associated with inflation. The amount of currency in circulation, for instance, shot up by more than 50 percent between 1983 and 1984, and again by close to 50 percent between 1987 and 1988 (Naughton 1995, 1098, Figure 5). In the process of escalating price increases and increased supply of currency, urban Chinese experienced the worst inflation in decades. In the late 1980s, urban China, as represented by the three provinces in Figure 3.2, lived through double-digit inflation year after year, reaching as high as 20 to 30 percent in 1988 and 1989.

Much of the early gains in nominal income were thus eaten away by the

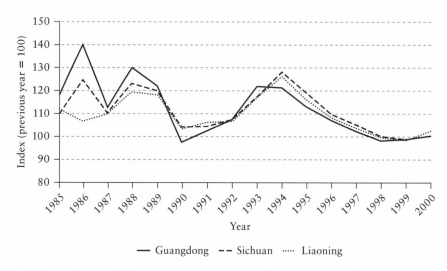

Figure 3.2   Changes in cost of living, urban China, three provinces, 1985–2000

rampant inflation that followed price reforms. There was a modest increase in nominal income between 1986 and 1987, but that increase was more than offset by inflation at levels of 10 percent and higher. Real income (measured in 1986 yuan) decreased in all three provinces between these two years. The following year, 1988, saw a sharp increase in nominal income, coinciding with the intensification of price reforms. At the same time that nominal income rose by more than 20 percent for Sichuan, 40 percent for Liaoning, and more than double for Guangdong, cost of living also skyrocketed, with an annual inflation rate of around 20 percent in Sichuan and Liaoning and 30 percent in urban Guangdong, as shown in Figure 3.2. These high inflation rates continued for all three provinces in 1989. As a result, even though nominal income continued to grow in 1989, in real income terms, urban employees in both Liaoning and Sichuan suffered a net average income decrease compared with 1988. Although most urban residents may have gained economically during these initial years of rampant inflation, not all reaped the gains equally. In fact, it was between 1987 and 1989 that urban China saw its first drastic increase in income inequality. Price reforms and enterprise reform measures benefited some much more than others. The combination of hyperinflation, a sudden increase in income inequality, and a temporary net decrease in income all contributed to a deep sense of dissatisfaction and insecurity among urban Chinese. The anger, disgust, and fear were all well displayed in the streets of Beijing and other cities in the spring of 1989.

Due to an official austerity program imposed in the late 1980s, the two years after the 1989 turbulence represented a quiet break before the next big move. Increases in nominal income continued at a modest level, and inflation was suddenly brought under highly effective control. The increase in cost of living was no more than 5 percent in 1990, and about 7 percent in 1991, a sharp contrast to the double-digit inflation in the earlier years. Even the degree of income inequality, which will be discussed in detail in the next chapter, reversed its upward trajectory. The three years between 1992 and 1994 formed another phase of drastic increase in nominal income and concomitant hyperinflation, to a degree comparable to that between 1987 and 1989. Nominal average income for urban employees nearly doubled between 1992 and 1995, and inflation rates rose again to over 20 percent annually for both 1993 and 1994. But unlike what happened following the first spike in inflation in 1988 and 1989, real income did not fall this time; in fact, it increased after 1991. The population at the same time was also better prepared psychologically to live under the cloud of hyperinflation. Hyperinflation eventually became history by 1996, when China entered a period of low inflation, even deflation, after implementing monetary controls in the mid-1990s and even more so following the Asian and the global economic slowdown at the end of the 1990s (see Figure 3.2).

It is during the second half of the 1990s that real income levels for urban Chinese had the largest increase. As shown in the last two rows of Table 3.4, while nominal income for all three provinces rose much more during the nine years between 1986 and 1995 than during the five years of 1995 and 2000 (left columns), in terms of real income (right columns), in both Liaoning and Sichuan the net gain during the five-year period (1995–2000) is about the same as that during the nine-year period of 1986 to 1995. In five years, average real income levels in all provinces rose by about 40 percent. Even in Guangdong province, where real income increased much more than in the rest of China in the early years of urban reforms, the pace of real income growth maintained its level during the second half of the 1990s.

Changing Income Sources

Along with the rise in income level, an important change in urban residents' income was an increasing diversity in income sources. First of all, no longer

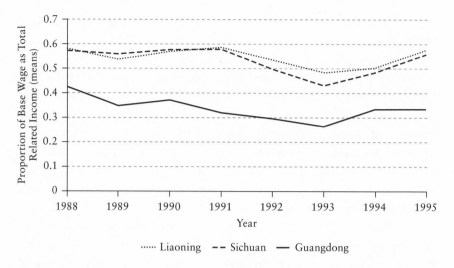

Figure 3.3   Declining importance of base wage among state and collective employees

was it the case that almost all urban residents relied solely on the state or the collective for employment and income. As a result of diversification in employment, shown in Table 2.1, an increasingly larger proportion of urban employees began working for non-state- or non-collective-owned organizations or as self-employed. Even among those who continued working in state- or collective-owned firms, there was an important change in the sources of their income.[8] Over time, the base wage, which is stipulated by government regulations, began making up a smaller share of the income employees received from their employers. In contrast to this decline, the income share coming from other labor-based sources, including bonuses, subsidies, and other wage incomes from employers, gained importance. Unlike state-stipulated wages, these work-organization-based incomes were directly linked to the economic performance of a worker's organization, with distribution mostly determined by the failure or success of the work organization. Figure 3.3 shows changes in the sources of labor-based incomes for the three provinces separately. Among employees of state- and collective-owned firms, all three provinces saw a decline in the share of base wage as total labor-related income. The decline was most pronounced in the early 1990s. In Liaoning and Sichuan, the share of base wage as total labor-based income dropped from close to 60 percent in 1991 to less than

50 percent in 1993, before a rebound in 1995. In Guangdong, as early as 1988, the share of base wage was already below the 50 percent line. The base wage share dropped further, to below 30 percent, in 1993.

The large share of income coming from state- and collective-owned work organizations not only represented an increasingly more important source for urban employees' rising incomes, it also has extremely important implications for the pattern of income inequality in urban China. As locales and work organizations are increasingly differentiated in their economic resources, and as these categories possess more and more economic power, they play an important role in income distribution, and therefore income inequality. This is the subject that will be further examined in the following chapters.

Another important source of income and income change is income-in-kind provided by the Chinese state and urban Chinese work organizations to their employees and their families. The income system under the socialist planned economy in China was essentially what the Chinese called a "low income, but high welfare" system. The low and relatively equal nominal income did not reflect fully the actual standard of living in urban China, because a much higher proportion of real income was provided in the form of welfare. Such welfare included free housing, free medical care, childcare, education, subsidized food in cafeterias at the workplace, entertainment (from reading materials to movies), pension, and even funeral expenses. Though varied from one workplace to another, in-kind income augmented urban residents' overall income by a large margin (Lardy 1984; Khan and Riskin 1998; Bramall 2001).

While collective welfare was a well-known feature of the urban Chinese socialist system, the exact amount of such income-in-kind was often difficult to measure, not only because of the numerous kinds and forms in which it appeared, but also because of the difficulty in attaching a fair market value to every subsidy received. Surveys of household income and expenditure, used in this study as a main data source, contained questions about the detailed sources of income. These surveys, however, still miss a major part of income-in-kind. One set of estimates of the difference between nominal income and actual income is provided by results from two large-scale income distribution surveys conducted in China in 1988 and 1995 (Griffin and Zhao 1993; Khan and Riskin 1998; Li Shi et al. 2000).[9] A wider definition of income, including more subsidies or forms of income-in-kind, led to an increase of 55 percent in the estimated per capita disposable household income over the official statistics in 1988 (Khan et al. 1993).[10] Similarly, by including housing subsidies, rental value of owner-occupied housing, and other net subsidies, the per capita household income level in 1995 was found to be 33 percent higher than that based on a more narrowly defined income definition (Khan and Riskin 1998, 233).

Urban economic reforms, while aimed at increasing the role of the market in distributing resources, were by no means effective in substantially reducing the role of subsidies in urban residents' overall income in the first decade of reforms. One analysis reports that, for instance, while urban per capita income rose by 2.83 times between 1990 and 1995, subsidies paid to urban residents also increased by 2.58 times during the same time period. As a result, the share of subsidies in total estimated income remained almost unchanged, at a level of 44 percent of the nominal income in 1990 and 41.74 percent in 1995 (Bramall 2001, 701).[11] What did change, however, was that welfare provision increasingly became associated with the degree of success of one's work organization, instead of the previously uniform allocation by the state. Such a change assigned a greater role to categories such as local cities and work organizations in distributing income to their members and thereby further increased the importance of these categories in creating urban income inequality. I shall return to this subject in detail in Chapters 4 and 5.

Housing and Consumer Durable Goods

The decade after 1985 was one of drastic income increases for urban Chinese but, more important, of real increases in the standard of living. The real benefits of rising income can be seen concretely in items that are closely related to urban residents' quality of life, such as housing space, quality, and ownership of consumer durable goods. In the mid-1980s, residents in most Chinese cities lived in crowded housing with few if any modern facilities. For the three provinces selected for detailed analyses, the average per capita living space in 1986 was barely above eight square meters. An average household of four, in other words, had two rooms on average, each 16 square meters in size. By 1995, the average per capita living space increased to 9.5 square meters, a 17 percent improvement, and by 2000, to 11.7 square meters, a 44 percent increase in a 15-year time span (see Table 3.5). The three provinces also differed, depending both on the absolute income level and the pace of change

TABLE 3.5
Improvements in housing space, three provinces, urban China, 1986–2000

Year	LIAONING		SICHUAN		GUANGDONG		COMBINED	
	Mean	S.D.	Mean	S.D.	Mean	S.D.	Mean	S.D.
1986	6.50	3.06	9.01	4.90	9.11	4.71	8.15	4.46
1987	5.79	2.64	9.27	5.05	10.33	6.05	8.40	5.08
1988	6.10	3.01	8.88	4.36	10.98	6.75	8.61	5.23
1989	6.25	2.83	9.30	4.30	11.49	6.89	8.99	5.31
1990	5.99	2.34	9.52	4.73	11.42	7.00	9.04	5.48
1991	6.31	2.82	9.79	5.04	12.50	7.41	9.47	5.88
1992	6.58	2.83	9.21	4.97	11.33	6.52	8.76	5.13
1993	6.68	2.93	9.48	5.21	11.84	6.67	9.11	5.39
1994	6.98	3.31	9.60	6.25	12.52	7.13	9.46	6.08
1995	7.19	3.39	9.95	5.76	12.65	6.86	9.56	5.73
1996	7.43	3.39	10.14	5.73	13.57	7.26	9.97	5.94
1997	7.53	3.46	11.06	5.62	13.65	6.96	10.39	5.85
1998	8.01	3.82	11.25	5.68	13.80	7.12	10.66	5.94
1999	8.29	3.85	11.32	5.63	14.17	7.45	10.88	6.02
2000	8.86	4.35	12.28	7.16	15.14	8.18	11.70	6.99

during the decade and a half. Liaoning remained the most crowded, with 6.5 meters at the beginning of the period and slightly below nine square meters per person at the end. Guangdong started with a lower density of 9.1 square meters per capita, a level achieved by the three provinces combined only a decade later, and ended with 15.1 square meters per person. By the end of the 1990s, the average urban resident in Guangdong had almost twice the living space as the average urban resident in Liaoning.

Not only did living space expand, the quality of housing also increased remarkably. One indicator of housing quality is whether the housing unit has sanitary facilities such as a toilet or a bathroom. In 1986, private toilets and baths were still a luxury in urban China, with only 12.7 percent of households in the three provinces having them. Three times as many, 37 percent of the households surveyed in these three provinces, did not have *any* toilet facilities. By 1995, nearly half (49.3 percent) of these households had acquired a private bath and toilet, and the percentage of households without access to toilet facilities had dropped to only 13 percent. By 2000, 58.9 percent of the surveyed households in these provinces had their own bath and toilets, and the percent without toilet facilities dropped to 7.3 percent.

Another indicator of housing quality, which is equally if not more important than sanitary facilities for a Chinese household, is a kitchen for its exclusive use. In 1986, one in seven (14 percent) of Chinese urban households lived in housing units with no kitchen facility, and 7.3 percent shared a kitchen with others. By 2000, these numbers had declined to 1.4 and 1.6 percent, respectively. Within urban Chinese kitchens, cooking also became easier and cleaner, as a major shift occurred during the decade in the type of fuel used by urban Chinese households. In 1986, the majority (64.3 percent) of urban Chinese households in these three provinces relied on coal for cooking inside their homes. By 2000, only 8.4 percent still used coal, and the majority of households had shifted to natural gas and propane as cooking fuel. These numbers, however, depict only the beginning of an upward trend in housing improvement in urban China.

Within urban Chinese homes, furniture and consumer durable goods also became common items. In 1985, only 17.21 percent of urban Chinese households owned a color TV and 6.58 percent owned a refrigerator; by the mid-1990s, color TV ownership virtually saturated urban Chinese households and two-thirds of households owned a refrigerator.[12] Most important of all private belongings is no doubt housing. In 1986, about 11 percent of the urban households surveyed in the three provinces reported that they owned their houses or apartments. By 1995, even before the major push to privatize urban housing, private housing ownership had risen to 37 percent of all surveyed urban households. By 2000, following the completion of housing reforms in 1998, nearly three quarters (74.2 percent) reported owning their housing units. This level of housing ownership based on three provinces is very close to the national figure for urban China based on the 2000 Population and Housing Census, which gives 72 percent for 2000 (Wang 2003).

GROWTH WITH INEQUALITY

Popular perception of rising inequality in post-socialist China derives largely from media reports that focused on the extremes: the richest and the most impoverished. The contrast between the two groups indeed depicts a picture of staggering differences in income and consumption. In a country where private ownership was virtually eliminated for decades and personal wealth was literally unknown until the early 1980s, *Forbes* magazine in 1994 could identify 17 individuals in mainland China with personal wealth over 100 million yuan (Yang 1997, 35). By the late 1990s, the average urban employee received a yearly income in the range of 15,000 yuan or less (less than 2,000 USD), whereas the richest urban Chinese are believed to possess personal wealth in the range of 10 billion yuan (over 120 million USD). Those urban Chinese who are trapped in the bankrupt state-owned enterprises and who could not find alternative employment received as little as 80 to 320 yuan per month, or less than 4,000 yuan per year (Yang, 2000).

Most residents in urban China, however, fall outside of the extreme ends of distribution. In this study, I focus on urban income inequality not among those at the extremes but those who make up the overall majority of the urban population. While the contrast between the very extremes tends to generate more social envy and ignite a sense of injustice, it is the experiences of those who form the majority of a society that best informs the magnitude of social and economic change. By relying mainly on household income and expenditure survey data, I examine in the following sections the trend, timing, and local variations in income inequality among the three provinces for the period between 1986 and 2000. In addition to income, another important measure of economic well-being is housing. Housing distribution occupied a particularly important position in well-being distribution under the socialist redistributive economy regime. Measures of housing inequality will also be included in this study.

Measuring Between-Group Income Inequality

Income inequality can be measured for different population groups and in many different ways (Allison 1978; Jenkins 1991; Deaton 1997). Evaluations of inequality level and trends can also differ, depending on the study population and inequality measures used. In order to make results truly comparable, consistency is required both in the study population and in measures. First of all, it matters who or what is the unit of the analysis, that is, whether it is the household as a whole, household member, or working persons (employee) in the household. Income differentials among different households result from earnings per household member and are subject to the influence of household demographic compositions. Measurement of per capita income, while taking into consideration the number of household members, does not reveal accurately income inequality in the workplace. Whereas using income among current employees avoids the problems associated with the other two units of analysis, it has its own limitations. Not all income derives from employment, and a person's true economic well-being is perhaps more closely associated with per capita income in the household than with per wage earner income.

Second, it also matters what measure is utilized. There are several measures for income inequality, but not all of them are equally useful (Allison 1978).[13] Among the most commonly used measures are the coefficient of variation (V), the Gini index (G), and the Theil index (T). Whereas all three provide a measure of inequality, the Gini index and the Theil index are used more frequently. The Gini index is popular due to its relationship to the Lorenz curve and has a bound between 0 and 1, where 0 means total equality and 1 means absolute inequality (i.e., all income possessed by one person or one group).[14] To allow comparisons, especially between urban China and other settings and time frames, this study uses the Gini index as one of the main income inequality measures.

To measure between- or inter-group versus intra-group inequality, this study relies more on the Theil index of income inequality. Developed by Henri Theil in 1967, such a measure allows the decomposition of inequalities (Allison 1978).[15] Unlike the Gini index, which is relatively insensitive to transfers at the extremes, the Theil index is more sensitive to transfers at the low end of the distribution. More important, because the focus of this study is not on the level but on the pattern or the distribution of rising income inequality, the decomposition feature of the Theil index is especially desirable. Overall inequality level can be decomposed into those between categories, such as between ownership types, industries, and locales, and those within each of the categories. In addition to these two measures, Gini and Theil, I will also use other measures, such as the ratio between the top and the bottom percentiles, which is an especially useful measure to examine the extremes of the income distribution.

Rising Inequality Level

The decade after 1985 was no doubt a decade of great reversal from China's earlier pursuit of equality. Results based on China's Urban Household Income and Expenditure Survey in the three provinces under study confirm those reported from other sources and reveal a drastic increase in income inequality in a decade's time. Tables 3.6 to 3.8 present year by year inequality measures calculated for each of the three provinces between 1986 and 2000, and for three separate study populations: all current employees, all residents (per capita), and all income earners. In addition to the commonly used Gini index, inequality measured by the Theil index is also given for each of the study populations, with all three provinces combined.

TABLE 3.6
Income inequality among urban Chinese employees, 1986–2000

	GINI INDEX				THEIL INDEX
Year	Liaoning	Sichuan	Guangdong	Combined	Combined
1986	0.1833	0.1829	0.2783	0.1992	0.0671
1987	0.1833	0.1843	0.2809	0.2143	0.0746
1988	0.2122	0.2220	0.2645	0.2601	0.1192
1989	0.2515	0.2186	0.2874	0.2941	0.1532
1990	0.1932	0.2209	0.2809	0.2713	0.1300
1991	0.2195	0.2074	0.2606	0.2841	0.1428
1992	0.2126	0.2245	0.3010	0.3067	0.1648
1993	0.2382	0.2639	0.3239	0.3507	0.2147
1994	0.2468	0.2883	0.3179	0.3696	0.2138
1995	0.2748	0.2635	0.3206	0.3639	0.2158
1996	0.2951	0.2672	0.3389	0.3828	0.2430
1997	0.3146	0.2756	0.3457	0.3821	0.2494
1998	0.3151	0.2891	0.3450	0.3877	0.2588
1999	0.3246	0.3090	0.3222	0.3951	0.2657
2000	0.3414	0.3199	0.3627	0.4012	0.2757

The rising trend in income inequality is clearly evident by any measure. Income inequality among current employees, measured by the Gini index, rose from 0.2 in 1986 to over 0.35 in 1995, an increase of 75 percent. Between 1995 and 2000, it went up further, to 0.4, doubling the level in 1986 (Table 3.6). The Gini index for all income earners and for household members rose even more, as both doubled in a decade's time (Table 3.7 and Table 3.8). While the overall trend suggested by these three measures is similar, the level of inequality differs depending on the study population or the unit of analysis.

Inequality is the highest among all income earners. The Gini index among this population shot up from 0.2 in 1986 to 0.4 by 1989, and by 1994, it reached a high level of 0.44 (Table 3.8). This measure shows the highest inequality because the study population (those with income) included income earners who were outside the labor force and whose incomes were more at the extremes. Income earners not only included employees in work organizations but also retirees, whose income tended to be lower, and persons with only non-employment sources of income, such as interest, rents, and transfer income.

Income inequality among current wage earners also rose quickly during the late 1980s. At the beginning of the period, income inequality within the

TABLE 3.7
Income inequality among urban Chinese residents, 1986–2000

| Year | GINI INDEX | | | | THEIL INDEX |
	Liaoning	Sichuan	Guangdong	Combined	Combined
1986	0.1630	0.1690	0.1594	0.1684	0.0479
1987	0.1562	0.1841	0.2190	0.2018	0.0731
1988	0.1640	0.2024	0.2357	0.2328	0.0930
1989	0.1707	0.2008	0.2454	0.2521	0.1107
1990	0.1478	0.1993	0.2368	0.2380	0.0995
1991	0.1767	0.2052	0.2342	0.2568	0.1141
1992	0.1772	0.2128	0.2666	0.2816	0.1466
1993	0.2016	0.2449	0.2796	0.3212	0.1841
1994	0.2261	0.2704	0.2815	0.3366	0.1997
1995	0.2374	0.2476	0.2718	0.3309	0.1698
1996	0.2406	0.2419	0.2805	0.3360	0.2003
1997	0.2533	0.2502	0.2919	0.3345	0.1998
1998	0.2574	0.2554	0.3041	0.3408	0.2073
1999	0.2607	0.2751	0.2809	0.3442	0.2053
2000	0.2839	0.2941	0.3123	0.3474	0.2075

workplace was quite low, at 0.20 measured by the Gini index. It rose to 0.26 in 1988 and to 0.29 in 1989, with an increase of nearly 50 percent in three short years (Table 3.6). Workplace income inequality increased further after 1990, reaching 0.37 by 1994 and 0.40 by 2000. Given that workplace inequality is more traceable, namely that it is linked to both individual and workplace characteristics, it is the best candidate to use in studying the structure of income inequality. This measure will therefore be our focus in the later parts of this study.

The absolute level of income inequality is lowest for per capita, or per household member, income. The Gini index was extremely low, at 0.17 in 1986. It rose to 0.25 by 1989, to 0.33 in 1995, and further to 0.35 by 2000 (Table 3.7). Such a relatively lower level of inequality in comparison to the levels for the other two populations shows the welfare equalizing effect of the household. The effect may be explained by households with fewer income earners nevertheless including more high-income-earning members per household than households with more income earners in total. It could also be because households with fewer income earners were also the ones with fewer members to support.

A comparison between the two measures of inequality, the Gini and Theil indices, reveals to some extent the underlying dynamics of the rising

TABLE 3.8
Income inequality among urban Chinese income earners, 1986–2000

| Year | GINI INDEX | | | | THEIL INDEX |
	Liaoning	Sichuan	Guangdong	Combined	Combined
1986	0.2325	0.1837	0.1893	0.2004	0.0684
1987	0.1833	0.1843	0.2809	0.2143	0.0746
1988	0.4133	0.2556	0.3271	0.3623	0.2449
1989	0.4527	0.2422	0.3829	0.4029	0.2965
1990	0.4084	0.2447	0.3242	0.3644	0.2429
1991	0.4108	0.2285	0.3248	0.3754	0.2586
1992	0.3860	0.2490	0.3937	0.4038	0.3064
1993	0.3937	0.2813	0.4069	0.4296	0.3374
1994	0.3939	0.3081	0.4092	0.4404	0.3497
1995	0.3976	0.2795	0.3953	0.4248	0.3260
1996	0.3874	0.2796	0.3978	0.4251	0.3288
1997	0.3803	0.2916	0.3941	0.4156	0.3143
1998	0.3734	0.3088	0.3811	0.4175	0.3137
1999	0.3669	0.3275	0.3510	0.4185	0.3099
2000	0.3761	0.3369	0.3799	0.4186	0.3116

inequality. As the numbers in Tables 3.6 to 3.8 show, for every study population, the rise in inequality measured by the Theil index is *much larger* than that measured by the Gini index. For every study population, the Gini index at most doubled over a 10-year period, but in all three cases the Theil index quadrupled or more than quadrupled. Recall that the Gini index is more sensitive to changes in the middle of the income distribution, whereas the Theil index is more sensitive to changes in the extremes, especially income transfers from the very poor to others in the population. What this comparison suggests, therefore, is that the process of polarization shaped rising income inequality in urban China *much more* than what is revealed by the Gini index. If measured by an index that is affected by income transfers between the extremes, as is the case with the Theil index, income inequality in urban China rose much faster than is suggested by using the Gini index. In the last section of this chapter, I will return to the issues of the poor and the rich.

Temporal Variations in Income Inequality

Rising income inequality in post-socialist urban China did not follow a linear trajectory. Two peaks of rising inequality stand out when we examine the contour of the rising income inequality in urban China after 1985.

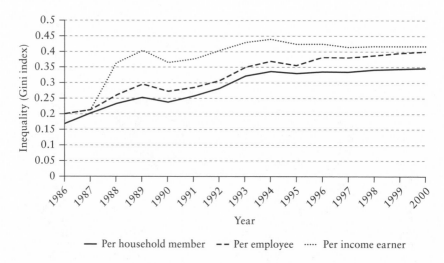

Per household member   – – Per employee   ····· Per income earner

Figure 3.4   Trends in urban income inequality, three measures, China 1986–2000

To facilitate detection of any trend, Figure 3.4 plots the Gini index for the combined sample for the three different study populations: employees, all residents, and income earners. As shown in Figure 3.4, the largest increase in income inequality occurred in the late 1980s, and then again after 1991. These two time periods also corresponded to the periods of most rapid income increase and heightened inflation. In other words, periods with more drastic reform efforts were also the ones that had highest inflation, income growth, and, most relevant to our investigation, inequality. Periods of radical economic reorganizations, in other words, also resulted in intense economic and social restratification.

The first rapid increase in inequality took place during the price reform and hyperinflation period in the late 1980s. In three short years from 1986 to 1989, the Gini index for urban employees' income rose from 0.20 to 0.29, an increase of 45 percent, and the Theil index, a measure that is more sensitive to income changes at the extremes than the Gini index, rose from 0.067 to 0.15; that is, it more than doubled (Table 3.6). For two consecutive years, 1988 and 1989, cost of living in the urban sectors of the three provinces also rose between 20 and 30 percent annually (see Figure 3.2).

Inequality rose not only because some urban residents were further left behind than others during the period of price inflation, but also due to a widely perceived increase in corruption associated with the price reforms.

Whereas some workers in profitable organizations received a share of the surplus income in the forms of bonuses and welfare provisions, their gains paled when compared with those few individuals who had access to power and control over resources at different levels. For the latter, they used their access to power and resources to obtain goods in government-set prices, and then sold these goods at the higher, market prices. The price reform thus gave rise to a new economic organization called the "briefcase company" and a new profession in the transitional economy, "handlers." These handlers differed from the earlier small vendors who moved goods from one locale to the other and made profits. For many of them, there was never the need to see the goods or to have the capital or a warehouse; all that was required was the ability to have the paperwork done. Not surprisingly, most of those who made a fortune by Chinese standards at the time were people who had access to redistributive powers. And not surprisingly, a disproportionately large number of those who had access were children, relatives, and friends of government officials and factory managers. The gains made in this designed loophole were sizable—an estimated 100 billion yuan in 1988 alone—and 70 percent of it went into the pockets of these individuals (He Q. 1998, 20). To put this estimated number into perspective: in the same year, 1988, the total wage bill for the 136.08 million employees in urban China was only 231.62 billion yuan.[16] In other words, a small number of well-connected individuals made what was equivalent to 30 percent of all urban Chinese employees' income in that year. Given that only a small number of privileged people benefited from this windfall of new wealth, the speed and pattern of private capital accumulation was shocking to most Chinese people, whose recent memory was the socialist egalitarian years.

What followed this initial rise in inequality was a noticeable break, indeed a reversal in rising inequality, which occurred between 1989 and 1990. A drastic rise in income inequality in a short period in the late 1980s, coupled with runaway inflation and widely perceived corruption in association with the dual-track pricing system, contributed to the massive demonstrations in Chinese cities in the spring of 1989. Deliberate government measures followed in the wake of the 1989 protests to quell the fear of rising inequality. The government slowed down measures of reform, put a brake on currency circulation and therefore inflation, and increased salary and wages of government employees and workers. An across-the-board salary increase for employees in government organizations and nonprofit (*shiye*) organizations was implemented in the fourth quarter of 1989. Citing low income in these organizations as a reason, everyone working in these organizations received a salary increase by one grade. Certain officials who had not had a salary increase for some time received additional pay raises (Zhu 2001, 27). It is likely that such moves led by state organizations set off a wave of comparable wage increases for other urban employees. As a result, compared with a net decrease in real income in most of urban China in 1989 (Guangdong being the exception), urban employees saw a real income increase in 1990 (see Table 3.2). Between 1989 and 1990, the degree of income inequality decreased in all three provinces. Whereas 1989 marked the peak of income inequality in the 1980s, the level of inequality in 1990 dropped to the level in 1988, a substantial change for one year.

The halt on increasing urban income inequality was only temporary, however. After creeping up somewhat between 1990 and 1991, the years following 1991 witnessed another period of escalating increase in inequality. Between 1991 and 1994, the Gini index of income inequality among urban employees rose from 0.28 to 0.37, an increase of 32 percent. It is the increase during this short time period that secured China's membership in the league of unequal societies in the world. This second phase of increasing inequality in urban China also occurred during a period of intensified economic reforms. In the beginning of 1992, fearing that the economic reform was slowing down and that it might eventually be sidetracked in the wake of the 1989 crackdown on student demonstrations, Deng Xiaoping toured the Special Economic Zone of Shenzhen and called for more rapid reforms. Throughout the 1990s, with the exception of one year, 1995, when there was a small dip in inequality level, the degree of income inequality for current employees and for residents increased consistently.

Variation among Three Provinces

The process of rising inequality in post-socialist urban China did not unfold uniformly in different parts of China. Regional heterogeneity persisted. Even with detailed data for only three provinces, such regional diversity is easy to detect. Provinces, though themselves large and heterogeneous internally, are the second highest level of administration, directly below the central government. Whereas the geographic boundaries of some provinces have changed over time, most provinces, including the ones in this study, have remained more or less in their current shape for centuries, if not more. The main exception in the provinces included here is the separation of Chongqing city from Sichuan province, which took place in 1997. As a result of history, both prior and after the socialist revolution in 1949, provinces not only differ in their local dialect, culture, overall level of wealth, but also in political and administrative traditions. Though not the best geographic unit for comparison and analysis, provincial differences do reveal the effect of local tradition as well as of government policies.

Guangdong is such an example. The province is not only distinguished by its gastronomical (Cantonese cuisine) and linguistic (Cantonese) uniqueness but also for its historical overseas merchants and its local Chinese culture that emphasized the role of lineage and ancestor worship. During China's reform era, it was a province that was given the green light to reform earlier than other provinces and was permitted to conduct a more liberal economic policy in the early 1980s (Vogel 1989). As a result, this province had a higher level of inequality than the other two provinces throughout the decade and, given the correlation between reform and inequality noted, an earlier date of rising inequality as well. The rise in inequality in Guangdong predated the other two provinces, from 1986 to 1987, rather than from 1987 to 1988. By the time the second phase of substantial inequality increase occurred after 1991, however, Guangdong was not exceptional from the national trend (see Figure 3.5).

The contours of rising inequality differed between the other two provinces. In both Liaoning and Sichuan, inequality rose after 1987. In Liaoning, it rose two years in a row, while in Sichuan the rise was only for one year. Perhaps as a result of the extended increase in Liaoning, the drop in inequality in 1990 was also more pronounced in Liaoning province in comparison to both Sichuan and Guangdong. In Liaoning, state-controlled industry occupied a more prominent position in the overall urban economy than in other provinces, and state policies such as government-implemented wage increases could therefore have been more effective when a halt in inequality was called for in 1989. The same ownership and industrial structure also led to the predicament of Liaoning being the province that suffered the most among the three when state-owned enterprises fell further into debt and experienced closures in the late 1990s. Inequality increase in

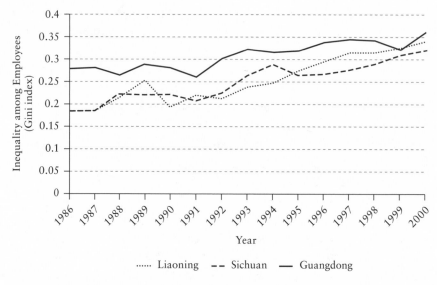

Figure 3.5 Trends in urban employee income inequality, three provinces, 1986–2000

Liaoning province was the fastest among the three provinces in the second half of the 1990s. What is also interesting is the lack of change in income differentials in Sichuan for most of the latter half of the 1980s. In fact, after an initial rise between 1987 and 1988, Sichuan was remarkably resilient to the pressures of increasing inequality for several years. Between 1988 and 1992, there were no substantial changes in income inequality observed among urban employees. It was not until after 1992 that Sichuan joined the other provinces in the march toward higher inequality.

There is a seeming inconsistency between the overall trend of the three provinces combined and the trends for different provinces in the rise of inequality. Whereas the overall trend is clear, marked by two periods of increases and one break, it is not so clear that every province followed the same stages, as shown in Figure 3.5. Moreover, when analyzed separately, the level of inequality for each province was also lower than that for the three provinces combined (see Figure 3.4). Such inconsistency is in fact a most fascinating feature of the rising inequality in China. The higher overall inequality level for the three provinces combined in contrast to each province alone is caused by inter-provincial inequality, a phenomenon that shall be examined in detail in Chapter 4.

HOUSING INEQUALITY

Although monetary income has been the most common measure used in the examination of social and economic inequality, under a socialist redistributive system where a "low wage, but high welfare" policy was pursued, welfare and especially housing provision is at least an equally important source of inequality. Studies of the state socialist system of redistribution often focused on housing rather than nominal income, because housing was the most important welfare item under state socialism and also the best measure to examine the redistributive processes under socialism (Szelényi 1978, 1983; Bian 1994). The logic, as first explained by Iván Szelényi, is that

> inequalities in administrative allocation, and inequalities arising from it, probably became inevitable when the wage policy was set. If wages are set officially to exclude the cost of housing and other public goods and services, then housing and other goods and services must obviously be allocated to all comers, including those with high incomes. If any of the services happens to be scarce—as new housing units must always be, since only a small fraction of the housing stock can be new each year—those scarce goods are always likely to be allocated to the most meritorious citizens in the most essential jobs, who tend to be those with the highest incomes. It could scarcely be otherwise. How could the state say to its rising managers and bureaucrats, 'If you get promoted you will reduce your housing chances'? (Szelényi 1983, 10)

In a pioneering study of urban inequalities under socialism, Szelényi and his colleagues were surprised to find that in Hungary in the late 1960s, newly constructed housing financed and built by the state was mostly allocated systematically by the government to the higher income groups (clerical workers, professionals, intellectuals, and bureaucrats). The bulk of the working class was conspicuously missing among the people who received housing allocation. Instead of fulfilling the socialist promise of providing housing to those who needed it, housing allocation clearly favored those close to the administrative or redistributive power. Individuals with higher occupational status occupied better housing units, were more likely to have bathrooms, and had better chances to upgrade their housing units, especially by receiving state-financed and state-built new housing units (Szelényi 1983). It was through the study of housing allocation in socialist cities, Hungary and elsewhere, that Szelényi and his colleagues came to the revelation and conclusion "that administrative allocation sometimes *reproduce[s]* the unequalizing market mechanism which it is supposed to replace and reverse" (Szelényi 1983, 9; italics by original author).

Welfare provision, including housing, similarly constituted a major portion of the total economic compensation package both before and during reforms for urban Chinese. As late as 1995, China's National Bureau of Statistics estimated that the average welfare benefits received per urban employee was 3,304 yuan, equivalent to 70 percent of the average yearly nominal income. Housing benefit was calculated at 1,960 yuan, by far the most important item among welfare provisions (Wang and Wei 1999, 539, footnote 1). Moreover, as it was in Hungary and other socialist countries, it is in housing that economic inequality generated by the redistributive system can be most clearly seen for urban China. In fact, the gap in housing benefit was greater than that in nominal income between officials and ordinary workers, not only under the planned economy system but well into the reform era as well. A survey conducted in 1995 by researchers at the Chinese Academy of Social Sciences found that the average wage income for heads in the public organizations was estimated 29 percent higher than that for the average technical workers. But the gap in housing benefits was significantly larger, 44 percent apart. The housing benefit received by those in the head's position would even make private entrepreneurs jealous: the benefits they received were 57 percent more than those enjoyed by the private entrepreneurs surveyed.[17] More telling, among the four categories of officials and technical professionals classified by the state, government officials enjoyed a more generous housing benefit than non-official professionals in every category. The estimated housing benefit difference between high-level cadres (department or *si/ju* level) and senior professionals and scientists (who belong to the same government stipulated category) was 44 percent; between middle-level cadres (division chief or *chu* level) and middle-level professional and technical personnel 11 percent; and between low-level officials (branch or *ke* level) and low-level technical personnel, 5 percent.[18]

Housing inequality over time can be examined by using a measure that is crude but useful: per capita housing space calculated from the household survey data. This measure captures only one dimension of housing conditions, namely space, but not other important dimensions such as location, construction materials, design, age, facilities, all of which reflect the quality of the housing. In the absence of a housing market prior to the mid-1990s

TABLE 3.9
Housing inequality in urban China

	GINI INDEX FOR PER CAPITA HOUSING SPACE			
Year	Liaoning	Sichuan	Guangdong	Combined
1986	0.2478	0.2608	0.2654	0.2712
1987	0.2350	0.2394	0.2900	0.2854
1988	0.2362	0.2374	0.2966	0.2885
1989	0.2188	0.2303	0.2966	0.2852
1990	0.1986	0.2301	0.2989	0.2946
1991	0.2272	0.2560	0.2975	0.3030
1992	0.2174	0.2615	0.2879	0.2826
1993	0.2248	0.2630	0.2865	0.2877
1994	0.2427	0.2767	0.2893	0.2981
1995	0.2317	0.2662	0.2744	0.2866
1996	0.2288	0.2677	0.2722	0.2894
1997	0.2314	0.2622	0.2549	0.2836
1998	0.2388	0.2598	0.2519	0.2795
1999	0.2409	0.2618	0.2570	0.2797
2000	0.2470	0.2894	0.2582	0.2928

SOURCE AND NOTE: China Urban Household Income and Expenditure Survey sample data. Only one person per household (head) is included for calculation to avoid problem of unequal weighting due to variations in household size.

in which price or value of the housing unit could be used to gauge housing inequality, space was among the few pieces of information that could be used. Such a measure was certainly useful, or at least more useful than it is after the mid-1990s, for two reasons. First, during most years prior to the mid-1990s, housing shortage was widespread for urban Chinese. Having a place to live, or to have a few extra square meters of living space, meant a lot more then. Housing space, in other words, represented the foremost criterion for housing condition. Second, while difference in quality certainly existed, for most urban Chinese, housing facilities were few and simple and quality of housing did not vary greatly before the mid-1990s. It was not until the late 1990s, when most urban housing returned to the hands of the individuals and when modern apartments and houses were built, that large differences in housing quality became prominent in urban China.

Similar to the diversity in rising income inequality, housing inequality also increased at a different pace and to different levels in different Chinese provinces. In Table 3.9, the Gini index for housing inequality for the three provinces for the years 1986 to 2000 is presented. Unlike the rapid increase in income inequality, however, a quick read of the results in the table reveals little change in housing inequality after 1985. The Gini index

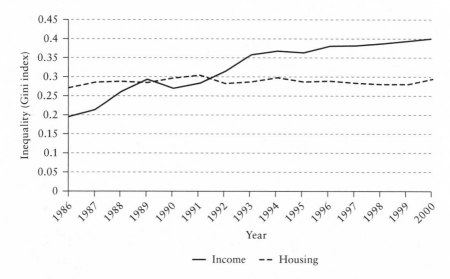

Figure 3.6   Divergence in housing and income inequality, urban China, 1986–2000

for per capita housing space stayed more or less constant around 0.30. Significant improvements in housing space (more than 40 percent overall; see Table 3.5) and conditions, in other words, were not accompanied by the same degree of rising inequality as in income up to the mid-1990s. As the numbers in Table 3.9 show, the Gini index for housing inequality went up somewhat between 1986 and 1987 but stayed largely unchanged in the following years. This trend holds for all three provinces combined and for each province individually. Moreover, unlike provincial differences in income inequality, where Guangdong stands out as the more unequal province compared with the other two, the differences in housing inequality by the mid-1990s were still much less pronounced across provinces compared to that in income.

The divergent trajectories of housing versus income inequalities during the decade can be seen more clearly when the two trends are plotted together, as shown in Figure 3.6. This figure reveals several important and interesting facts about the pattern and trend of urban inequality in China. First, it is important to notice that housing inequality at the beginning of the urban reforms was significantly *higher* than inequality in income. At the beginning of our study period, the Gini index for per capita living space was close to 0.3, whereas for per capita income it was only 0.17. For per capita income, it was not until 1992 that the Gini index rose to 0.28. Though the two measures, per capita housing space and annual income, are different in many aspects, the fact that there was more inequality in housing, the main welfare provision under socialism, than in nominal income confirms features of inequality under the socialist redistributive systems.[19] While both housing and income were determined by the socialist redistributive system, the redistributive bureaucracies controlled housing allocation much more closely, the single most important benefit. The inequality by design is clearly shown here.

Second, during the decade of reforms after 1985, while somewhat giving up control over income distribution, the redistributive bureaucracies in urban China continued their administrative grip over housing allocation. Although housing conditions in general improved, there was no clear sign of major changes in the mechanisms of public housing allocation. The same hierarchy remained.[20] Due to its prominence as the most expensive benefit, housing allocation was also the most sensitive issue and under more public scrutiny than income (it is easier to hide under-the-table income than extra apartments). Most work organizations published criteria for housing distribution and posted in the public lists of names that received new apartments. In many work organizations, both housing allocation criteria and selection of housing recipients were also submitted to the Labor Union or the Committee of Employee Representatives for approval or consultation.

Third, given the pattern of housing inequality both under and after socialism, it is highly unlikely that recent urban housing reforms will reduce the degree of urban inequality. In fact, if there is any major change, the privilege is likely to go to those with greater access to the redistributive power. This is so because only a very small fraction of the urban population, the truly rich, can afford to buy houses or apartments directly in the market at market prices. The price difference between market, or commodity, housing and the internal price, at which government and work organizations sell housing to their employees, was estimated at 7.69 to 1 in 1995 for 11 Chinese provinces. The ratio was 7.99 to 1 in Beijing, 5.47 to 1 in Liaoning, 12.50 to 1 in Sichuan, and 12.07 to 1 in Guangdong.[21] Among the average urban Chinese, those who were able to purchase housing, and especially to purchase large housing units, still needed to rely on heavy subsidies from their employers as of the mid-1990s. State-owned enterprises and organizations, therefore, were the main buyers in the housing market.

In Beijing, for example, over 85 percent of the sales in housing before 1995 went to these organizations. Even in 1996, 76 percent of the sales went to the public organizations (Wang and Wei 1999, 540). With privatization of urban public housing based on existing occupancy and current administrative rank, current inequality in a user's rights is being transformed into permanent inequality of ownership, including transfer right. Increasing housing inequality as a result of housing reforms has therefore put a permanent mark on inequality for future generations of the Chinese population.

THE RICH AND THE POOR

Rising inequality in urban China also led to the creation of the extreme groups in income distribution: the rich and the poor. The changes at the extremes are not merely a part of the overall inequality; they reveal the degree of economic polarization in the society. Given the limitations in the household survey data, namely that the richest and the poorest are both likely to be excluded in the sample, profiles of the rich and the poor in this study are no doubt understatements of the true contrast. Even with this limitation in data sources, however, much can still be learned by looking at the households and individuals who are between the two extremes of the surveyed households. The poor, in particular, is the group that merits the most attention, not only from the social scientists and policymakers but also the general population. The coexistence of great wealth on the one hand and abject poverty on the other raises a practical question concerning the lives of the poor but also an ethical question regarding social justice (Sen 1973, 1992).

Poverty can be conceptualized and understood in different ways. Poverty has been defined in many ways and by using different measures, such as income, consumption, or welfare, and defined as absolute compared to an established poverty line or as relative compared to the average state of the population. One common measure used in measuring absolute poverty in transitional socialist societies is the headcount of population falling below a poverty line, such as a minimum per capita income of US $4 per day (Milanovic 1998; Hutton and Redmond 2000). Another measure that has been applied for urban China is to calculate from income the calories needed to maintain a level of daily food energy: 2,100 kilocalories per capita per day for urban China in 1995, equivalent to 2,291 yuan annual income (Khan and Riskin 2001, 79–80).

Among the many measures of poverty, one used commonly and the one I shall rely on here is a measure of relative poverty. Unlike measures of absolute poverty, such as those measured by minimum income per day or amount of income needed to maintain a basic standard of food consumption, a relative poverty measure relates more closely to the concept of "prevailing standards of necessities," which has been elaborated on and advocated by political economists from Adam Smith to Amartya Sen. To Smith, who wrote in 1776, "Under necessities, therefore, I comprehend not only those things which nature, but those things which the established rules of decency have rendered necessary to the lowest rank of people." For Sen: "the measurement of poverty must be seen as an exercise of description assessing the predicament of people in terms of prevailing standards of necessities. It is primarily a *factual* rather than an ethical exercise when facts are related to what is regarded as deprivation" (quoted in Hagenaars 1991). In the following I shall focus on two measures of polarization and poverty: the average income at the two poles of income distribution, and changes in the population who fall under a relative poverty line.

Polarization

One common way to examine economic polarization is to compare the ratio of average income among those at the top 10 percent of the income distribution with that of those among the bottom 10 percent of the distribution. Figure 3.7 plots this ratio for urban employees for the period between 1986 and 2000. The figure gives the trend for the three provinces combined, as well as for each province. Given the large difference in income among the provinces (as shown earlier in this chapter), it is more meaningful to follow the change in each province, rather than the combined trend (e.g., one could be comparing top income earners in Guangdong with bottom earners in Liaoning).

The 1990s was a decade of emerging economic polarization in urban China. Beginning in 1991 and 1992, there was a clear trend toward further polarization. The income ratio between the top and the bottom 10 percent of wage earners rose from less than 3 in 1992 to more than 4 percent in 1995 and nearly 6 percent in 2000 for Liaoning; from 3 in 1992 to 5 percent in 2000 in Sichuan; and from slightly above 3 to almost 6 percent in Guangdong.

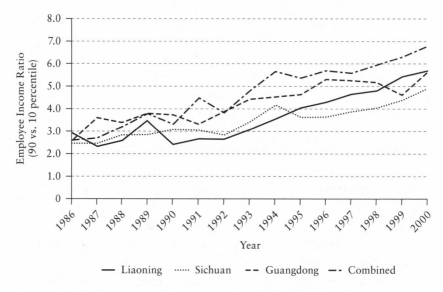

Figure 3.7   Changing income disparity, urban China, 1986–2000

The overall trend of income disparity between the top and bottom income earners, however, differs from that of income inequality. Throughout most years until 1992, while overall income inequality rose substantially in urban China, the ratio between the average incomes of top and bottom income earners remained relatively stable at 3 to 1. Similar to the income inequality trend, the overall level was higher in Guangdong than in Liaoning and Sichuan, and there was a sudden increase in the ratio for Liaoning and Sichuan for 1989 as well.

The quickening of economic polarization among urban Chinese employees was caused primarily by a faster income increase of the top income earners compared with those at the bottom, rather than an absolute decline of income among those at the bottom. As shown in Table 3.10, after 1992, income increase for the top 10 percent earners was in most cases much larger than the increase in the bottom 10 percent. The difference in several cases was 2 to 1 or more than 2 to 1. In Liaoning province, for example, the average annual income for the top 10 percent income earners rose by 24 percent in 1993, 43 percent in 1994, and 23 percent in 1995, compared with 7, 24, and 7 percent, respectively, for the bottom 10 percent for those years. Similarly, in Sichuan, the comparison between the two groups was 32 to 10 percent in 1993, 41 to 16 percent in 1994, reversed to 12 to 30 percent

TABLE 3.10
Income growth at the top and the bottom of the distribution
(rate of change over the previous year)

Year	LIAONING		SICHUAN		GUANGDONG		COMBINED	
	Top 10%	Bottom 10%	Top 10%	Bottom 10%	Top 10%	Bottom 10%	Top 10%	Bottom 10%
1987	−7	17	0	−1	42	−1	8	4
1988	44	29	30	14	74	85	58	34
1989	16	−14	10	9	31	19	24	5
1990	7	54	11	2	5	5	5	18
1991	6	−4	22	23	18	33	49	12
1992	14	15	6	14	44	23	−5	10
1993	24	7	32	10	38	20	39	10
1994	43	24	41	16	39	36	40	19
1995	23	7	12	30	18	15	17	23
1996	11	4	10	9	20	4	13	7
1997	11	2	14	8	9	11	6	8
1998	8	5	8	4	7	9	9	3
1999	8	−4	13	5	5	17	10	3
2000	25	19	8	−3	10	−9	9	1

in 1995, and 13 to 5 percent in 1999. When the there provinces were combined, the comparison between the two groups was 39 to 10 percent in 1993 and 40 to 19 percent in 1994, before dropping to 17 to 23 percent in 1995. In the late 1990s, the rate of income increase among the top 10 percent was generally twice that of the bottom 10 percent. Rising inequality, therefore, was driven mostly by the rich getting richer at a faster pace than the poor suffering a net decline in average income. Indeed, in only very few cases did the average nominal income for the bottom income earners decline in the decade.

Emergence of Urban Poverty

Whereas the income ratio between the rich and the poor shows the gap between the two groups in the society, the prevalence of poor or the degree of poverty shows another important aspect of a great social concern. This is so because an overall inequality measure could be produced by many different underlying distributions, such as one with more people near the lower end of the income distribution, and therefore more poverty, and another with more people in the middle but also more at the higher end of the distribution. What often matters is not only how unequal the income distribution is but also how many people live under conditions of poverty.

The relative poverty measure I adopt here is the percent of households

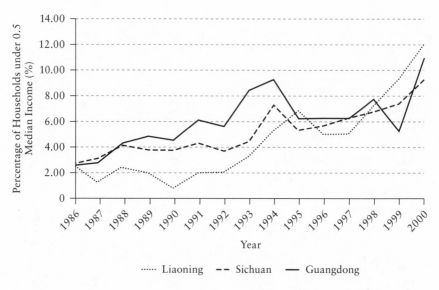

Figure 3.8   Rising urban poverty, province as reference, China, 1986–2000

who have less than 50 percent of the median income in the population. The 50 percent of median income is often used as the demarcation line for the poor (Hagenaars 1991; Smeeding 1991). Among several industrialized Western countries, for instance, the average percentage of poverty measured in such a way was 9.4 in the 1980s (Smeeding 1991, 48–49).[22] To calculate the prevalence of urban poverty in China after 1985, I use per capita household income of each household and compare that income to two references: the provincial and the city median income of a particular year. The household is used as the unit of analysis, as we assume the standard of living of an average urban resident is most closely related to this measure. Households with per capita income falling below the 0.5 provincial or city per capita household income median lines are aggregated, and the aggregated numbers are compared with the numbers of all households.[23] Provincial and city references, instead of that for the whole sample, are used because of the large income differences among provinces and cities. Using the national median income would lead to less than meaningful results. One such example is a study that estimated the urban poverty index (headcount ratio) for China. By using the national median income as the standard, the results show no change in national poverty rate between 1988 and 1995. At the

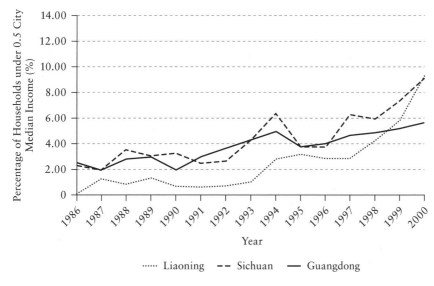

Figure 3.9   Rising urban poverty, city as reference, China, 1986–2000

same time, however, in the low-income Shanxi province, over 20 percent of the urban households were classified as in the poor group, whereas in high-income Guangdong province, less than 1 percent fall into the poor group (Khan 1999, 369).

Along with the overall increase in income inequality, urban relative poverty also emerged, as shown in Figures 3.8 and 3.9. At the beginning of the time period, poverty was at an extremely low level in urban China, at 3 percent or less for 1986 and 1987. The poverty measure rose subsequently, especially in Guangdong. It was not until the 1990s, especially after 1992, however, that urban poverty saw its first rapid increase. The measure rose from 6 percent in 1992 to above 9 in 1994 before a drop in 1995 in Guangdong, and from 3 to more than 7 percent for Sichuan. For Liaoning, a province that maintained a very low level of poverty throughout the 1980s, the rise in poverty since 1992 was not only consistent with the rise elsewhere but also the most rapid. In three years, the poverty ratio using the provincial reference line more than tripled from 2 to 7 percent (Figure 3.8). Urban poverty took another sharp upward turn after 1997. By 2000, the poverty ratio in the three provinces rose to 10 percent or a higher level.

Given the large income difference among cities within each province, a poverty ratio using the city median income as the reference point makes more sense in gauging the living conditions of the poor. These city-based ratios, as shown in Figure 3.9, portray a level of poverty that is somewhat lower than the province-based calculations, as one might expect. The trend, however, is generally very much the same. For most years during the decade after 1986, poverty measured by the indicator here remained low. For Guangdong and Sichuan, the prevalence was mostly only between 2 and 3 percent until 1991 (until 1992 for Sichuan). The rise in poverty in these two provinces occurred mostly after 1992, when the prevalence level doubled or more than doubled to 5 percent and above. Liaoning followed a somewhat different trajectory. Poverty prevalence remained at an extremely low level of about 1 percent until 1993 and then shot up to over 3 percent by 1995 (Figure 3.9).

The rise of urban poverty up to the mid-1990s in these three provinces, especially in Liaoning, was only the beginning of a worsening trend. Enterprise reforms and bankruptcies of state-owned enterprises only started at a large scale around the mid-1990s. An estimate by China's National Federation of Trade Unions gave the number of 6.92 million workers whose wages were stopped or reduced or who were forced into early retirement as of 1995. Reports of unemployment after 1995, though vastly diverse in their estimated numbers, all confirm a rapidly rising trend (Solinger 2001a). One estimate argues that if one takes into consideration the pervasive disguised unemployment in urban China, the real unemployment in the late 1990s was already at 10 percent, not the 2.8 percent of the official unemployment rate (Zhang and Wei 1999, 413). Unlike private entrepreneurs or rural migrant labors who are self-selected to enter the urban labor market, the combination of personal life experiences of the urban laid-off workers and the failure of the state in providing effective support have made these workers' reentry into the labor market extremely difficult (Solinger 2002). Along with the rise in overall inequality, urban poverty, fueled by rising urban unemployment, became a prominent feature of the urban social scene and a major concern for policymakers as well as the population.

The closing years of the twentieth century indeed saw sharp increases in poverty in urban China. Such a rapid increase in poverty removed China from the group of most egalitarian countries in the world. As shown in Figure 3.9, in Guangdong province, using the city median as the reference line, the poverty measure rose from 4 percent in 1996 to 6 percent in 2000. In

Sichuan, urban poverty rose from 4 to close to 10 percent. The most rapid increase was in Liaoning, a province hardest hit by reforms. Urban poverty shot up from 3 percent in 1996 and 1997 to close to 10 percent in 2000. Such poverty levels in urban China by the end of the 1990s were well above those of the Nordic countries (mostly below 7 percent), roughly the same as those of Canada (11.4) and Spain (10.4), and approaching those in Italy (13.9) and the United Kingdom (13.2) but still below those of the United States (17.8) (Smeeding, Rainwater, and Burtless 2001, 186). Whereas urban China's poverty levels did not experience the kind of rise as those which occurred in a large number of Eastern European countries due to income decrease in those countries,[24] its record of poverty containment in the context of rapid economic and income growth was by no means admirable. Urban China's poverty level at the end of the 1990s, using comparable measures, was only on par with what was found in Hungary (9.0), Slovakia (10.9), Bulgaria (12.6), and Poland (13.5) in the early 1990s (Emigh, Fodor, and Szelényi 2001, 18).

The decade after 1985 was a decade that fundamentally changed the equality nature of the urban Chinese society. At the beginning of the decade, the features of the socialist redistributive system were still clearly evident: a very low level of income inequality among urban employees and their family members, coupled with a higher degree of inequality in welfare provision such as in housing. Over the decade, income inequality rose rapidly, between nearly doubling to quadrupling, depending on the measure used and the location examined. In the latter half of the 1990s, measures of income inequality, especially measures of polarization and poverty, showed a further worsening trend. All signs, regardless of measure and location, confirm the fundamental shift in the degree of inequality in urban China.

The trajectory of escalating income inequality dovetailed closely with the unfolding of economic and social reforms, which aimed to dismantle the socialist planned economy system in urban China. The two short time periods within the decade during which income inequality increased most significantly occurred first between 1987 and 1989 and then again after 1992. The first of these periods coincided with reforms in the price system, and the second followed adoption of drastic reform measures, allowing public organizations to operate their own businesses and encouraging the rise of non-public economic sectors. Income inequality also rose earlier and remained at a higher level in Guangdong, a province that reformed earlier and with a greater depth, than in Sichuan and Liaoning. By the end of the decade, however, the level of inequality quickly converged for the three provinces examined in this study, and Liaoning province, with its heavy economic baggage associated with a large number of insolvent state-owned enterprises and rising urban unemployment, registered the fastest rate of increase, in both income inequality and in urban poverty.

What lies underneath this quick shift from equality to inequality has yet to be explored. Have the sweeping changes mandated by the economic reform measures affected everyone in urban Chinese society equally? What has happened to the pre-reform era institutional arrangements that defined urban inequality under socialism? Have they been swept away, or have they morphed into and reemerged in new forms? With the rapid rise in inequality, what categories serve as the institutional basis of urban inequality now? Moreover, what do the changes in social categories that define inequality in the Chinese case tell us about social inequalities in general? It is through the answers to these and other questions that we begin to understand the patterns and structures of social inequality. And it is the answers to these questions that form the topics for the subsequent two chapters of this book.

CHAPTER FOUR

Enlarging Inequality: Categories

What truly defined the trajectory and pattern of rising inequality in China was not just the inequality as manifested in the rising numbers of the rich or poor but the drastically enlarged income gaps across different social categories. Chief among these social categories are urban and rural China, the two sectors that effectively followed two different economic and social systems under socialism. Within the urban sector, which is the focus of this book, other categories largely defined the extent of and trend in income inequality. As introduced in Chapter 2, these categories include different locales, ownership types, industries, and most importantly, work organizations; they also include social categories that transcend geographic and institutional boundaries, such as gender, seniority, and occupational group. These category-based inequalities represent the most salient features of rising inequality and are key to understanding the underlying political economy and social structures that define inequalities in post-socialist China.

Relying primarily on data collected for the urban sector of three Chinese provinces, this chapter decomposes the rising income inequality in urban China into that *between* categories with clear geographic and institutional boundaries and that *within* these categories. A clear picture emerges that the most prominent feature defining rising income inequality in urban China during this time period was the rising importance of categories. This chapter also examines in detail what categories, with or without clear geographic boundaries, affected income inequality and how their roles changed over time.

To examine the roles of social categories in enlarging urban inequality in China, I divide the task into two parts in this chapter. The first part is what can be called descriptive, with the aim of establishing the fact that inter-group inequalities accounted for an important and increasingly larger portion in the overall rise of urban income inequality. The second part can be viewed as more analytical, where I present results of statistical analyses under the heading of the patterns of inequality. In order to ascertain the roles of the categories in creating income inequality among individuals, the task here is to differentiate the effects of categories, such as locales, work organizations, and gender, from that of individual characteristics, such as educational attainment, age, and length of employment. It is in this part where the sociological interpretations are examined against the more economics-oriented interpretations of rising inequality, as reviewed in Chapter 1.

TRENDS IN CATEGORICAL INEQUALITY

The examination of categorical sources of inequality in this section encompasses the following categories: urban versus rural sectors, provinces, cities, ownership sectors, industries, and work organizations.

Urban/Rural Differences

Before moving into examinations of categorical sources of income inequality in urban China, it is important, for the purpose of understanding categorical sources of inequality in general, to review briefly recent changes in the most glaring categorical difference in income in China. This is the difference between urban and rural sectors, the two largest groups in China.[1] After more than two decades of reforms, this most prominent gap has yet to close. In fact, the urban-rural divide remains the largest divide in contemporary Chinese society. Excluding the huge subsidies to urbanities in terms of housing, food, medical insurance, pension, and urban infrastructure, official figures of yearly per capita income at the eve of economic reforms, 1978, were 343.4 yuan for urban households and 133.6 yuan for rural households—a ratio of 2.57 between urban and rural households (NBS 2000, 312). This income gap narrowed initially, following the government policies of increasing prices for agricultural goods and of allowing peasants to engage in non-collective income-generating activities. In 1985, the income gap between urban and rural Chinese dropped to below 2 by 1985, as shown in Table 4.1.

TABLE 4.1

Annual per capita household income, urban and rural China, 1985–2000

| | NOT ADJUSTED FOR INFLATION | | | | | ADJUSTED FOR INFLATION | | | | |
| | INCOME (YUAN) | | | ANNUAL CHANGE | | INCOME (1985 PRICES) | | | ANNUAL CHANGE | |
Year	Urban	Rural	Ratio U/R	Urban (%)	Rural (%)	Urban	Rural	Ratio U/R	Urban (%)	Rural (%)
1985	739.1	397.6	1.86	—	—	739.1	397.6	1.86	—	—
1986	899.6	423.8	2.12	22	7	840.7	399.4	2.10	14	0
1987	1002.2	462.6	2.17	11	9	861.0	410.5	2.10	2	3
1988	1181.4	544.9	2.17	18	18	841.1	411.6	2.04	–2	0
1989	1375.7	601.5	2.29	16	10	842.2	380.9	2.21	0	–7
1990	1510.2	686.3	2.20	10	14	912.9	415.7	2.20	8	9
1991	1700.6	708.6	2.40	13	3	978.2	419.5	2.33	7	1
1992	2026.6	784.0	2.58	19	11	1073.3	443.4	2.42	10	6
1993	2577.4	921.6	2.80	27	18	1175.7	458.5	2.56	10	3
1994	3496.2	1221.0	2.86	36	32	1275.7	492.3	2.59	9	7
1995	4283.0	1577.7	2.71	23	29	1337.9	541.4	2.47	5	10
1996	4838.9	1926.1	2.51	13	22	1389.3	612.6	2.27	4	13
1997	5160.3	2090.1	2.47	7	9	1437.0	648.5	2.22	3	6
1998	5425.1	2162.0	2.51	5	3	1519.9	677.5	2.24	6	4
1999	5854.0	2210.3	2.65	8	2	1661.6	703.2	2.36	9	4
2000	6280.0	2253.0	2.79	7	2	1782.5	716.8	2.49	7	2
1999/1985	8.5	5.7	1.50	—	—	2.4	1.8	1.30	—	—

SOURCES: Income: NBS 2000, 312; NBS 2002, Table 10-2. Price: NBS 2002, 290, Table 9-1.

The trend of narrowing urban and rural income inequality seen in the late 1970s and early 1980s was soon reversed. Urban economic reforms brought in an unprecedented flow of capital investment, almost exclusively to Chinese cities, beginning in the early 1980s. At the same time, these urban reforms gradually allowed and even encouraged urban-based institutions to use their organizational resources to benefit their employees. Partly as a result of these changes, income increase among urban Chinese soon far outpaced that of rural Chinese. As the official statistics presented in Table 4.1 show, between 1985 and 2000, annual increase in income was faster in urban than in rural areas in 10 out of the 15 years when inflation is not taken into account, and in 9 out of 15 years when inflation is taken into consideration. Moreover, due to large discrepancies between the magnitude of income increase in the mid-1980s and again in the early 1990s between urban and rural China, the cumulative income gains for urban Chinese over the 15 years was an over 8 times increase in nominal income, compared with a less than 6 times increase for rural Chinese. Adjusted for inflation, urban Chinese saw its citizens' real income increase by more than double, or 2.4 times, compared with 1.8 times for rural Chinese. By the mid-1990s, the urban-rural income gap had returned to that of the pre-reform era of the late 1970s.

The persistent and indeed increasing income gap between city and countryside is the most important source of *overall* income inequality and *increasing* inequality for China. As reported in a World Bank study, for China as a whole, "the rural-urban income gap explained one-third of total inequality in 1995 and one-half of the increase in inequality since 1985" (World Bank 1997, 3). If urban public subsidies, which could augment urban incomes by as much as 80 percent, are included in the calculations, "rural-urban disparities accounted for more than half of total inequality in 1995 and explain even more of the increase since 1985." Inequality between urban and rural China is staggering, as the World Bank study comments, "Internationally, the urban-rural income ratio rarely exceeds 2.0—as it does in China—and in most countries it is below 1.5." Moreover, because of the extensive urban public subsidies, "even China's high ratio fails to capture the full extent of disparities in living standards between city dwellers and rural residents" (World Bank 1997, 3). Results from two multi-province surveys, one in 1988 and another in 1995, confirm this conclusion. As two principal scholars responsible for these surveys, Khan and

TABLE 4.2
Income inequality within China's two largest
groups: rural and urban (Gini index)

Year	Rural	Urban	Ratio (rural/urban)
1979/80	0.31	0.16	1.94
1988	0.34	0.23	1.45
1995	0.42	0.33	1.25
2001	0.38	0.32	1.19

SOURCES AND NOTE: 1979/80: World Bank 1983, 83–95.
Later revised estimates by the World Bank put rural level at 0.32
for 1978, 0.28 for 1979, and 0.26 for 1980 (Ahmad and Wang,
1989); 1988: Khan et al. 1993, 61; 1995: Khan and Riskin 1998,
237, 241; 2001: Khan and Riskin 2005, 382.

Riskin, concluded: "Inequality between urban and rural China dominates inequality within both populations in 1995, as it did in 1988. That is, the Gini ratio for China as a whole is higher than it is for either rural or urban China" (Khan and Riskin 1998, 247).

After a decade-long increase in inequality in both urban and rural areas, urban China as a whole still enjoys a greater degree of equality than rural China. This comparison is shown in Table 4.2. Although the urban-rural gap in the degrees of *within-group inequality* has been closing in the two decades since 1980, urban China as a whole has always been more equal than rural China. On the eve of China's urban reforms in the late 1970s, income inequality within urban China was only about half of that in rural China, 0.16 versus 0.31, as measured by the Gini index. Urban inequality has risen faster than rural inequality in recent years, however, as recently as in 2001, urban China as a whole was still the more equal segment of the society. Moreover, inequality within Chinese cities, or intra-city inequality, accounted for only a very small portion of the overall income inequality in China. A World Bank study estimated that in 1995, inequality within urban areas accounted for only 10 percent of overall income inequality (World Bank, 1997). Due to rising urban-rural income gaps, China's overall income inequality level remained unchanged in the second half of the 1990s, despite an observed small decline in the level of inequality both within rural and urban areas, especially within China's rural sector (Khan and Riskin 2005, 358).

The difference between urban and rural China is largely a function of the differential social and economic systems in China, as discussed in

Chapter 2. In urban China, a more egalitarian system was implemented with the backing of the state-run economy. In rural China, by comparison, local variations in natural environment and hence in agricultural production under a collective economy inevitably meant a greater degree of income differential. The relatively higher degree of equality in urban China, moreover, testifies to the success of China's socialist system in the past in creating an egalitarian society within this segment of the society.

Inter-provincial Inequality

A major source of inequality and the rise of inequality in urban China can be explained by inequalities between other lower-level categories. The first subnational category is the province, a category often used to describe the widening regional disparities (e.g., Hu, Wang and Kang 1995). The 1997 World Bank Report concludes that inter-provincial inequality accounted for *over a quarter* of the total inequality in 1995 and *over a third* of the increase in inequality between 1985 and 1995. These numbers convincingly show the dominance of the largest groups, urban versus rural areas and provinces, in shaping inequality in China. Together, urban-rural and inter-provincial sources account for *over half* of all inequality in China in 1995 and over *80 percent* of the rise in inequality since 1985. What these numbers also suggest is that if one lives only in an urban or only in a rural area, but stays in the same province, the inequality one observes or feels within his or her social space is *no more than half* of what the overall inequality measures imply.

Within China's urban sector, a similar pattern as that which drove the national inequality increase has emerged. Rising income inequality in urban China is largely a product of rising inter-category inequality. Figures 4.1 and 4.2 show the rising importance of inter-provincial income inequality among urban employees in China for the 15-year period under study.[2] Inequality not only sharpened between different regions, as shown in the World Bank numbers (which included both urban and rural sectors) but also among the urban sectors of different provinces. Among China's 30 provinces covered by the urban household survey, the share of inter-provincial inequality as total income inequality among Chinese urban employees increased from 9 percent in 1986 to 26 percent by 1993 (Figure 4.1). Inter-provincial inequality stayed at this level for several years, until the end of the 1990s, when it began to show some signs of decline. Among the three

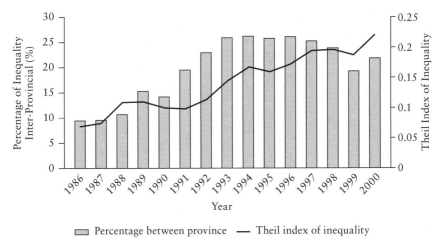

Figure 4.1   Rising inter-provincial inequality, urban China, 1986–2000

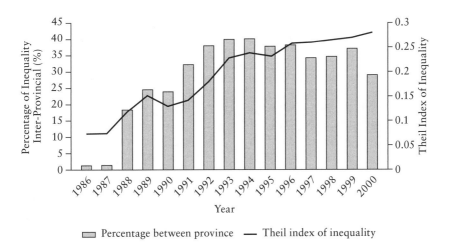

Figure 4.2   Rising inter-provincial inequality, three urban provinces, 1986–2000

provinces examined in detail in this study, the share of inter-provincial income inequality as overall income inequality rose even more drastically, from less than 2 percent in 1986 and 1987, to close to 25 percent in 1989, to over 40 percent in the early 1990s, and stayed at a level of between 30 and 40 percent in the second half of the 1990s (Figure 4.2). One main reason for the more rapid increase among the three provinces is the province of

Guangdong. Over the decade after the mid-1980s, Guangdong stood out as a province with an average urban employee income well above most other provinces in China, including Liaoning and Sichuan, examined in detail in this study (see Chapter 3, Table 3.4).

Inter-city Inequality

Unlike provinces whose population size varies from a few million to nearly a hundred million in China, cities are much smaller and more meaningful political economy units that both generate local economic growth and maintain boundaries in shaping inequality. Chinese cities were largely products of a socialist urbanization process that served primarily the need of a socialist industrialization program. Under socialism, formerly existing cities grew or withered and new cities emerged according to the need of the planned economy. Cities, in other words, existed largely as units of socialist production. The fact that cities existed as such means, on the one hand, that their role as organizational units for economic development continued or actually expanded in the post-socialist transformation. On the other hand, cities as products of socialist industrialization also pre-defined each city's relative position vis-à-vis others in both economic growth and income distribution.

Post-socialist transformations have resulted in not only much increased economic differentiations among Chinese cities but also in a pattern of inequality in which inter-city inequality makes up a major portion of the overall inequality level. Moving below the large provincial categories to cities, a similar if not more pronounced trend of increasing inequality between categories emerges. As shown in Figures 4.3 and 4.4, at the same time that the overall inequality index (the Theil index) increased by three- to fourfold—from less than 0.07 to over 0.19 for all cities and to 0.27 for cities in the three provinces in a decade's time (follow the right vertical axis)—the share of inequality that is inter-city also doubled for all cities—from 17 in 1986 percent to 33 percent in 1996 (Figure 4.3).[3] Among cities in the three provinces, the inter-city share rose even more, by fivefold, from 10 percent in 1986 to 50 percent in the mid-1990s (follow the left vertical axis in Figure 4.4). By the mid-1990s, in other words, *one-third to one-half of all urban income inequality could be accounted for by the city's geographic location alone.* In the latter half of the 1990s, the share of inter-city inequality as total income inequality among urban employees remained at a

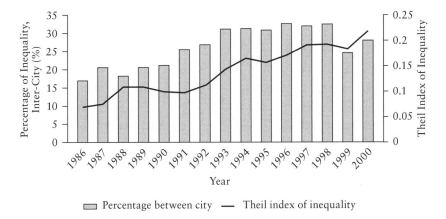

Percentage between city   — Theil index of inequality

Figure 4.3   Rising inter-city inequality, urban China, 1986–2000

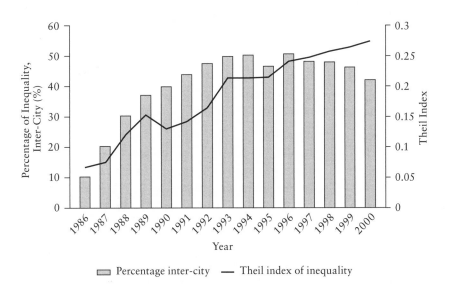

Percentage inter-city   — Theil index of inequality

Figure 4.4   Rising inter-city inequality, three urban provinces, 1986–2000

high level of 30 percent for all cities, and 40 to 50 percent for cities in the three study provinces.

Such a high level of geographic segregation is one of the most salient features of the emerging pattern of inequality in post-socialist urban China. What is most spectacular is not that cities have grown apart in their economic levels or that all urban Chinese no longer enjoy the same chances of employment and the same level of economic well-being but that a major source of inequality can be traced to the role of the cities. Cities have emerged as a political economy unit in engineering growth and as a more prominent social category in defining inequality. The role of the city as an income-determining category exists regardless of the characteristics of the individuals living in them, as will be shown in a later section of this chapter. The city's role as an increasingly prominent political economy unit will also be further examined in the next chapter.

Inter-ownership Type and Inter-industry Inequality

Two other categories in urban China also play important roles in shaping the pattern of urban income inequality: ownership type of a work organization, and the industry one belongs to. These two categories were central channels for resource allocation under the planned economy system (as discussed in Chapter 2) as well as important institutional sources of inequality in the post-socialist era. Table 4.3 gives the share of these two factors in the decomposition of urban income inequality after the mid-1980s for the three provinces.

Ownership type accounted for a significant share of urban income inequality, though considerably less than does the role of geographic location. For the three provinces combined, the share of income inequality index accounted for by ownership type was about 6 percent in the mid-1980s. The share dropped to below 4 percent at the end of the 1980s and edged back to over 7 percent by the middle of the 1990s. The three provinces differ, however, in the importance of this categorical variable. In both Liaoning and Sichuan, ownership type played a more important role than in Guangdong. In these two provinces, ownership type alone accounted for around 10 percent or more of income inequality. Moreover, whereas the earlier inter-ownership income differences were mainly due to the advantage of the state sector over the collective sector, by the mid-1990s, inter-ownership income inequality was driven both by higher incomes in the non-state and non-collective sectors and by the differences between the state and the collective sector (see also Chapter 2, Table 2.2).

Industry also served as an important category in shaping urban income inequalities in China. Its share in overall income inequality dropped from around 8 percent in the mid-1980s to around 4 percent throughout most of the decade. It rose in 1994, then dipped again to around the 5 percent level

TABLE 4.3

Shares of income inequality (percentage of Theil index), ownership type and industrial sector, urban China, 1986–2000

Year	OWNERSHIP TYPE				INDUSTRY			
	Liaoning	Sichuan	Guangdong	Combined	Liaoning	Sichuan	Guangdong	Combined
1986	11.3	5.4	6.8	6.3	13.4	7.6	6.8	6.4
1987	5.3	13.3	4.1	6.3	3.0	7.6	6.6	4.5
1988	13.0	11.0	3.0	5.6	4.9	2.9	4.8	1.8
1989	8.6	11.0	2.8	3.4	2.2	6.3	4.4	3.4
1990	9.8	14.6	2.8	3.6	2.2	7.1	4.9	3.4
1991	7.5	10.5	1.5	3.6	2.8	3.9	3.5	2.5
1992	10.4	16.7	2.7	5.2	4.3	5.0	3.8	4.6
1993	12.2	14.3	3.5	7.1	3.1	5.5	4.5	4.3
1994	9.9	14.0	6.0	7.1	5.4	12.1	9.2	6.7
1995	8.7	12.5	5.1	6.8	3.4	10.2	7.4	4.6
1996	7.5	11.8	7.6	7.9	4.9	7.1	5.9	4.0
1997	9.6	6.6	6.5	7.9	5.1	5.5	4.5	2.1
1998	8.1	9.1	7.2	7.2	4.4	10.9	6.3	3.5
1999	8.1	9.7	7.3	7.1	8.0	14.2	5.5	3.6
2000	9.9	12.2	5.5	7.7	7.3	13.3	4.3	4.8

for all three provinces combined. The degree of inter-industry inequality also varies by province. Similar to inter-ownership-type inequality, urban Sichuan province again appeared to be the most segregated across different industries. Starting in 1994, inter-industry inequality in most years accounted for over 10 percent of the total income inequality. In Guangdong province, inter-industry inequality was also highly prominent in 1994, accounting for nearly 10 percent of the overall inequality level in that year.

Work Organizations

Of the categories that define income inequality in urban China, work organization is no doubt the one that is the most intimately relevant. Work organizations are the foci where both income generation and welfare distribution take place. Chinese work organizations, as discussed in Chapter 2, were largely the creation of the socialist planned economy overlaid on the Chinese collective-oriented society. During China's post-socialist transformation, work organizations, while reducing their roles in social control and political mobilization, have expanded their roles in income generation and distribution as independent economic organizations with much increased freedom compared with the socialist planned economy era.

In contrast to the relatively rich data sources that allow the examination of inequality within and between geographic and industrial categories as shown here, much less suitable data are available to track systematically the changing roles of work organizations. While cases demonstrating the role of work organization in income distribution are abundant, as will be shown in the next chapter, there are only a few surveys that included information on both individuals and their work organizations. What these limited data sources show, nevertheless, is a picture not unlike the one we have just seen. Work organizations are a crucial source of income determination.

Among the few existing data sources that are available to evaluate the role of work organizations in income determination by decomposing inequality into between- and within-organization sources is a survey conducted in 1993. The survey of Chinese work organizations covered nearly 100 work organizations in 10 cities across China (10-City Survey), with about 40 employees interviewed from each work organization.[4] By partitioning the variance of individual incomes into within-organization and between-organization components, we find that 53 percent of the total variance in income was at the individual level, and 47 percent at the organizational level.[5] Work organizations, in other words, were as important as different individual characteristics in accounting for income differences, such as a person's political affiliation, work experience, and educational background. In the next section of this chapter, I will return to a more in-depth examination of the sources of inter-organizational income differences. In particular, I will address the question of the relative extent to which the inter-organizational difference is due to having individual employees of different traits or to the organizations themselves. Moreover, I will examine why and how work organizations play their roles in creating and maintaining inequality.

Another more in-depth study designed specifically for testing the role of work organizations in inequality is the doctoral dissertation research by Wang Gao (1998).[6] The study was based on a survey conducted in 1996 that covered 20 out of the 80 medium- to large-sized enterprises in the city of Mudanjiang in Heilongjiang province, a province in Northeast China that is adjacent to Liaoning, included in this study. Wang's study collected information on work organizations as well as on 1,209 employees in these organizations. Using multilevel analytic models, Wang reported a similar finding to that of the 100 work organizations already mentioned, but in this case restricted to one city. Of the total variance explained among these employees' incomes in 1996, over 50 percent could be attributed to work organizations and the rest to individual characteristics.[7] Work organizations in this case, as in the earlier 10-City Survey carried out in 1993, similarly form a prominent source of income and inequality generation. What matters in post-socialist urban China is not just the traits such as educational attainment and skills an individual possesses but also in what organization the individual is employed.

PATTERNS OF INEQUALITY

The income differences shown here across locales, ownership types, industries, and work organizations are nevertheless *not* sufficient to demonstrate fully the role of categories in defining income inequality in urban China. With the exception of the few analyses that explicitly separate group from individual effects, it is not clear to what extent the observed income differences among categories are due to the roles of these and other structural locations, or "empty places," and to what extent they are due to individuals who happen to occupy these structural locations. For instance, it is entirely plausible that the higher incomes observed in certain cities, industries, or work organizations originate from the fact that better endowed and more productive individuals work in them. The higher incomes of these categories, in other words, could be merely a reflection of the aggregation of higher-earning individuals who are disproportionately represented in these categories.

To understand the pattern of inequality, and in particular to appreciate the roles of categories in defining changing inequalities, one needs to separate income inequality associated with categories from that associated with individual characteristics and to examine whether the relative importance of the category has declined in terms of the characteristics of the individuals during the course of China's rising inequality.

City as a Source of Income Inequality

To further examine the roles of social categories in determining urban income inequality in China, I analyze in more detail data from the Urban Household Income and Expenditure Survey. Though such data do not contain information on work organizations, they allow the separation of individuals from locales and industries. In this analysis, I rely on a relatively simple method, the analysis of variance (ANOVA), because it allows the breakdown of all the variance in the dependent variable, in our case income, into different sources.[8] For example, it tells us what proportion of the income difference among individuals is due to their gender or to their educational attainment. It *also* tells us what proportion of the variance, if any, is due to the individual's employment sector or to the geographic location of employment and residence while *controlling* for the effects of other individual or categorical characteristics.

Three different income types of currently employed individuals are used as measures of income: total annual income, income that is from base salary or wages, and other types of labor income. The separation of income sources is based on the consideration that the two separate income sources—base salary or wages versus other types of labor income—are subject to different degrees of state jurisdictions. In contrast to base salary and wages, which are subject to more state regulations and standards, other types of labor income, including bonuses, job subsidies and allowances,

TABLE 4.4

Categories as explanatory variables: urban income inequality, China, 1988 and 1995

Model	1988			1995		
	R^2	df	F	R^2	df	F
1. Base: "Education, Gender, Employment length, and Occupation"	0.3529	69	—	0.1908	66	—
2. Model 1 plus "Ownership type" and "Industry"	0.3722	87	1.34	0.2559	84	3.67
3. Model 2 plus "Province"	0.4750	89	17.43	0.4470	86	29.72
4. Model 2 plus "City"	0.5471	117	45.18	0.5091	107	55.19

overtime pay, and income from secondary employment, depend more on the economic performance of an employee's work organization. In the decade after the mid-1980s, as shown in Chapter 3 (see Figure 3.3), these other types of labor income became an increasingly important source of overall labor income, accounting for nearly half or more of the total income.

In order to separate the role of city as a structural location in income determination from other factors affecting income, I include in the analysis various controls that are commonly used in studying income determination, such as gender, educational attainment, seniority (indicated by the length of employment), and occupation. Ownership type and industrial sector, two category variables, are also included in the analytical model. To observe changes over time, analyses are carried out for two time frames: 1988, the first year we have individual data by income categories, and 1995, a point when cross-locale inequalities peaked.

Results of analyses summarized in Tables 4.4 and 4.5 show the relative importance of categories in affecting the income of urban Chinese employees. Table 4.4 summarizes results that only compare different models: models including only control variables (education, gender, employment length, and occupation) versus models including category variables that have clear geographic and institutional boundaries (province, city, ownership type, and industry) as well. Only total income of the employee is used in the comparisons. Table 4.5, by contrast, presents more detailed information on the relative importance of each and every variable in determining urban employees' incomes. All three income variables are transformed into their log form in the analyses here. Whereas results in Table 4.4 provide evidence supporting the general argument that category variables beyond the control

TABLE 4.5
Relative importance of the determinants of income, urban China, 1988 and 1995

1988	TOTAL INCOME			BASE SALARY			OTHER LABOR INCOME		
Source	Partial SS	df	MS	Partial SS	df	MS	Partial SS	df	MS
Gender	6.67	1	6.67	2.16	1	2.16	15.67	1	15.67
Education	1.82	5	0.36	2.03	5	0.41	16.12	5	3.22
Length of employment	223.14	45	4.96	254.62	44	5.79	230.05	45	5.11
Occupation	16.13	18	0.9	10.51	18	0.58	24.72	18	1.37
Ownership type	15.62	5	3.12	9.63	4	2.41	92.03	4	23.01
Industry	1.6	13	0.12	2.298	13	0.18	8.066	13	0.62
City	221.76	30	7.39	68.27	30	2.28	680.38	30	22.68
Model	693.79	117		537.72	115		1371.41	116	
Residual	574.38	4217		400.2	4049		1901.73	4186	
Total	1268.18	4334		937.92	4164		3273.13	4302	
Adjusted R² (%)	53.45			56.12			40.29		

1995	TOTAL INCOME			BASE SALARY			OTHER LABOR INCOME		
Source	Partial SS	df	MS	Partial SS	df	MS	Partial SS	df	MS
Gender	16.61	1	16.61	13.62	1	13.62	12.87	1	12.87
Education	15.09	6	2.52	14.70	6	2.45	22.98	6	3.83
Length of employment	178.69	47	3.80	140.88	47	3.00	160.55	47	3.42
Occupation	8.96	12	0.75	9.98	12	0.83	15.20	12	1.27
Ownership type	40.29	6	6.72	110.64	2	55.32	59.19	6	9.87
Industry	29.27	12	2.44	9.32	12	0.78	74.48	12	6.21
City	670.38	23	29.15	292.70	23	12.73	1357.62	23	59.03
Model	1348.12	107		874.39	103		2068.02	107	
Residual	1300.16	4886		1555.05	4693		3893.70	4724	
Total	2648.28	4993		2429.45	4796		5961.73	4831	
Adjusted R² (%)	49.83			34.59			33.21		

NOTE: With the exception of the effect of "Industry" in 1988 for total and for other labor income, all MS are statistically significant at 0.05 or higher.

variables significantly increase the explanatory power of the model, results in Table 4.5 allow comparisons of different variables concretely.

At least as early as 1988, categories played an important role in determining income inequality among urban Chinese employees. Such a conclusion is supported by the results in Table 4.4, which is a comparison of different models facilitated by an F-test.[9] This test statistic is based on the difference in R-squared of the successive models. For instance, in 1988, the "base" model (Model 1) that includes only an employee's educational attainment, gender, length of employment, and occupation, has an R-squared value of 0.35. This means that these four control variables can explain 35 percent of the income variation among employees in 1988. These control variables, though conventionally assumed to be individual-level factors, can be argued to represent social categories as well. Gender, for instance, can be easily treated as a category, not as an individual trait. Under the Chinese gerontocracy system, it can be argued that age represents not just personal job experience and skills but also entitlement that follows seniority. More discussions will follow in this chapter on these factors. For the moment, however, they are treated as individual-level variables as commonly used in economic studies of income determination.

In Model 2, two group membership variables are added: "ownership type of the work organization" and "industry." Adding these variables increases the R-squared from 0.35 to 0.37. The F-statistic resulting from the comparison of these two models, 1.34, suggests that there is no statistically significant difference between the explanatory power of the two models. In other words, in 1988, "ownership type" and "industry" did not have a significant impact on income, once the four variables at the individual level are controlled for.[10] This is not the case, however, for the other two group membership variables, "province" and "city." When compared with Model 2, each of them (Models 3 and 4) has a greater explanatory power in explaining income differentials. Overall, for 1988, both "province" and "city" can add significantly to the understanding of income differences. Adding "province" to the base model increases the R-squared, the proportion of income variance explained, from 0.37 to 0.48, a 28 percent increase, and adding "city" increases the explanatory power of the model by 47 percent, from 0.37 to 0.55.

Between 1988 and 1995, the pattern of income determination changed, as the importance of group membership variables increased further. First of all, the explanatory power of the four factors traditionally regarded as individual-level factors in Model 1 decreased in 1995 compared with 1988. Instead of explaining more than a third of income differences among urban employees, in 1995 these factors accounted for less than one-fifth of the variance (R-squared decreased from 0.35 to 0.19). At the same time, adding "ownership type" and "industry" increases the explanatory power of income significantly, as shown in the F statistic for Model 2 in Table 4.4. Adding "province" increases the explanatory power by 75 percent, from an R-squared of 0.26 (Model 2 for 1995) to 0.45, and adding "city" nearly doubles the variance in income explained. The importance of these categories in explaining income inequality, as shown in the earlier section of this chapter, clearly still holds after controlling for the other commonly used factors of income determination.

The prominent roles of categories, especially that of the "city," can be seen in more detail from results presented in Table 4.5. These results show the changing relative importance of income determining factors not only for total income, but also for incomes broken down into "base salary" and "other labor income." A note is in order to explain how to read the results in Table 4.5. The first column of Table 4.5 gives the sum of squares (SS), or the variances in income that can be accounted for by a particular source/ variable. The second column gives the number of degrees of freedom (df), an indicator of how many categories a particular variable possesses. Our real interest lies in column 3, the mean sum of squares (MS), which is equal to the sum of squares divided by the number of degrees of freedom. This measure can be viewed as the mean variance explained by each independent variable, and it is more suitable for comparison than simply the sum of squares, because a large number of categories tends to result in a large amount of variance, other things being equal. Another useful result is the Adjusted R^2, which gives the percentage of total variance in the dependent variable explained by all independent variables included in a particular analysis.

Two sets of comparisons can be made, one within each year across different categories of income, and the other across time, between 1988 and 1995. Within each year and across different income categories, the variable "city" plays the most significant role in income determination, as a variable with the largest mean sum of squares (MS). Additionally, its role is much more important in determining "other labor income" compared to "base salary." The difference in MS between the variable "city" and the next most important variable is much larger in the "other labor income" model than in the "base salary" model.[11] In other words, local city plays a much larger role in determining the portion of the income that is less subject to state control.

Over time, the role of the city became much more important. In terms of total income, in 1988, the ratio between the most important variable, "city," and the second most important, "gender," was only 1.11 (7.39:6.67). Even for "other labor income," the ratio was only 1.45. In 1995, these ratios rose to 1.75 and 4.59, respectively. Clearly, whereas the total variance in income that was accounted for by all these variables decreased somewhat, the role of geographic location increased substantially.

What does city mean or what city-level characteristics account for the inter-city income differentials among urban Chinese employees? To answer such a question, one can take an explicitly contextual approach, treating income differentials among individuals as a result of both their individual characteristics and the economic characteristics of the cities they live and work in. The analytical strategy used here is the Hierarchical Linear Models (HLM) or multilevel modeling, which allows explicit modeling of group and individual effects separately, to estimate simultaneously equations at both the group and the individual levels (Raudenbush and Bryk 2002).

In contrast to the main data source used in this study, which contains individuals from cities of different sizes in only three provinces, the data source used in this section to examine city versus individual effects on income variation includes only large cities but covers all China, based on a large-scale survey conducted in 1999 by China's National Bureau of Statistics. This survey covered 35 of the largest cities in China, including all provincial capital cities of China, plus a selected few other large cities that experienced rapid economic growth.[12] Survey data on individual workers are combined with published statistics for cities where the individuals are drawn. Recognizing that there are no simple and perfect measures of economic and market reform measures, I have chosen four city-level measures as indicators: population size, level of local economic output (per capita gross domestic product), per capita foreign direct investment, and the recent rate of economic growth (1998 GDP per capita divided by 1992 GDP per capita). Local GDP per capita is a good indicator of development, and given the rapid pace of urban development in the post-socialist period, the change from 1992 to 1998 may adequately identify those cities with more

TABLE 4.6

Individual- and city-level factors of income differentials, large cities in China, 1998

	(1)	(2)	(3)
Intercept	6.570***	6.542***	6.469***
Population (Ln)	—	—	0.025
GDP / Capita (Ln)	—	—	0.529***
FDI / Capita (Ln)	—	—	−0.006
GDP growth 1992–98	—	—	−0.083*
Population (Ln)	—	—	0.011
GDP / Capita (Ln)	—	—	−0.043+
FDI / Capita (Ln)	—	—	0.015*
GDP growth 1992–98	—	—	−0.004
Level-1 controls	None	All	All
Variance components			
Intercept (τ_0)	0.047	0.049	0.016
Level-1 variance (σ^2)	0.328	0.256	0.256
Intra-class correlation	12.4%	16.0%	6.0%

NOTE: $^+ p < 0.10$; $^* p < 0.05$; $^{**} p < 0.01$; $^{***} p < 0.001$ (two-tailed tests).

or less steep development trajectories. Further, foreign direct investment (FDI) is often considered a key measure of the degree of market reforms in transitional economies, especially in China (see for example Bandelj 2002, 2007; Bian and Zhang 2002; Huang 2003; Gallagher 2005; Shu and Bian 2003).[13]

At the end of the 1990s, a significant share of income differentials among employees in China's largest cities, 12.4 percent, was due to inter-city difference (labeled as "intra-class correlation" for Model 1 in Table 4.6). Table 4.6 presents results of multilevel regression analyses of city-level factors of income differentials.[14] One of the unique features of the multilevel model is that the total variance in income can be decomposed into variance between cities (labeled as the intercept, τ_0, at the bottom of Table 4.6) and variance within cities, or the individual-level variance (σ^2). Inter-city differences persist when individual characteristics are controlled (Model 2), with 16 percent of the remaining variance in income occurring between cities.[15] Such a share is substantially smaller than the inter-city share for the three provinces already shown (50 percent) and for the national sample of over 100 cities (around 30 percent). The differences are likely caused by the data used. Whereas earlier analyses in this chapter include large as well as small cities, the present analysis includes only employees in large cities. These large cities form a more homogeneous group of cities compared with cities of all sizes. At the same time, intra-city variation in income is also expected to be larger for large cities than for smaller ones.

City-level economic growth characteristics explain a large share of the observed inter-city income differences, but not all. As shown by results under Model 3 in Table 4.6, the four city-level measures explain two-thirds of inter-city income differences, with inter-city variance dropping from 0.049 (Model 2) to 0.016 (Model 3). After controlling for city-level economic growth and individual level factors, 6 percent of the income variance among individuals remains to be inter-city difference. The strongest effect of city-level measures is GDP per capita, with average incomes drastically higher in cities of higher GDP per capita levels.

Such a result is expected, since GDP is essentially a measure of average income. At the same time, however, the positive effect of average GDP level in the city on individual-level income is somewhat tempered in cities with rapidly growing economies, as shown by the negative effect of GDP growth. Moreover, the magnitude of this effect stays largely the same regardless of controls at the individual level (results without individual-level controls are not shown in the table). Thus, the advantage of living in more developed cities does not occur just because workers are more likely to have higher education or work in better occupations, industries, or sectors in those cities. In addition, inter-city income differentials are not all due to differences in economic growth and market development across Chinese cities.

Ownership Type and Industry as Determinants of Inequality

The roles of the other two category variables, "ownership type" and "industry," also deserve mention. "Ownership type" has always been an important factor in determining income, but its role relative to other factors in 1995 was much greater in the "base salary" than it was for "other labor income." Such a pattern is consistent with our knowledge of the wage distribution system in China. During the period of the socialist planned economy, employees of state-owned organizations enjoyed an overall higher level of income than those employed in collective-owned and other non-state-owned enterprises. Following the reforms, the picture became more complicated as the number of ownership types increased and a new ordering emerged in their relative privileges. For instance, those working for joint venture and foreign-owned companies received incomes on average higher than those working for state-owned or collective-owned firms. But wages in state-owned organizations in general still surpassed those in collective-owned firms in urban areas. Organizations owned by the state were not only the first to benefit but also tended to be the last to go bankrupt. The basic conclusion that can be drawn is the same, which is that ownership type continued to play a role in income determination up to 1995.

The continuing importance of work organization ownership type through the mid-1990s is supported by the evidence given here and by other independent surveys as well. Surveys conducted by All-China Federation of Trade Unions report that compared with collective-owned work organizations, in 1992, employees in state-owned units on average received 20 percent higher income, and those in foreign/overseas and in Chinese/privately invested companies received 90 percent more. In 1997, these figures were 20 and 70 percent, respectively (Lu 2002, 156).

There is also evidence that the role of the industrial sector in income determination increased during the decade under study. In 1988, similar to what is revealed in Table 4.4, the variable "industry" was hardly an important factor at all when other factors affecting income are taken into consideration. In 1995, "industry" not only became significant but rose to be one of the most important factors. It ranked fourth among seven variables, after "city," "gender," and "ownership type," in determining "non-base salary income." It was more important than education, occupation, and seniority, all highly important factors in determining income in most settings. This is another indication of how segmented groups increasingly dominated the distribution of income beyond the state-stipulated base salary and wages.

The Role of Work Organizations

At the work organization level, available data show that after controlling for individual-level factors, the prominent role of the work organization persists. Moreover, income differentials persist after a number of characteristics of work organizations that potentially contribute to its economic performance are taken into account. Such an unexplained effect of the factor of "work organization" suggests the independent roles of work organizations in urban employees' income determination. To illustrate this important relationship, I use multivariate analysis results based on yet another data source different from the urban household surveys,[16] namely, the Survey of Chinese Work Organizations carried out in the early 1990s.[17] The most noticeable advantage of this dataset is that its research design generated a sample of individuals that are nested within work organizations.[18]

The survey also simultaneously collected data on characteristics of both individual employees and work organizations, thus allowing the kind of Hierarchical Linear Models (HLM), or multilevel modeling, similar to the examination of city-versus-individual effects presented earlier in this chapter. The analytical strategy used here, in other words, allows explicit modeling of group and individual effects separately, to estimate simultaneously equations at both the group and the individual levels. This analysis uses logged yearly income as our dependent variable. The independent variables include both individual characteristics and organizational attributes. At the individual level, they include variables that have been most widely used in previous studies.[19] At the organizational level, a number of variables that characterize a Chinese urban work unit are used.[20] Moreover, this analysis also includes "city" as a control variable since, as shown earlier, income differences across cities were pronounced. Table 4.7 provides further details based on results of multilevel models.

Work organizations are a clear source of inequality. As mentioned earlier in the chapter, decomposing income variance among individuals reveals that nearly half of all variance is due to that between work organizations. In the first model (Model 1), only predictors at the individual level are included, and in the second and third models (Models 2 and 3), characteristics of work organizations are added to examine their effects on the intercept (group mean income) at the organizational level. Results in Model 1 are almost the same as those reported in numerous other studies of income inequality in urban China based on individual-level analyses: among employees in our sample, the older male employee who was a Communist Party member and had a college education was most highly rewarded in terms of income. We also observe that our variables explain more than one-fourth of the income variance at the individual level (13 percent of the total variance), not too dissimilar to what we learn from other studies.

Could work organizational differences in employees income be due to economic performance of the organizations and, moreover, due to different cities where the work organizations were located? To answer these questions, one needs to move to the next two models in Table 4.7. In Model 2, organizational size, ownership type, rank, and profitability are introduced

TABLE 4.7

Individual and work organization factors of income differentials, 10 cities, 1992

	(1)	(2)	(3)
Intercept	7.962***	7.456***	8.232***
Individual level			
Male	0.035**	0.035**	0.036**
Age	0.039***	0.039***	0.039***
Age²/100	−0.032***	−0.033***	−0.032***
Party member	0.058***	0.057***	0.057***
Senior high school (vs. below)	0.003	0.003	0.003
College+ (vs. below sr. high)	0.052*	0.052*	0.052*
Work organization level			
Size 300−500 (vs. <300)		0.192**	−0.018
Size 500+ (vs. <300)		0.083	0.019
Public (vs. collective)		0.287**	0.163*
Private (vs. collective)		0.506***	0.277***
High rank (vs. low rank)		0.121+	0.071
Nonprofit (vs. low performance)		0.105	0.178**
High performance (vs. low)		0.189*	0.208***
Percentage of variance explained by the model			
Within work organization	27	27	27
Between work organization	—	18	69
City controls	No	No	Yes

into what is called a level-2 equation that predicts the intercept (group mean income). Size, ownership type, and rank are important indicators of a work organization's position in the redistributive economy (Bian 1994; Zhou 2000; Wu 2002). Together with profitability, these factors are expected to explain a significant portion of the average income of an organization's employees. This is indeed the case. Adjusting for variables at the individual level, our results show that medium-sized work units (in contrast to small-sized organizations), state and private ownership (versus collective ownership), higher rank in the bureaucratic hierarchy, and higher economic performance all contributed significantly to individual income differences. Overall, however, these variables explain only about 18 percent of the variance at level-2, the organizational level.[21]

Organizational size and rank are also sensitive to the city effect because large-sized and high-ranked organizations also tend to locate in large cities. Similarly, more private firms are located in Southern coastal cities than in others. In Model 3, the variable city is added to the list of variables used in Model 2, given the large inter-city variations in income. The effects of work organization size and rank disappear, while ownership type and profitability remain as important organizational traits. Comparing with those in Guangzhou, individuals in other cities earned one-fifth to three-quarters less (detailed results are not shown in the table). Private firms and public work organizations added 28 percent and 16 percent premiums, respectively, for their employees. Individuals in low-performance firms not only earned 21 percent less than those in high-profit firms but also 18 percent less than those in nonprofit agencies (government-funded). The fact that these nonprofit public organizations (*shiye danwei*) did almost as well as the high-performance production work organizations highlights an important feature of the transitional Chinese society: organizations that were close to the political power and possessed unique resources also benefited equally if not more than organizations that had market advantages. Compared with Model 2, the proportion of between-organization variance explained in Model 3 also increases from 18 percent to 69 percent, leaving 31 percent of the total variance at the organizational level unexplained.[22]

It is important to acknowledge the significance of the proportion of inter-organizational income difference that is not explained by the work organizational characteristics. Given that we have controlled for the conventionally used organizational characteristics, the residual portion of the variance is likely due to the unobserved factors that are unique to each of these work organizations. The premium of being associated with a work organization is therefore sizable given such an organizational effect revealed here.

Gender Inequality

In addition to the categories already examined, which are easily discernible due to their relatively clear geographic or institutional boundaries, there are other inequality-generating categories that transcend geographic and institutional boundaries and permeate the whole society. A most common and important social category of this type and a perennial source of inequality in every society is gender, or the separation of males and females in political, economic, and social life. Gender discrimination against women constituted one of the central tenets of the Chinese social stratification order. One of the main efforts to achieve overall equality under socialism consequently focused on reducing gender inequality, especially in spheres such as urban employment and income, where the socialist state had more direct control (Stacey 1983; Honig and Hershatter 1988; Whyte and Parish 1984; Bauer et al. 1992).

Against the backdrop of what has been observed as an overall retreat in gender equality in recent years in China, as evidenced by reports of explicit discrimination against women in the labor market and by the prominent increase in prostitution and crimes against women, what is the evidence in urban employment over which the state had the most direct control and influence? Among other factors, one difficulty in assessing gender inequality in China is the lack of comparable data for a comparable realm over time.[23] With available data here over a decade's time, straddling both pre- and post-reform periods, we can begin to examine the trend in gender inequality as it manifests itself in one segment of the society, income from urban workplaces.

There was a clear trend toward worsening gender income inequality in China's post-socialist transformational process. Figures 4.5 and 4.6 show the trends of gender penalty in income in urban China during the period between 1986 and 2000, in terms of percentage difference between female and male urban employees in annual income. Figure 4.5, labeled "unadjusted," shows the "crude" percentage difference in income, without taking into consideration other gender-specific factors also affecting income, such as education, occupation, and industrial sectors. The three lines in Figure 4.5 plot female employees' relative income disadvantage in total annual income, and by two separate sources of income—that from base wages or salaries and from other labor incomes. The latter two are for the years between 1988 and 2000, since it was not until 1988 that income data by sources were collected in the survey. The differentiation by source of income allows examination of organizational sources of changing gender inequality.

Gender penalty in income is most clearly seen from the line representing "total income." The female disadvantage in income increased from a 15-percent deficit compared with men in the mid-1980s, to a 20-percent one by 1993, and to 25 percent in 2000. Also seen in this figure is the gap in gender penalty in income for female urban employees between base

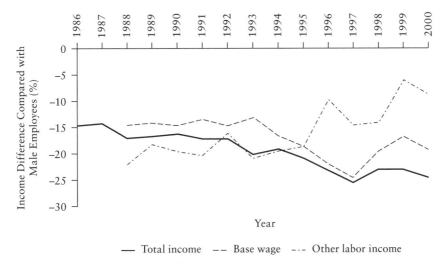

Figure 4.5   Gender penalty in income, urban China, 1986–2000 (unadjusted)

wage and income derived from other sources. Such a discrepancy is to be expected, as the base wages and salaries were set by the state wage system, while other forms of labor income were left more in the hands of localities, and mostly of enterprises. Up until 1993, there was only a 15 percent difference in base wages and salaries, whereas with few exceptions, the gender difference in income from other labor-related sources was mostly around 20 percent. By the mid-1990s, however, this earlier pattern was reversed. While gender penalty for "other labor income" improved compared with the decade before, female income disadvantage from wages and salaries increased. It is this source of income inequality that was driving the continued downward trend in income equality between female and male urban Chinese employees.

A substantial portion of such "crude" gender difference in income as seen in Figure 4.5 can be attributed to outcomes of a cumulative process of gender-specific "routing" in the Chinese society: gender-specific childhood education, different length of employment in part due to an earlier stipulated retirement age for women, different levels and specializations in educational attainment, different occupations, and different industries (Honig and Hershatter 1988; Bauer et al. 1992; Evans 1995). Once these factors are controlled for statistically, what emerges can be read as the "net" effect

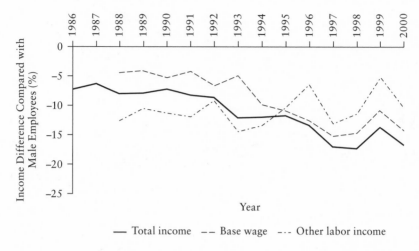

Figure 4.6   Gender penalty in income, urban China, 1986–2000 (adjusted)

of gender discrimination in income. It is "net" only in the sense that this difference is the income disadvantage for women compared with men with the *same* seniority, *same* educational attainment, holding the *same* position (occupation), and working in the *same* industries. Figure 4.6 shows the trend in gender inequality adjusted for these and other factors.[24]

A pattern of worsening gender inequality in income, similar to that in Figure 4.5, is shown in Figure 4.6. In less than a decade's time, the net gender penalty in income rose from 7.3 percent in 1986 to 12 percent by 1993. It increased further in the late 1990s, to over 15 percent in most years. Whereas there was always a gap in the degree of gender penalty between "base wage" and "other labor income," with the latter being twice or more than that of the former, the degree of deterioration in gender equality was more noticeable in "base wage" where the state used to exert a direct influence in promising women the same pay as men in the same jobs.

Prior to 1993, in areas where the socialist state had more direct influence, namely in basic wages and salaries, the gender gap was only around 5 percent after controlling for other factors, a respectable if not perfect record given the government's promise of equal work for equal pay. After 1993, the gap in this income source suddenly enlarged, to as high as 15 percent, contributing directly to the overall worsening in gender equality in income in the 1990s.[25] Increasing inequality in this income source indicates a shift toward a "hands off" policy in the state's relation to gender equality in the workplace. Increasing gender inequality, as shown here, was clearly an important contributing factor to the increasing urban income inequality throughout China's transition away from socialism. Rising gender income inequality was especially pronounced during the 1990s.

Seniority, Education, and Occupation as Sources of Inequality

Three other factors figure prominently in the determination of income and income inequality in post-socialist urban China. They are seniority, education, and occupation (Walder 1990; Wang and So 1994; Bian, Logan, and Shu 2000; Wu 2002; Zhou 2000, 2004). In most economic and sociological literature on income determination, these factors are considered individual characteristics. Seniority, or length of tenure, which is often measured by chronological age, is regarded as an indicator of the skills an individual has accumulated along the path of life, especially through employment. Educational attainment is considered an indicator of an individual's possession of human capital. And occupation is regarded as an individual trait because it shows where a person ends up, based on his or her credentials and through individual efforts. All these factors are considered individual traits not only because they reflect more clearly individual effort in obtaining them but because they are attached to individuals and therefore can be measured at the individual level.

However, while it is true that these factors are associated more closely with individuals than categories that have geographic or institutional boundaries, the fact that they are also social categories should not be neglected. Take seniority as an example. Chinese society, by no means unique in this regard, is an age-based society in which older age used to be associated with honor and privilege. Not only does Chinese cultural tradition emphasize respect for the aged, the Chinese political system until this very day clearly resembles a male gerontocracy. Even with the transformation from an agrarian to an industrializing society, Chinese employers, including the state during the planned economy era, continued to honor seniority as one of the bases in determining wages. In the most recent wage policies for state employees announced in 1993 by the Chinese government, for instance, seniority remained one of the explicit factors, together with position, rank, and base wages, in determining the overall wage level. This explicit compensation by seniority, however, is very small, with one yuan added to each additional year of employment (Zhu 2001, 28). The rationale of using seniority as one of the bases in wage determination is not as explicit in the Chinese case as that developed in Japan, where age is used with an explicit consideration of an employee's responsibility for a family's living costs. I discuss more of the Japanese case in Chapter 6.

Education and occupation are two social categories that have received the most intense scrutiny and much theorizing recently in studies of China's transformation toward a market-oriented economy. This is the case not because China is becoming increasingly more of a "credentialed" society where the intangible importance placed on education in the past is now equated to merely holding a diploma in one's hands, and not because occupational stratification was once a pillar of social stratification in China's agrarian past. Education and occupation have received close attention because they are each assigned a role to represent a different stratification regime.

Educational attainment is seen as a form of individual human capital, with its importance in income determination associated mostly with a market economy. The rising importance of educational attainment in generating economic returns, therefore, has been interpreted to indicate the success in the transition toward a market economy. In comparison, occupation, particularly the privilege associated with being a cadre, has been seen as an indicator of possessing redistributive power. Its declining importance has been correspondingly interpreted as a sign of the waning of state socialism. Studies of transitional socialist societies in the past decade, not just in China but other societies as well, have often focused on these two factors and have produced mixed empirical findings on their changing roles (e.g., Nee 1989, 1991, 1996; Róna-Tas 1994; Bian and Logan 1996; Walder 1996; Xie and Hannum 1996; Gerber and Hout 1998; Cao and Nee 2000; Zhou 2000).

The difficulties involved in such studies of transitional socialist societies, in addition to differences among scholars in their theoretical approaches—over what should be the proper units/agencies of analyses, the nature of causal relations, and issues of measurement—also lie in the lack of longitudinal data that can be used to track change over time. Most attempts to study change so far have therefore resorted to data constructed from surveys of life histories, in which respondents recall their characteristics in the past (Bian, Logan, and Shu 2000; Zhou 2000, 2004). The Urban Household

Income and Expenditure Survey data for the decade studied here, with their limitations, provide a series of cross-sectional longitudinal data that can be used to examine the changing importance of seniority, education, and occupation for income inequality. In Table 4.8, I present the results of analyses based on these survey data. The numbers in this table are percentage differences associated with the categories of interest.[26]

Seniority has been a highly important factor in determining income among urban employees, and its role in affecting income has hardly changed in a 15-year time span. In the results presented in Table 4.8, seniority is represented by two measures, length of employment since the first job (length), and a squared term of length (length^2), with the latter used to capture a tapering-off effect of age on income.[27] The percentages in Table 4.8 show the changes with one unit change in length of employment, in this case, one year. The prominent effect of seniority on income can be seen from a brief exercise here. For the year 1990, for example, person A, with a five-year employment length, had an income advantage of 25.2 percent over a person who just began working. Person B, with the same characteristics as person A except for a 10-year employment history, would have an advantage of 45.9 percent.[28] The difference, 20.7 percent, is thus quite substantial, given only a five-year difference in seniority. Over the 15-year period, the importance of seniority increased initially but then more or less stayed at the same level. By the late 1980s, income return associated with one additional year of employment was around 6 percent for overall income. Following a drop in the early 1990s to barely 5 percent, the seniority advantage in income edged up again in the late 1990s.

In most cases, the effect of seniority is more important for "other labor income" than for "base wage." The seniority effect for "other labor income" was as high as nearly 8 percent versus no more than 6 percent for "base wage" per additional year of employment. Such a difference suggests different income distribution principles for the two income sources. If income determination by seniority is seen as a measure of egalitarian distribution, then it is in "other labor income," which were generated and distributed locally, where income was more equally distributed.

The income advantage associated with education increased sharply after the early 1990s. Compared with urban employees with a junior high school education, who compose between 35 to 45 percent of the urban Chinese employees in these data, those with university and college education, rising

TABLE 4.8
*Changing importance of seniority, education, and occupation
in income, 1986–2000*

	TOTAL INCOME (%)					
Year	Length	Length 2	University	Cadre 1	Cadre 2	N
1986	4.82	−0.08	4.85	12.54	4.15	4175
1987	4.18	−0.06	7.68	11.06	2.91	4254
1988	5.99	−0.10	−0.35	16.48	−8.07	4335
1989	5.98	−0.10	2.58	16.98	7.02	4246
1990	5.49	−0.09	5.34	9.17	−4.90	3857
1991	5.38	−0.09	4.19	13.93	−1.69	4178
1992	4.77	−0.08	6.22	14.62	−6.27	5095
1993	5.40	−0.09	11.88	8.14	−11.70	4721
1994	5.13	−0.09	15.30	17.19	−5.38	4595
1995	5.03	−0.08	22.08	12.78	−1.00	4994
1996	5.23	−0.08	19.81	10.30	0.31	4889
1997	5.80	−0.11	25.50	29.19	12.95	4245
1998	6.30	−0.12	19.67	26.49	8.11	3934
1999	5.42	−0.10	22.30	19.18	−0.59	3703
2000	4.69	−0.09	29.39	52.00	30.48	3586

	BASE WAGE (%)					
Year	Length	Length 2	University	Cadre 1	Cadre 2	N
1988	5.80	−0.09	5.06	16.01	−3.38	4165
1989	5.86	−0.09	8.51	16.34	−5.83	4151
1990	5.38	−0.08	7.22	9.41	−5.84	3670
1991	5.03	−0.07	6.76	7.37	−5.53	4105
1992	5.05	−0.07	16.37	19.29	−6.15	5010
1993	5.18	−0.07	11.59	11.00	−9.10	4571
1994	5.52	−0.08	14.51	20.89	−0.27	4419
1995	3.27	−0.03	20.90	16.69	0.37	4797
1996	4.34	−0.07	17.94	10.03	2.62	4836
1997	4.88	−0.08	21.30	30.51	11.4	4189
1998	5.42	−0.10	21.60	33.21	11.8	3849
1999	4.91	−0.09	23.58	22.21	2.66	3563
2000	4.10	−0.08	37.86	54.00	29.2	3280

	OTHER LABOR INCOME (%)					
Year	Length	Length 2	University	Cadre 1	Cadre 2	N
1988	6.87	−0.14	−6.21	20.23	−13.26	4303
1989	6.93	−0.14	0.90	21.78	−11.12	4202
1990	6.90	−0.13	0.13	10.60	−6.28	3831
1991	6.50	−0.12	−0.53	24.86	1.45	4116
1992	4.89	−0.09	1.34	5.03	−12.97	5075
1993	6.02	−0.11	13.55	9.69	−9.58	4698
1994	5.16	−0.10	19.27	13.51	−7.39	4540
1995	5.64	−0.11	22.22	11.43	0.97	4832
1996	5.26	−0.10	30.63	41.07	15.04	4319
1997	7.80	−0.17	19.43	4.51	−5.91	3675
1998	7.01	−0.15	6.82	67.69	39.90	3245
1999	5.76	−0.13	25.04	−2.82	−18.61	2998
2000	5.47	−0.12	25.03	37.69	35.54	2831

from 10 to 30 percent of the total labor force, commanded a substantial income advantage, increasing from 5 to well over 20 percent for their income from all sources. The rising significance in educational returns was also most noticeable in "other labor income." Before 1993, the income differences between university/college educated and junior high school graduates were not only small but were all statistically nonsignificant, adding further evidence to a scenario in which income from such sources was distributed more according to other criteria, such as seniority and cadre status. After 1992, university- and college-educated individuals were much more handsomely rewarded than before in these income sources: 13.6 percent more in 1993, 22.2 percent in 1995, and 25 percent in 2000 (Table 4.8).

In contrast to the roles of seniority and especially education, where a clear trend can be detected over time, the trend of cadre status in commanding an additional income advantage is less clear-cut. In the analyses, with results presented in Table 4.8, two comparisons are made to examine the cadre advantage, first between cadres and production workers, and second between cadres and professionals. Cadres in these analyses are those individuals whose occupational status was listed as an official of mid-level (*chu*) rank and above. Compared with production workers, with the exception of one year (1993), in each year there was a substantial income advantage associated with cadre status, in the range of 10 to 30 percent.[29] Such an advantage can be considered a "net" advantage, as other relevant income-determining factors are all controlled for statistically.[30] At the same time as we observe a consistent advantage associated with a leadership position, however, it was not until after the mid-1990s that we see an upward trend in cadre income advantage over workers.

Another way to examine the cadre advantage as evidence of changing social stratification order, as argued by some, is not by the kind of the comparison made thus far, but by one between cadres and rising market-based

NOTES TO TABLE 4.8: The numbers are percentage differences in income associated with a particular income-determining factor. They are obtained from multivariate regression analysis using the log form of income as the dependent variable, by taking the exponential form of the regression coefficients. Length is length of employment (since first job); length2 is a squared term of length; university is compared with junior high school education, cadre (1) is compared with production workers, and cadre (2) is comparison with professionals. These percentages are converted from multiple regression coefficients, controlling for gender, industry, ownership sector, and city. With the exception of 1988, 1993, and 2000 for total income, 2000 for base wage, 1988 and 1992 for other labor income, all other cadre (2) effects are statistically nonsignificant. Other nonsignificant effects are cadre (1): total income 1993 and other income 1990, 1997, 1999, 2000; university: other income, 1988–1992, 1997–1999.

social groups, such as entrepreneurs and professionals.[31] Whereas the data up to 2000 used here do not yet allow the comparison between cadres and entrepreneurs, a comparison can be made between cadres and professionals, whose occupations are reported as engineers or senior engineers and professionals.[32] Unlike the clear cadre advantage over workers already described, there is little evidence of cadre advantage over professionals, once other factors are controlled for. In the 41 comparisons (15 for "total income," 13 each for "base wage" and "other labor income"), only six turned out to be statistically significant. There were, in other words, no significant income differences between the two social groups compared here. Though these results fail to lend support to the prediction of waning redistributive power, it should also be noted that this comparison is still not the best way to test the overall hypothesis of declining cadre advantage. More suitable tests should be based on direct comparisons between bureaucrats who have close ties to political power in redistributing economic benefits and entrepreneurs who have no or little tie to the political establishment.

It is clear from the analyses in this chapter that categories not only accounted for a large share of urban income inequality in China, but they also accounted for an increasingly *larger* share of the inequality during the decade and a half under examination. In other words, the importance of many categories increased, rather than decreased, along with China's urban reforms. These categories include some that have clear geographic and institutional boundaries, such as city and industry; they also include social categories that transcend geographic and institutional boundaries, such as gender and occupational group. While systematic data over time are still lacking to demonstrate the rising role of work organizations in defining income inequality, available data and case studies similarly reveal the significant role of the work organizations in defining income inequality.

The role of categories in structuring and explaining the rapidly rising income inequality in urban China cannot be overstated. By the mid-1990s, the geographic location of the city alone already accounted for a third to nearly half of all income inequalities among the urban individuals included in this study, depending on the geographic coverage of the study population. In the three-province sample, ownership type and industrial sectors accounted for an additional 10 to 15 percent. Even when all these category variables and individual variables are used together to examine income determination, there is an unmistakable pattern: not only did category variables account for a lot, they also accounted for more in the mid-1990s than they did a decade earlier. Without fully accounting for the critical roles of these various categories in defining income inequality, one risks missing the basic picture of understanding the structure of social inequality in post-Mao China.

What makes these categories so central to understanding the trend and patterns of income inequality in transitional China? What do these categories mean, and through what mechanisms do they generate and maintain inequality? Moreover, what are the implications of such a pattern of inequality for urban Chinese employees and their family members? In the next chapter, I turn to the examination of the meaning of these categories and their roles in structuring inequalities.

EXPLANATIONS

CHAPTER FIVE

Maintaining Equality: Boundaries

By accounting for nearly half and in some cases more than half of the overall increase in inequality, categories, especially cities and work organizations, have evolved into crucial structural bases of urban inequality. The previous chapter demonstrated the prominent role of categories in redefining urban inequality during the first two decades of China's transformations away from the socialist economic system. The primacy of these categories in explaining rising inequality also implies another important new social reality, that the rise of inequality *within* each category or a group is *much less* than that suggested by the overall increase. Categories, in other words, not only serve as basis of inequalities, they also serve as institutions for protecting the members within them, by maintaining equalities within their boundaries.

What is meant by the classification "city" or "work organization"? Are they truly socially meaningful and important categories that define inequality, or simply geographical locations and organizational workplaces where people happen to live and work? In this chapter, I turn to the question of boundaries, by exploring how inequality-generating categories are formed and maintained in China's post-socialist transformations. I examine, in other words, the political economy and social basis of these units of social and economic stratification. In addition, I also entertain the roles of culture—in particular the Chinese cultural beliefs of equality and inequality—and that of political organization, namely the continued permeation and governance of the Communist Party organization and other auxiliary organizations in maintaining equality.

LOCAL STATE CORPORATISM:
WHAT'S IN THE NAME OF A CITY?

One important feature of the rising inequality documented in this study is the increasing share of inequality accounted for by cities in different parts of China. Is inter-city inequality simply a geographic phenomenon that accompanies the process of economic reform and growth, often known as "uneven development," that may soon be washed away by the forces of the market? Or, is it an artifact of something more fundamental and enduring, reflecting the very nature of the political-economic basis of current Chinese society?

An easy explanation for rising income disparity among cities is that it simply reflects the vast differences in cost of living that have emerged over the past decades. Economic change in the two decades of China's post-socialist transformation indeed resulted in huge regional differences in income and in standard of living. It can be argued that higher incomes are needed to compensate for the higher cost of living in some cities. This is especially the case in this study. At one extreme, there are cities such as Shenzhen and Guangzhou in Guangdong province, where both costs of living and income levels are well above the national average. Among employees of the surveyed households, those in Shenzhen and Guangzhou had an average income level that was 2.5 and 1.4 times that of the whole sample with three provinces combined in 1990, moving up to 2.6 and 1.8 times in 1995. At the other extreme, there are cities such as Zigong and Nanchong in Sichuan province, where the levels are well below the national average. In 1990, surveyed individuals had an average income that was 13 percent below the whole sample in Zigong, and 22 percent below in Nanchong. By 1995, they sank further to 29 percent and 36 percent below the average of the three provinces.

Regional disparity in income levels and in different costs of living do not necessarily result in the kind of inequality distributions as seen in post-socialist urban China, where a significant portion of overall inequality resides in inter-city inequality. To examine the extent to which inequalities between cities are a function of cost of living, one can compare urban China with settings where income levels and costs of living also vary greatly within the same country. One case of comparison is the United States. To make the comparison at a similar scale with a similar number of cities, I use the 1990 U.S. population census data and draw a random sample of

32 cities from a total of 262.[1] Sample cities include both high-income and high-cost areas such as New York and Boston and low-income areas such as Wichita Falls, Texas, where the income level was only 60 percent of the national average in 1989, the year before the 1990 census. By applying the same method used for the Chinese sample in this study, I calculate income inequality among employees and decompose inequality into that between cities and that within cities for the United States in 1989.

The comparison between the United States and China and between China (for the three provinces) at the start and the end of a decade span are shown in Figure 5.1. In the case of the U.S. sample, 96 percent of total income inequality was within cities, whereas only 4 percent was between cities. At the national level in the United States, when all cities are used in the calculation, the same pattern persists, with inter-city inequality accounting for only 4 percent of overall income inequality (Cohen and Huffman 2003). By comparison, for urban China as represented by those cities in three provinces, there was a change in the shares of between- versus within-city inequality. The two shares changed from 10 to 90 percent respectively in 1986 to 47 to 53 percent in 1995. Clearly, variation in cost of living cannot be the only explanation for China, as it is not an explanation for the United States at all. In contrast to the United States where income inequality is evenly distributed within each geographical confine, in urban China it is both within and between cities. To understand the significance of city in income determination in urban China, we need to look for explanations elsewhere.

City as a Political Economic Unit

Localities, especially cities in contemporary China, are not just geographic spaces. Rather, they are political economic units. They are social spaces that are "patched together with physical space or geography," and in the words of sociologist Harrison C. White, "Localities are—contrary to common sense—complex and confusing accomplishments of human social structure" (1992, 130).

A salient feature of China's post-reform economic system is the growing strength and economic management responsibility of the local government. At a time when the central government has distanced itself from directly controlling individual enterprises, the ties between enterprises and local governments have become strengthened in an unprecedented way.

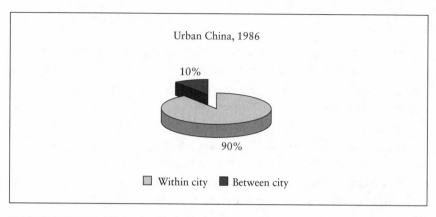

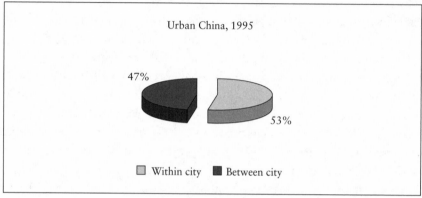

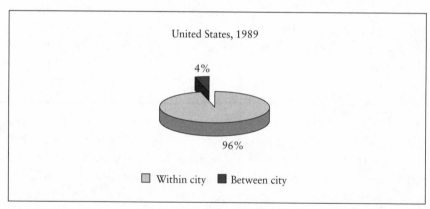

Figure 5.1 Decomposition of income inequality, urban China and the United States

SOURCE: Urban China based on individuals in roughly 30 cities in three provinces, collected in the Urban Household Income and Expenditure Survey; United States based on individuals in 32 randomly selected MSAs, contained in the 10% sample of the 1990 census.

Increasingly, local governments have not only been given more power and responsibility over enterprises within their jurisdiction, but the functioning of local governments has also relied on incomes drawn from these enterprises, and on economic entities created by local governments themselves.

A former senior economist at the World Bank summarized the ascendance of local government's power in urban China in the late 1980s as follows: "Perhaps the most surprising hypothesis emerging from recent World Bank work on China is that an unusual degree of local autonomy exists in urban areas. The central and provincial governments appear to have yielded to local governments the bulk of real authority in such diverse areas as the ownership and control of economic enterprises, the administration of the national tax system, and financing of urban and social infrastructure, and the policy and regulatory reforms necessary to improve cost recovery and the efficient management of public assets. To an extent unknown outside the developed world, China's cities are becoming their own masters except where very large investments are concerned (and particularly if an increasingly rare equity infusion from a higher-level government is required" (Hamer 1990, 240). Local governments, instead of being a bureaucratic force that obstructs market-oriented reforms, have often played the role of active participants in engineering market reforms (Lin 2001). In this regard, the Chinese experience of the state's role in market creation is not different from that of other market-based societies, such as that documented and espoused by Polanyi (1944/1957).

Two institutional arrangements underlie the rise of the power of local governments: the nature of China's property rights regime, and the fiscal reforms carried out by the central Chinese government in the mid-1980s (Granick 1990; Oi 1992, 1995; Lin 1995; Oi and Walder 1999; Walder 1992b, 1994, 1995; Wang 1995; Wong 1992). Unlike the former USSR or a number of former East European socialist countries, China has not carried out a wholesale privatization of public assets. Instead, the large-scale sale of state assets took place in a much more controlled way in China than in Russia and other countries. In urban China, significant disposal of state assets did not occur until the late 1990s. What happened prior to the late 1990s was mostly decentralization of control or a limited experiment in workers' ownership in the form of stock purchasing. During the two decades following 1978, the number of enterprises directly under the central government or its ministries declined drastically. Control was turned over to the enterprises, under the jurisdiction of various levels of local government.[2]

The property rights regime that emerged is what has been characterized as a multiple principals system, where multilevel supervision prevailed (Granick 1990). Although decentralization freed most firms from the hands of the central government, it did not transfer the property rights to enterprises in any explicit and holistic way. Rather, public ownership of the means of production with multiple masters continued. Within such an institutional framework, the local government and the enterprise could each claim to be the representatives of the public and therefore could claim joint custody of the assets. Each party had its own leverage.

The city or the local government was the greater public of the two and enjoyed a greater political power. In many cases, the local government still controlled personnel appointment power and other key resources, such as local banking finance, provision of local infrastructure, and increasingly, local regulations. In this sense, firms or enterprises were not totally free. But firms and enterprises had their leverage too. They possessed more direct control over the means of production, and for the local government to benefit from this property, firms or enterprises must make a profit. So the rights of the firm had to be recognized and respected too (Walder 1992b).[3]

Another institutional arrangement was the state fiscal system reform carried out around the mid-1980s. These reforms in the state fiscal system clearly tilted the balance of economic power from the central state to local governments up to the mid-1990s. Prior to the reforms, profits from state- and collective-owned firms were turned over to the state. In return, firms received allocations for labor and capital for production. The central government also made most revenue and expenditure decisions. After the mid-1980s, two important changes took place: the first in the relationship between the government and the enterprise, and the second in the bond between central and local governments. Enterprises, instead of submitting all their income to the state, were now under a system by which they only needed to pay state taxes and a certain portion of their profits.[4] As for local governments, they were not only allowed to keep taxes under their jurisdiction but also to keep a portion of other local revenue.[5] Both reforms were decentralization efforts, designed to generate more incentive at local levels and to take away the suffocating hands of the state that had micromanaged

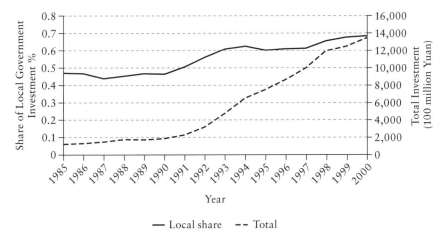

Figure 5.2   Increasing local government capital investment, 1985–2000
SOURCE: Calculated from NBS 2000, 174.

the economy. At the same time, this system was also supposed to guarantee the central government's revenue. Thus, local governments had a financial incentive and even imperative to exert strong control over local enterprises and to create new businesses.

One indictor of this shift was the investment made by different levels of government. During the decade after the mid-1980s, the central government's share in capital investment as a percentage of gross domestic products (GDP) stayed roughly constant, right below 10 percent, although the amount of investment increased as a result of the overall growth in GDP. Local government's investment, however, rose at a much faster rate. Its share of the GDP rose from 10 percent to close to 20 percent (Naughton 1995, 1094). As plotted in Figure 5.2, along with an exponential growth in the amount of total capital investment starting in the late 1980s, the share of local government investment as a percentage of total investment rose steadily in the first half of the 1990s, rising from 46 percent in 1990 to over 60 percent by 1994.[6] In the three provinces under examination in this book, local investment in 1996 accounted for 63.1 percent of total investment in Liaoning, 67.2 percent in Sichuan, and 81.6 percent in Guangdong province. These local investments were mostly local governments' investment in urban areas, as they did not include investments made by rural collectives and urban individuals (NBS 1996, 44).

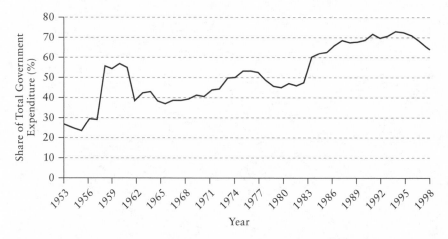

Figure 5.3   Trend in local government expenditure, China, 1953–1998
SOURCE: Calculated from NBS 2000, 268.

The rise of the local government's importance was not limited just to capital investment. Starting in the mid-1980s, local government's share of total government expenditure rose to an unprecedented level and stayed there. Figure 5.3 shows the trend of local government's share in total government expenditure for much of China's socialist and post-socialist history, between 1953 and 1998. Though past decentralizations resulted in an increase in the role of the local government, most noticeably the peaks in the late 1950s in association with the Great Leap Forward famine and a temporary hump in the late 1970s, the rising importance of the local government was unmistakable after the mid-1980s. By the early 1990s, local governments' expenditure accounted for over 70 percent of all government expenditure.[7]

The rising economic role of the local government is also seen in another kind of financial arrangement, "extra-budgetary" revenue and expenditure. These revenues and expenditures are outside the regular budget and traditionally stayed in the hands of local enterprises, administrative organizations, and governments. Local share in this financial source rose from around 60 percent in the early 1990s to over 80 percent in the mid-1990s (NBS 2000, 271; Wang 1995). To augment revenue, local governments, against repeated warnings from the central government, levied many different kinds of local fees and taxes against enterprises under their jurisdiction.

One estimate put local revenue from such sources at 500 billion yuan for 1996, amounting to about 7 percent of China's gross national product in that year. Most of that revenue was believed to have gone to income and welfare of local residents (Yang et al. 1997, 9).

Local officials, as active agents running the local governments, also have at least three rationales for their deep involvement in the economy. First, economic growth and improved standards of living have been the primary sources of political legitimacy in China after the Cultural Revolution. This is the case at every level of the Chinese communist bureaucracy. In the Chinese political system, local city mayors and party secretaries are appointed by the party organization at a higher level. Promotion decisions in post-Mao China have been increasingly linked to local economic growth records. Promotion criteria formulated by Chinese Communist Party's personnel organizational apparatus explicitly stipulated that "cadres should... be determined to carry out the reform and opening-up policy, be devoted to the cause of modernization, and work hard to build socialism and the making of concrete achievements."[8] Landry's recent analysis of promotion patterns among over 2,000 mayoral-level officials in the 1990s confirms that cadres with strong local economic performance records were indeed more likely to be promoted, especially to a position in a different city. Relying on ethnographic data sources, Yi-min Lin documented the same phenomenon: officials who fulfilled revenue contracts were promoted to higher-level positions (Lin 2001, 133). In addition, Wu Guoguang and Zheng Yongnian (1995) identify a new feature of the political system in the post-reform era: not only does the central government tend to promote officials from successful economic growth areas to higher-level government, local officials also use the economic performance of their local areas as bargaining chips to demand promotion.

Second, as pointed out by Oi (1995), the Chinese government is a bureaucracy that has a long tradition of engineering economic growth. Managing the economy is not something new to local Chinese governments. What has changed is the institutional context, from a more centrally controlled planned economy to a market-based economy. In comparison to the planned economy days, local officials have more power and also more responsibilities. At the end of the 1990s, for example, the city of Chengdu, the capital of Sichuan province, had over two dozen vice-party secretary or vice mayor-level city officials. Most of these city-level officials were in charge of managing a particular aspect of the local economy. The number of local government officials engaged in economic activities was thus far larger than during the days of the planned economy. This increase in the number of local officials apparently has caught the attention of the central government, and reform is reportedly under way to simplify local bureaucracies.

Last but not the least, the survival and growth of local administrative power depended increasingly on the local economy. Fiscal pressures and incentives led local governments to promote local industry vigorously, in order to use revenues from profitable enterprises to offset losses of the insolvent ones. Even the operation of the local government sometimes depended heavily on the local government's revenue, in the form of off-budget funds. In one city district carefully studied by Yi-min Lin, 11 out of 61 government departments were completely funded by such a source after 1987 (Lin 2001, 130). The rise of local governments' power resulted in what Christine Wong characterized as "problems of persistent overinvestment, duplication, regional blockades, and continuing bureaucratic management of industry" (Wong 1992, 198). At the personal level, local officials' welfare, from salary and bonuses and housing to sedan cars, banquets, cellular phone bills, and overseas trips, also depended on the local fiscal coffer, which was increasingly linked to the local economy (Walder 1995; Lin 2001).

Base on her observations of rural village and township economic and political organizations in the early 1990s, Jean Oi characterized the new economic development model as "local state corporatism." According to Oi, in the post-reform institutional context: "the state responsible for much of this growth is *local* governments that treat enterprises within their administrative purview as one component of a larger corporate whole. Local officials act as the equivalent of a board of directors and sometimes more directly as the chief executive officers. At the helm of this corporate-like organization is the Communist Party secretary" (1995, 1132; italics by original author). Within this new institutional context, local officials are fully "fledged *economic* actors, not just administrative-service providers as they are in other countries" (Oi 1995, 1137; italics by original author).

The "local state corporatism" model applies in principle to the nature of economic and social organizations in China's cities. Given the size and complexity of the economy, the reach of the government is much less effective in cities than in smaller villages and townships. Coordination and control of economic activities also differ significantly between cities and townships, due to the larger populations and more complex economic activities in cities than in townships. Similarities nevertheless exist between the economic and political institutions in cities and in townships (Lin 2001, 127–130). Officials in both settings face the same political mandate of economic development and the same moral expectations from citizens to maintain social order, largely through a growing local economy and low unemployment. In both settings, a significant portion of the local government's operating budget relies on local economic sources.

Maintaining Local Equality

As heads of the local corporation, local government officials participate in activities associated with economic growth, such as attracting capital investment and other resources. They are also expected to participate in distributing income, both directly and indirectly. They can exercise their power to redistribute resources directly by using the profits of richer enterprises to subsidize poorer ones, or by ordering banks to provide loans to failing enterprises. Indirectly, local governments can help to generate new employment opportunities or to provide needed social services by using surpluses from profitable enterprises and local taxes.

A telling example of such behaviors is an event I personally encountered during a trip through a medium-sized city in Shanxi province in September 2001. Topping the day's agenda for the city's mayor, who was going to have lunch with our group, was his visit to a local textile factory, where he was to buy a big piece of cloth made in that factory. The mayor's action took place under well-orchestrated publicity so that the citizens of the city, at least those on the government payroll, were expected to follow the lead to buy locally produced textile products. These activities and publicity stunts were organized with one important aim: to "buy local" and to save the local textile factory, which was on the verge of bankruptcy as it faced increased competition from cloth produced elsewhere. Closing down the factory and increasing the number of the unemployed would create new problems for the city. Though it was highly doubtful if such a measure actually saved the factory, what appeared was a familiar "nationalistic" behavior; emphasis was placed on purchasing local goods.

Local governments could protect members within their boundaries by reinforcing boundaries and by excluding non-members. One widely publicized example is how cities designed their own regulations in the 1990s to exclude rural migrants from certain jobs in the cities. Whereas rural migrants have been welcomed to cities to provide needed services, many large cities issued formal regulations to exclude migrants from certain jobs that appeared more attractive to urban unemployed people. These cities include Guangzhou in Guangdong province and Shenyang in Liaoning province (Solinger 1999, 2001b), as well as the capital city of Beijing and the largest metropolis, Shanghai (Wang, Zuo, and Ruan 2002). Such a practice, as documented by Solinger, began in the late 1980s when cities faced urban unemployment problems induced by the state's economic austerity measures (1999, 115). By the mid-1990s, when urban unemployment became more acute and widespread following the bankruptcies of state-owned enterprises, more cities put out elaborate regulations fencing out outsiders.

These city regulations not only specified job categories as reserved for urban residents, they also made explicit suggestions that urban residents not be underpaid compared with "outsiders." Employers who violated these restrictions faced stiff fines. The Labor Bureau of one of Beijing's city districts, for example, stipulated that at least 35 types of jobs should not be open to migrants. The Beijing Municipal Labor Bureau also made recommendations to local employers suggesting that wages for laid-off urban employees should not be below those of the labor cost of migrant laborers.[9] Employers using migrant laborers were required to contribute to an unemployment fund for each migrant laborer they hired. This fund, however, was created only to help unemployed *urban* laborers. In Shanghai, for instance, a contribution of 50 yuan per migrant laborer was required. Half the revenue from this source was to be centralized at the city level to be used for reemployment of Shanghai local resident laborers, and the other half was to remain with district labor bureaus (Wang, Zuo, and Ruan 2002). During the mid-1990s, in an attempt to alleviate urban unemployment and to facilitate reemployment, the city government of Shenyang ordered managers in over 100 work categories to hire urban surplus workers first (Solinger 2001b, 119).

The income-equalizing effect within localities, or intra-group egalitarianism, has been shown in several studies. Xie and Hannum's thorough analysis of data from a 1988 survey, for example, reports two important findings of relevance here: first, most of the positive regional economic growth effect on individual income came from the bonus share of the income, rather than from regular salary or wages. Second, at the same time, the distribution of this increased income was *not* strongly associated with individual characteristics, such as years of schooling, experience, party membership, or gender.[10] In other words, while income levels varied in different cities in China, distribution of income *within* these cities tended to be rather equal, as least at that time, according to the characteristics included in their study.[11] This is so because, in their words, "bonuses and subsidies are distributed to workers mainly for their affiliations with profitable work units" (Xie and Hannum 1996, 983).

Analyses of China's Urban Household Income and Expenditure Survey data in this study reveal similar results. As reported in Table 4.5 of the previous chapter, for both 1988 and 1995, the effect of "city" in explaining income variations among urban employees was much larger for "other labor income" than it was for "base salary." Unlike "base salary," which was subject to state regulations, "other labor income" was more subject to local policies and practices. In 1988, the contrast of the city effect between "other labor income" and "base salary" was 22.68 to 2.28, and in 1995, it was 59.03 to 12.73 (in mean sum of square terms). Whereas "city" was a key variable in explaining income differentials among individuals for both types of income, its role was much more prominent in the portion of income that was generated and regulated locally.

THE MINOR PUBLIC: WORK ORGANIZATION OWNERSHIP

A greater source of income stratification in urban China originates from an organizational level lower than the city. This is the Chinese work organization, or *danwei*. Under socialism, better work organizations (*danwei*) meant better welfare provisions and higher prestige. In the era of reforms, the role of the *danwei* has become more crucial to many urban residents, often serving as a lifeboat. Chinese urban work organizations were central to social and political organization under the planned economy system because they were the controlling arms of the state. They now have an increased role in economic organization and welfare provision because they have been liberated from the hands of the state.

Workers and their entire families become urban poor when their enterprises go broke. At the same time, those working in profitable work organizations continue to enjoy collectively provided benefits, from higher pay, better pension plans, more employment opportunities for their children, to better and cheaper housing. Based on interviews in Chinese cities in 1993 and 1994, Dittmer and Lü (1996) observed that while the political control function of the *danwei* was attenuated with reforms, the welfare functions of the *danwei* were strengthened. One of the most ironic consequences of China's urban reforms is therefore the strengthening of the *danwei* system in its economic, though not political or social, functions.

The New Property Rights Regime

Key to understanding the increased role of the work organization is the nature of the Chinese property rights regime following the reforms. Drawing from previous literature on property rights, Walder and Oi identified three types of rights: use, appropriation of returns, and transfer; they concluded that the most important change in China was a downward reassignment of use and appropriation rights (to lower levels of government hierarchy, to firms, and to households), with the state retaining control over transfer rights (Walder 1994; Walder and Oi 1999).

Though claiming to be publicly owned, the means of production under socialism was never so controlled. Public ownership under socialism was effectively collective ownership, segmented into different regions, sectors, and work organizations. Differently endowed work organizations did not have the rights to transfer and to dispose of the collectively owned property during the era of central planning, but they possessed certain rights to derive income. Even before the recent reforms, the unequal status of *danwei* in the Chinese economic and political hierarchies formed a basis for intergroup inequality. Naughton puts it this way: "Even though the *danwei* was required to turn over virtually all its surplus to the government, the reality was that the *danwei* had at least initial control of a large revenue stream, and the diversion of even a small proportion of that revenue could have a significant impact on the workers' standard of living. ....'Collective' benefits were seen as being ideologically preferable to individual wage increases" (1997, 175). Walder (1992a) argues similarly that it was this segmented property right under the socialist planned economy that served as the key institutional basis for the redistributive economy. Chinese urban work units therefore were "minor public" structures, as compared with the state, the "major public" (Lü 1997).

Creating minor publics is one of the most important institutional changes in China's post-socialist transformations so far. Recent urban reforms, especially enterprise and ownership reforms since the early 1990s, have expanded the scope of property rights for the previously existing minor publics or *danwei*'s. Starting in late 1993, there was an intensified effort to experiment and to change the old state ownership of enterprises. Such reforms initially aimed at "clarifying property rights, responsibilities and rights, and separating administrative and business decisions, and achieving scientific management." [12] As an outcome of these enterprise reform measures, multiple forms of ownership emerged. A 1998 survey of 2,562 key enterprises by the National Bureau of Statistics found that 1,943 (75.8 percent) had completed the ownership reform. Among them, 768 became limited liability corporations, 612 shared holding firms, and only 563 (29 percent) remained as solely state capital firms (Wang 1999, 87).

Reduction in state ownership, however, should not be equated with an expansion of the private economy. For instance, reading from official Chinese statistics after 1995, one gets the impression of a drastic decline in public ownership of the urban economy. The number of employees in state-owned units dropped from 109.55 million in 1995 to 83.36 million in 1999, a whopping 23.9 percent decline in four short years (NBS 2000, 126). Almost all this change, moreover, occurred in a *single* year, between 1997 and 1998, when the number declined from 107.66 to 88.09 million. Such a change was clearly more the outcome of administrative fiat than a real change in ownership.

Most of the employment reduction in state-owned units turned up in a category called "limited liability corporations," which registered an increase in the number of employees from zero in 1997 to 4.75 million in 1998 and to 5.88 million in 1999. Another category is "share holding units," for which the number of employees rose from none on paper in 1997 to 1.33 million in 1998 and 1.99 million in 1999 (NBS 2000, 126). Together, these two categories alone accounted for nearly a third of all the employment reduction in state-owned sectors. The rate of increase in these two groups also far exceeds the changes in other non-state-owned sectors.[13]

Moreover, enterprises that have undergone ownership restructuring have by no means all been turned into privately owned firms. Based on China's survey of ownership restructuring among state-owned industrial enterprises conducted in 1998, Yi-min Lin and Tian Zhu (2001) reported that only about one-quarter of over 4,000 restructured enterprises turned into private (including foreign) ownership, with the remaining majority still controlled by the state or institutional and collective owners. In over 80 percent of the restructured enterprises, the government was involved in selecting the CEOs.[14] Thus they concluded that, "the state retained a pre-dominant ownership stake in over half of the restructured enterprises; the financial and personnel liabilities were not significantly reduced among the restructured enterprises; and the blue-print of reform and the actual organizational features of restructured enterprises" (Lin and Zhu 2001, 305).

China's post-socialist hybrid property rights regime is not dissimilar to those found among other formerly socialist societies. Preceding the peak days of Chinese property rights reforms in the late 1990s, in Hungary there was similarly a drastic reduction in the number of state enterprises, about 60 percent, between 1988 and 1994, and a phenomenal increase in the numbers of incorporated shareholding companies (20-fold) and limited liability companies (175-fold) during the same period. In most of these corporatized firms, however, research revealed a close marriage between public and private ownership (Stark 1996). The majority of shares in the case of Hungary were held by the State Property Agency or the State Holding Corporation that was created later (Stark 1996, 1001). In addition, there was also a high degree of inter-enterprise ownership embedded in different forms of interlocking networks.

Who Owns Taxi Companies in Beijing? Three Examples

The complexity and intricacies of the post-reform property rights regime can be seen in the examples of taxi companies in Beijing. The origins of these companies are telling examples of the kind of property regime that emerged in the 1990s. In the 1990s, about 60,000 taxis were roaming the streets of Beijing. The majority of the taxi drivers belonged to some kind of company, which numbered around 1,000 in the early 1990s when the taxi industry boomed. Though almost all drivers operated as individuals, bearing almost all the economic risk, few taxis were registered as individually owned (*ge-ti*).

There are different reasons for taxi drivers to associate with a company, even though many of the drivers in fact own their taxis. Drivers normally refer to two reasons. First, to start the company and to purchase cars require a sizable amount of capital. Individuals, after a period of hard work and with borrowing, can come up with enough funds to buy one vehicle, but few have enough to buy many and to start a company. Second, with a company owned by a government institution, it is much easier to deal with bureaucratic rules and paperwork. Such paperwork includes various kinds of tests, exams, and permits. Affiliation with a company also updates one on city regulations and important events. For instance, in the 1990s many drivers were still required to participate in weekly studies, which normally lasted a half day. Taxi drivers not only lost earning time, but also needed to incur additional expenses.[15]

The three examples that follow illustrate three different forms of the new property rights regime, all seemingly private: one in which public funds were used to start a company, one in which public and private funds were merged to form a new non-state-ownership company, and in the third, public assets disappeared and became private properties.

Case 1: The Forsci Taxi Company is a company that was registered by one of China's major research academies in Beijing around 1993.[16] The company had 25 small and inexpensive taxis.[17] To start such a company, at least 1.25 million yuan capital was needed, as each vehicle cost about 40,000 yuan, and registration plus various fees added up to another 10,000 per vehicle. The company bought these vehicles and rented them out to individual drivers. Each driver was required to pay 3,000 yuan (increased to 3,300 in 1995) a month to the company. The company, in addition to providing the vehicle, was also responsible for the registration fee (about 1,000 a year) and insurance (which costs about 2,000 a year). The company, in other words, collected a net of 3,000 yuan a month from each driver to cover for the capital of the vehicle and for the management that amounted to very little.[18]

Case 2: The Ocegar Taxi Company, established in 1993, belonged to the Communist Party Committee of one of Beijing's major districts. The company also had 25 cheap taxis. One driver informed me that when he joined the company, he was told that the funds were from the personal pockets of retired senior officials of the committee. So a profitable operation of the company was considered a nice way to pay tribute to the old cadres who had served the people of the district. It is highly doubtful, however, that the old cadres of this district could and were willing to raise the 1.25 million yuan needed to start such a company. Annual income of these retired cadres in 1993 could in no way exceed 8,000 to 9,000 yuan per person. It would take over 100 cadres with that kind of high retirement income who were willing to risk their investment in a taxi company to raise the capital, and it is doubtful whether the district had that many high-income retired cadres.[19] It is clear that this non-public taxi company had received initial capital from a group of individuals with common ranks and institutional affiliations, and it is likely that the funds contributed by them alone were not sufficient and that other funding sources were involved.

Case 3: Ocesafe Taxi Company is the largest of the taxi companies I encountered. The driver I talked to used to be an employee with a branch of the government's transportation bureau in one of Beijing's districts. This branch was established in the 1950s. For years it had both horse-pulled carts and automotive vehicles. The company mainly served the area where major clients were premier Chinese research institutions. Some employees in this company enjoyed state-owned status, some were classified as collective, and some were workers converted from farmers. The last category consisted of farmers in Beijing suburbs whose land was appropriated in the process of urban expansion. As a compensation for their lost land, some farmers were given non-farming jobs.

The publicly owned transportation company was not doing well for years prior to the early 1990s, at which point a new opportunity emerged. For a variety of reasons, including outdated equipment, increasingly intense competition, and poor management, this publicly owned enterprise could not make any profit and was on the verge of collapse. To save the company, its management sold one of the two parcels of land on which the company was located. It was not clear how and under what terms the land, which was state property, was sold. In any case, the land was sold for 30 million yuan. That amount of cash was then used to purchase close to 100 vehicles.[20] A taxi service company was thus born. Employees of the old publicly owned transportation company were given two choices: to stay with the new company as hired laborers on contract, or to leave. Those who decided to stay rented vehicles from the company and paid the same amount of rent as taxi drivers from outside the company.[21] Outwardly, this new taxi service company appeared no different from other taxi companies.

Who had control of the new capital and the new company? The head of this company was the head of the old publicly owned enterprise, and he was a good friend of the District Transportation Bureau. The Bureau still had control over the company, and appointed the head of this company. It was not clear to the workers of this taxi company how the new leaders ran the business or what salaries or bonuses these new leaders received.

The ambiguous nature of the new property rights regime among urban Chinese work organizations is by no means limited to these low-tech and service-oriented firms. China's high-tech sector, for instance, has been from its inception dominated by spin-off enterprises from public organizations, endowed with resources from the state. In 1989 and 1990, of all high-tech firms registered in China's high-tech zones, 80 percent were found to have been launched by government agencies and public institutions (Francis 1999). Similarly, among the 81 mostly publicly owned, large-scale enterprises in Shanghai studied by Guthrie (1997), 40 percent engaged in diversification into the service sector in the mid-1990s, either for survival or for income augmentation benefiting from privileged positions in the redistributive economy.[22] These new economic organizations, often with ambiguous property rights arrangements, have become a major source of employment and income inequality in urban China.

What these numbers and case studies show is that in the process of economic reorganization, what emerged in urban China up to the mid-1990s was not an economy dominated by private ownership but a mixed economy with both public and private ownership, and most commonly, with what Stark labeled as a "recombinant" property rights regime, in which the separation between private and public ownership of an organization cannot be easily if at all distinguished. Drawing from research based on the ownership structure of Hungary's 200 largest corporations and top 25 banks and other materials, Stark identified an emerging property form that was characterized by a "triple boundary blurring": the boundaries of public and private, of enterprises, and of justificatory principles. What emerged in post-socialist Hungary was a property regime in which "actors respond to uncertainty in the organizational environment by diversifying their assets, redefining and recombining resources" (Stark 1996, 997). In the Chinese case, at the same time that the central state was no longer fully and directly responsible for the employment and welfare of urban residents, it did not relinquish its nominal control over public property in most cases.

Devolution of public ownership from the state to work organizations resulted in a rapid increase in the economic resources of the minor publics. An example to illustrate this point is the changing source of revenues reported to the government. One revenue source that underwent the greatest increase within the category of "extra-budgetary" revenue was from "administrative and institutional units" (*shiye-xingzheng danwei*). Though designated as nonprofit and nonproductive, these units became the most impressive moneymakers. In 1985, the combined revenue from such units was 23.32 billion yuan; by 1990 it doubled to 57.7 billion, and by 1995 it literally quadrupled again, to 223.5 billion (NBS 2000, 267). The pace of increase doubled that of the increase in overall government revenue, which was only 46.6 percent between 1985 and 1990, and 2.13 times between 1990 and 1995 (calculated from NBS 2000, 267).

Implications for Income Distribution

Such a new property rights regime bears important implications for income distribution and inequality. Because private individuals do not legally own most workplaces, employees in the minor publics, which still employ the majority of urban workers, feel a sense of common ownership and entitlement. At the same time, even though managers of the firms have more power than they did in the past, their hands are still tied when it comes to the transfer and disposal of public assets. Urban Chinese work units use the resources they possess first to protect the welfare of their employees and their families. The early signs of the rising importance of *danwei* can be traced back to the early 1980s when the *ding-ti* (replacement) practice emerged. Children were allowed to replace their parents and to be employed in the same work unit. Capable work organizations also created their own enterprises to employ their employees' children.

When deciding income distribution within the work organization, equal entitlement was still an important consideration, as the examples in Lin's (2001) and Lin and Zhang's (1999) study of "backyard profit centers" run by government agencies show. In Wang Gao's study of 20 enterprises in the city of Mudanjiang, he showed that almost all the differences in average income between work organizations could be explained by ownership type, enterprise's capital and technology advantage, enterprise type (whether designated as a large enterprise), and magnitudes of redundant workers and old pensioners, whereas bureaucratic rank of the enterprise did not have the effect it did under the planned economy system (Wang 1998, 149–152). Wang concluded that as of 1996, while market forces affected income distribution at the macro level in determining an organization's profit level, intra-organizational income distribution among individuals still followed the principles of bureaucratic coordination.[23]

The same pattern, that of relatively equal income distribution within a work organization, persists well into the first decade of the twenty-first century, and characterizes income distribution even in high-profit, often state-sanctioned enterprises in virtual monopoly industries. In 2004, for example, the national average annual wage for urban employees was 16,024 yuan per capita, with those in the state-owned sector at a slightly higher level of 16,729 yuan (NBS 2005, Table 5-21). Yet in a number of state-controlled, large organizations in monopolizing industries, such as banking, electric power generation or distribution, and mobile communication, the average income was drastically higher. At the Bank of China, the average yearly income for its over 200,000 employees in the year 2005 was 88,548, more than five times the national average for all state employees. In two power-generation companies, Datang and Huaneng, the numbers were 103,500 and 105,828 for their 10,300 and 23,500 employees, respectively. At China Mobile, the average for its 47,400 employees was 143,292 yuan, amounting to 8.5 times the national average.[24]

A study of income distribution in a particular enterprise that enjoys a monopoly position similar to those listed reveals a high degree of within-organization equality. In 2004, the average wage income in this organization was 41,836 yuan, two and half times the national average. For 206 individuals included in the study who were employed continuously in the same organization, their average wage increased by 47 percent in two years, well above the pace for the whole country, which was about 30 percent. Within-organization distribution was extremely equal, with calculated Gini index of inequality below 0.1 for all three years. In the year that employees experienced the largest income increase, the Gini index was even lower. In 2004, the six individuals in leadership positions in the organization made an average of 65,155 yuan per person, whereas the lowest-paid individual in the sample had an income of 17,283 yuan, suggesting a gap between the two extremes of no more than four times. Equal distribution of wage income was even more pronounced in the distribution of bonuses than in basic wages, and educational level of the employee played no role in differentiating wage incomes (Luo 2006).

Labor market segmentation by firms, together with segmentation by

urban and rural sectors and by local residents and migrants, characterize China's post-reform emerging labor market (Knight and Song 2005).[25]
Analyzing income data from two large surveys in the 1990s, economists
Knight and Song reported that while firm-level profitability became more
closely associated with urban Chinese employees' incomes in 1999 than
in 1995, profit sharing within firms remained equal, due to what they interpreted as rent sharing.[26] In 1995, only employees of higher seniority at
state-owned enterprises were found to benefit more from a firm's higher
profitability. By 1999, even that pattern could not be established. Firm
profit, in other words, affected the overall income level for employees in
the firm, but its distribution did not reward individuals differently within
firms. Equal profit sharing was more prominent in 1999 than in 1995 and
was especially the case for profit-making enterprises.[27]

Similarly, Wu Xiaogang's study of income differentials among urban
Chinese employees could not provide evidence to support the market transition hypothesis that predicts an increased income advantage with more
education. The lack of added income advantage associated with higher education, he argues, is due to the fact that a major proportion of employees'
income comes from bonuses distributed by work organizations, and this
distribution, unlike the state-stipulated base wages, is distributed much
more equally within the work organization and is not closely related to an
employees' educational attainment. Wu attributes the inter-organizational
inequality to a firm's market position and to the work units' increasing
autonomy (Wu 2002).

Despite a bad reputation assigned to state-owned enterprises due to
their alleged inefficiencies and their risks of being closed down, as recently
as in the late 1990s state-controlled work organizations were still preferred
over foreign or privately owned businesses by many urban Chinese. A 1997
national employee survey reported that an overall majority of urban employees listed government agencies, public organizations, and state-owned
enterprises as their top choices if they were going to choose a work unit
again (Tang 2005, 145–146). Moreover, some urban employees, especially
those in public-owned work organizations, continue to hold a belief in their
right to welfare provision from their employers and to equal distribution of
income. In a mid-1990s survey of factory workers in Guangzhou, the majority of respondents still expected their employers to provide retirement,
medical, and housing benefits. Moreover, over 80 percent of respondents

in public-owned factories believed that there should be an upper limit for managers' income.[28]

Opportunity hoarding and rent seeking based on the new property rights regime not only prevail in previously state- or collective-owned enterprises but also in government organizations. State public agencies have converted, created, or adopted their "backyard profit centers" by using resources at their disposal. Such centers, like the taxi companies in Beijing illustrated earlier, rely on the government for their economic existence, and in turn supply income to their government sponsors. The income from these centers, as documented by Lin and Zhang, "are used in three major areas: consumption-oriented spending, reinvestment, and supplementary resources for covering the gaps in budgetary allocation" (Lin and Zhang 1999, 217). They cite a study showing that in 1993, some one-quarter of the income of state agency employees came from the supplementary resources of their work units. Income generated by *danwei*-owned profit centers tends to be equally shared among the members of the *danwei*.

As Lin and Zhang note, "consumption-oriented spending is often shared—although not necessarily in an equal fashion—among the members of an agency. This can take many forms, including cash income supplements, free or subsidized consumer goods, the provision, improvement, or expansion of communal facilities (e.g., housing, kindergartens, bathhouses, canteens, and cable TV), group consumption (e.g., banquets, junkets, and entertainment), and the addition or upgrading of office property that can easily be put to private use (e.g., automobiles, telephones, fax machines, and photocopiers)" (Lin and Zhang 1999, 218).

One well-publicized case is the Ministry of Water Resources officials' misuse of a $72 million fund in the 1990s. Instead of using the fund for its intended purpose, namely for building and repairing canals, reservoirs, and dams to prevent flooding and to facilitate irrigation, the leaders of this central government ministry diverted the fund to construct an expansive building they expected to use for the benefit of employees of the ministry. The 28-story Water Resources Administration Building was supposed to be built to house some offices of the ministry. But an important use of the building was to make it into a conference center, equipped with restaurants and fancy hotel rooms, with the income going into the "private" coffer of the ministry.[29] This case is but one example of a widespread practice among government organizations at various levels. China's National Audit Bureau reported that as much as $15 billion in government funds was squandered in 1999.[30] This amount equals about one-fifth of China's state treasury income and is almost twice the national defense budget in 1995.

Embezzling state funds for work unit collective benefits is a continuing phenomenon well after the mid-1990s. In 2002, for instance, the State Audit Agency reported that out of the over 100 billion yuan in state-allocated funds the agency audited, 10.4 percent was misused. One staggering new case is the Beijing Railway Bureau, which misused 470 million yuan (US $56.8 million) earmarked for equipment updates to build a four-star hotel, equipped with an indoor swimming pool and sauna rooms. Originally requested and approved as a recreational activity center for its employees with a construction area of 15,000 square meters, it exploded into a 60,000 square-meter facility of a quite different nature. The rationale used by the Bureau was that this hotel facility was built for the benefit of their employees. In a television interview, the head of the State Audit Agency admitted that such practices were common, and they were mainly driven by the interests of "small groups"—work organizations.[31]

What is worth noticing in these cases is that such diversion of the central government's allocated funds differs fundamentally from embezzlement of public funds by individuals. The funds diverted did not go into the pockets of the leaders who called the shots to cheat the central government. Rather, such decisions were often made in the name of the employees of the work organization. Income generated from diverted funds can be used to benefit the members of the organization, by purchasing apartments, subsidizing incomes, and distributing other welfare items. In Beijing, for instance, government agencies, large corporations, and military organizations made up the bulk of the buyers of newly built housing units. In 1996, they bought 75.6 percent of all apartments, with 88 percent of their purchased units located in the more desirable residential areas (Li and Li 2000, 39).

Work-unit welfare is not limited to former state- or collective-owned enterprises; they are emulated by other work organizations as well. For example, Anita Chan observed a continuation of welfare provisions among joint ventures in Beijing in the mid-1990s. She cited a survey of 140 joint ventures that found 72 percent of them provided housing subsidies, 88 percent medical insurance, and 92 percent retirement and unemployment insurance (Chan 1997, 105). Corinna-Barbara Francis' study (1996) of 11 high-tech companies in Beijing similarly reported that as of late 1993 these new economic entities in the marketized sector of the economy routinely provided housing, medical care, pensions, and other perks that were comparable to the traditional *danwei*. Instead of introducing managerial, institutional, and cultural innovations, these new economic organizations emulated the *danwei* system by reproducing the practices of work organizations. Managerial staff in these work organizations attributed such emulation not only to the need to compete for labor but also to the legacy of the *danwei* welfare system and the normative expectations from employees.[32]

Just as better-endowed and better-positioned work organizations may bring benefits to all their members, less fortunate ones bring all their members down when the organization fails. The urban work organization, in other words, functions as a boat that carries urban employees and their family members. Enterprise losses and bankruptcies are often more important sources of urban unemployment and poverty than are individual layoffs within the organizations.

One factory I personally visited in the summer of 1995 serves as an example to illustrate this point. This is a story of the reversal of fortunes of a chemical factory in a large city in Liaoning province. This organic chemical plant was a state-owned enterprise established in 1958. Created from five smaller plants all related to chemical processing, this factory started with about 1,100 workers and expanded to 2,800 employees by the early 1990s. With close to 40 years in operation, the plant had also generated over 1,400 retired persons on its payroll. The main products of the plant were calcium carbide, choleric products, and pesticide. The factory was a major contributor to the state in profits and taxes until the early 1990s, when it began borrowing funds from the state. By 1993, it had a net loss of over 20 million, and an accumulated debt–to–capital ratio of 1.8:1. In other words, even if all the capital of the plant was liquidated, it was not enough to pay off its debts. This plant, while highly profitable until 1992, was named in 1994 as number one on a list of 10 enterprises to go bankrupt in Liaoning province. With help from the local city government, this plant survived the threat of bankruptcy as of 1995.

The factory was killed, or almost killed, by its total dependence on the state, from obtaining production materials to selling products, nurtured over a period of four decades under the socialist planned economy system. There were many factors that had brought the factory to the verge of bankruptcy in a short two years, including the common culprits attributed to the poor performance of state-owned enterprises, such as inefficient management, outdated infrastructure and technology, and lack of capital to improve production. But the most important reason in this case was the sudden withdrawal of state support. The experience of this factory is an example of how victims are created and at the same time condemned both by the old planned economic system and the current "transition to the market economy."

Up until 1992, most products from this factory were in short supply, partly due to rural economic growth in China. One of its main products, pesticide, was a state-controlled item. The factory had no authority to sell any of it directly; it had to go through the Provincial Bureau of Chemical Production.[33] In 1992, an important change occurred. The Provincial Chemical Production Bureau told the factory leaders that the time of market economy had arrived and the Bureau itself was not going to purchase from and distribute pesticide for the plant. Instead, the Bureau was going to import pesticide directly from Russia, where pesticide much cheaper than the domestically produced product had suddenly become available. With the abrupt withdrawal of the state as a customer, such a change in the macroeconomic environment dealt a devastating blow to the whole industry: nationally only three out of over 40 pesticide factories survived the influx of cheap Russian products. Most domestic factories failed overnight because they did not have direct sales networks. They could not compete with such massive importation of cheap Russian products at such short notice, and they had no capital to change their line of production.

This factory in Liaoning was allowed to close down in the fall of 1993. By October 1993, only 700 of 2,800 employees were kept to maintain the offices and facilities of the factory. By November 1993, in order to save heating costs, the number of employees kept in the factory was further reduced to 400.[34] The winter of 1993 must have been one of the most miserable for employees and their families. Not only was there no wage payment, the factory also lacked money to run its furnace to provide heating to factory housing where most families of the factory lived in this bitingly cold city in Northeast China. For many families, the factory was the sole source of employment and income. Both husband and wife, and for some, even children, were all employed by this same plant, another by-product of the Chinese socialist planned economy. There were few job alternatives outside the factory.[35]

In 1994, pesticide imports from Russia stopped. Demand for domestic pesticide surged again. Moreover, all together 14 kinds of products that could be produced by this factory were in short supply in the market. The factory could produce and make profit, but one problem remained. It needed operating capital. With its virtually bankrupt status, however, no bank would lend money to the factory. The factory owed the state bank 107 million yuan, with a monthly interest payment of 1.2 million. In addition, it owed its employees back pay of 12 million, employee investment 4 million, and medical expenses and housing relocation expenses 2 million. It also owed other factories and suppliers a total of 60 million, but roughly the same amount could be collected from others as well. The city government came to the rescue. By the summer of 1995, the city government had injected a total of 15 million-plus yuan to help the factory restart. Workers were gradually brought back to work. In the summer of 1995, about 800 workers, less than a third of the total, were still "on leave." The factory was operating with a monthly profit of 900,000 yuan. At that rate, the funds from the city government could be recovered in two years.

Matching Exterior and Interior Categories

Even within urban work organizations, boundaries have been erected along the lines of membership based on property rights. Two examples illustrate such within-organizational boundaries, one separating the rights and benefits between "regular" and "migrant" workers, and the other between "old" and "new" employees. Since the mid-1980s, there has been a rapid increase in migration across rural and urban boundaries in China. Such increased migration, however, has not brought a corresponding desegregation between urban and rural Chinese. On the contrary, a number of studies have shown consistently how boundaries, in the form of invisible walls, have been erected to prevent rural migrants from settling in cities (Chan 1997; Solinger 1999; Wang, Zuo, and Ruan 2002). Newly arrived rural migrants are not only separated spatially from urban residents in terms of employment and residence, but even when they work side by side with urban residents in the same urban work organization, they are still treated by urban employees as outsiders. Exterior categories, in other words, are transplanted into interior categories within work organizations.

A case to illustrate such category matching or boundary maintenance is exhibited by the labor policies implemented in a construction company in Guangdong province in the late 1990s. The company, originally under the control of the Transportation Bureau of the province as a nonproductive (*shiye*) unit, was reclassified as a productive (*qiye*) *danwei* in 1992. In an experiment with enterprise reform, it became a limited liability company in 1994. This was a large company that built expressways and highway bridges for Guangdong.[36] In this company, there were two types of workers: about 2,500 regular employees (or *zhigong*) and two to four times that many migrant workers (or *mingong*), depending on the time of the year and the amount of work. These were clearly two different categories of workers, as shown by the differences in their respective income and benefits. For regular employees, the company not only provided housing in the form of apartments ranging from 75 square meters for junior employees to 100 square meters for top managers but also paid a big bill for the education of employee children. In order to get about 80 primary-school-age children of the regular employees into a nearby school, the company paid about five million yuan. Migrant workers, as outsiders, were paid less and not entitled to any benefits.

Matching exterior and interior categories was not limited to migrants but also existed between urban "early" comers and "latecomers." In a university guesthouse in Beijing, two maids worked side by side, performing exactly the same job. Ms. S., a temporary employee (*lingshigong*) in her early 40s and Ms. C., a regular employee of similar age, however, received quite different pay and benefits. Ms. S. was a laid-off worker who formerly worked in a brand-name shirt factory in Beijing before the factory closed down in 1996.[37] As a temporary worker, she was making 14 yuan a day, paid by the day and with no benefits. She belonged to the majority of the workers in the guesthouse. Ms. C., as a regular worker (*zhengshigong*), was paid about 1,000 yuan a month by doing exactly the same work (cleaning the same rooms). Moreover, on special occasions, she as a regular employee also received bonuses (e.g., 2,000 yuan on National Day, and another 1,000 yuan on Mid-Autumn Festival, etc.) as part of profit sharing by being a member of the organization and an old-timer. Her income averaged about 2,000 per month, four times that of Ms. S. Ms. S. is understandable of this vast disparity because this was what was meant by membership and entitlement. "They picked a good job years ago, back then my job was better." At the same time, she was also keenly aware of her own advantages over another group of people, namely migrants. She was also conscious of maintaining a boundary between people like herself and migrants, whom she perceived as outsiders. She complained about urban neighborhood committees for renting out their space to migrants, which allowed migrants to stay and to make competition between locals and the migrants more intense. She clearly preferred that local neighborhood committees use laid-off urban workers instead of migrant workers.[38]

CHECKS AND BALANCES: OLD AND NEW FACTORY INSTITUTIONS

In addition to a sense of shared public property that forms the economic basis of welfare distribution within Chinese work organizations, there are also socially and factory-based institutions that serve to curb the extreme forms of unequal income and welfare distribution in some Chinese work organizations. Workers, whose power and job security have seen a drastic decline, may still exert their influence both by their claim to ownership and by the support of the remaining factory institutions in their favor. Thus, the dynamics set in motion in the early days of urban Chinese income distribution reforms within work organizations, as observed by Walder, are still fully applicable to some organizations a decade later. This dynamic relationship, as summarized by Walder, is that "managers have always hoarded and evaded fiscal controls, but now they have greater freedom in disposing of factory resources, and the amount of resources they control has increased too. Workers, similarly, have always engaged in obstructive work practices, haggling, and other behavior designed to protect their interests, but not until recently has there been a large incentive fund in factory coffers to serve as the objective of their attempts at influence" (Walder 1987, 41).

The most prominent political legacy of post-socialist China is that China has been under the continued rule of the Chinese Communist Party. Political reforms in the two decades following China's reforms have drastically reduced if not totally eliminated daily political participation of ordinary citizens and have reduced the direct involvement of local party organizations in daily economic decisions. The Chinese Communist Party has nevertheless retained its monopolized control over important personnel decisions, ideology, and major policies. Communist Party organization branches remain omnipresent, reaching and remaining in not only publicly owned but also some privately owned work organizations. Membership of the Chinese Communist Party has seen a further growth in the 1990s, rising from 51 million in 1991 to 70 million in 2004, accounting for an ever larger proportion of the total population (Lü 2000). The continued rule of the Communist Party relies on its large membership, and its organizational reach. Continued organizational reach of the Communist Party, at the same time, has also to some extent perpetuated the *danwei* system (Li 2004).

In the wake of enterprise reforms in the 1990s, institutional relationships between the "three old committees" versus the "three new committees" have emerged. The three old committees are the Communist Party Committee, Workers' Union, and the Workers' Representative Committee. The three new ones, products of the reforms, are the Representatives of Stock Owners, Board of Directors, and Committee of Supervisors. Though the three old committees are not fully functional in all factories that have undergone reforms, many still provide a check to the power of the managers, especially in the areas of income and housing distribution.

In one state-owned company that was in the process of changing into a joint-stock company in Chengdu, Sichuan, factory managers described how the power of the managers was limited by various factory-based institutions. In addition to major investment and technological innovation decisions, the contract of profit sharing between factory managers and the "factory," which specified the income of managers, required approval by the Committee of Workers' Representatives. Distribution of factory-purchased housing also had to be publicized to all members of the factory and approved by the Workers' Representative Committee. The role of these old institutions seemed to be on the rise, and according to the managers interviewed, such an institutional check was not limited to only a few companies.[39]

Another case to illustrate the presence of such checks is a large beer company in Guangzhou. One of the largest beer production companies in China, this company is also a telling case of urban economic reform and property rights regime change. Founded in 1985 as a state-owned enterprise with an initial production capacity of 50,000 tons of beer annually, it had grown by the end of the 1990s to a company with 2,600 employees that produced 700,000 tons of beer, with over 200 million yuan net profit per year (after taxes). Though a state-owned company, by the end of the 1990s it had acquired several other smaller, collectively owned beer factories and bought stock in two other beer companies outside Guangdong province with a controlling share of stocks in one of them. Capital that originated in a state firm had not only expanded but had extended into other non-state companies. As workers in a growing and profitable company, employees at this firm were much better paid than others in the same city. In 2000, their average income was about twice of the norm in Guangzhou city. Intra-company income distribution follows a "multiplier" (or coefficient) system. Mid-level managers were paid about 2.5 times that of ordinary workers, and top managers five to seven times that of ordinary workers. The "multiplier," which was constructed by taking into consideration an employee's administrative position, technical requirements of the position, and his/her structural position (i.e., how important the position is in the process of production), required discussion and approval by the Workers' Representative Committee.[40]

Even after the transition from a state-owned to a joint-stock company, the managers' power in the factory was still under checks by both the old and new institutions. The Stock Owners' Committee included members of other publicly owned organizations that received a share of the stocks. Representatives from these other organizations sometimes functioned like representatives of higher-level government or Party organizations. The Committee of Supervisors, at the same time, was required to have representatives from the Workers' Union.

As late as the end of the 1990s, many top managers of large urban firms were still appointed by state-controlled organizations. This was said to be the case for over 80 percent of state-owned enterprises and for a substantial number of non-state-owned firms as well. The percentage of firms with leaders appointed by a higher-level government/party organization was around 30 percent of non-state-owned firms, and 59 percent of shared stock companies. There was, in other words, still a high degree of intermarriage between government and economic organizations as of the late 1990s.[41] The bottom line was that the power of managers was still limited in many previously state-owned organizations.

MORAL CONSTRAINT: COMPETITION VERSUS HARMONY

Another important factor that contributed to the more equal distribution of income and benefits within work organizations was a morally based inclination toward equality and an emphasis on harmony and stability. Though often criticized in the Chinese media simply as an egalitarian mentality incompatible with the pursuit of a market economy, there was much more to it than just a desire among Chinese urban residents to share resources and welfare equally. Recent changes in Chinese history, from the pre-socialist inequality to equality under socialism, and then to inequality after socialism, reflect deeply rooted social sentiment in Chinese society regarding equality and social organization. This social sentiment, embedded in the Chinese social and cultural tradition, serves as an important context for understanding both the equality attempted under socialism and the pattern of inequality that emerged after socialism.

The Paradox of Equality and Inequality in Chinese History

Balancing inequality and equality has always been a central tenet of the Chinese social and cultural tradition. For over two millennia, the Chinese lived in a cultural and social system instilled with a fundamental paradox of inequality and equality. On the one hand, their society has always been highly stratified with clearly defined hierarchies, differentiating people by political power, economic resources, occupation, education, family background, age, generation, and gender. On the other hand, the population has also believed deeply in a fundamental right of equality and the possibility of upward social mobility.[42] Both sides of this paradox are necessary and crucial to understanding this populous country. Whereas hierarchy and stratification have been highly valued for maintaining social and political orders, the deeply ingrained belief in social mobility has provided the spiritual engine for Chinese society throughout its history. China, depending on one's perspective and social position, was at once both a very unequal and a very equal society.

The Chinese examination system, no doubt a pillar of China's political system and one of China's great cultural inventions, is such an institution that has perpetuated both equality and inequality. The national competitive civil-service examination system, which was firmly in place by the Tang dynasty (AD 618–907), served as an almost uninterrupted institution to select and promote officials based on merit and performance until its abolition in 1905.[43] In his magisterial study of social mobility in late imperial China, based on over 35,000 records of national and provincial exam candidates of China's last two dynasties, Ping-ti Ho (1962) discovered a high degree of social mobility during the period he studied. For instance, among over 12,000 candidates who passed the highest-level (national) examinations, between 30 to 40 percent had no privileged academic or political backgrounds within three generations, whereas only less than 6 percent had a family background of high officials within three generations. Studies of other historical time periods by other scholars have reached a similar conclusion; between 30 to 50 percent of degree holders always came from families with no privileged backgrounds (He, H. 1998). Social mobility measured by achievements other than holding a degree exhibited a similar pattern in historical China. Utilizing longitudinal household register data for populations in Northeast China spanning from the late eighteenth to the early twentieth century, James Lee and Cameron Campbell report that while having a privileged family background bestowed a clear advantage for obtaining a title, there was substantial downward mobility among the title holders that opened up opportunities for men from undistinguished backgrounds (Lee and Campbell 1997; Campbell and Lee 2003). Such a high level of social mobility was unparalleled among major societies before the industrial revolution.

Spatially, economic equality in traditional Chinese society was local, confined to one's social group. Defining one's position in society by group membership was therefore always a salient feature of the traditional Chinese social configuration. Social groups are omnipresent in every society, but there is an important difference between the Chinese sense of grouping and that of some other societies, as noted by the Chinese sociologist Fei Xiaotong. According to Fei, who first wrote about this difference in the 1940s, a defining feature of traditional Chinese society was what he labeled the concentric grouping (Fei 1948/1985). In contrast to groups in Western societies where individuals joined groups voluntarily and enjoyed a more or less equal status, Fei described the Chinese concentric circle or grouping as self-centered and hierarchical. Each person constructs one's own group by placing him or herself at the center, defining the importance of others in their relationship to the ego. These perceived circles of networks formed one's social space.

The basis for defining relationships in traditional Chinese society, Fei argued, was the blood relationship. There was a strong sense of insider versus outsider, and a strong sense of belonging to a relatively rigid grouping. The traditional Chinese social stratification system was therefore highly ascriptive, differentiating individuals not only by traits at birth, such as gender, age, and ethnicity, but also by one's location in social circles defined by blood relationships. Recent empirical research by Cameron Campbell and James Lee has shown that in addition to parental background, having a prominent kin in the descent group was also an important facilitator in upward social mobility (Campbell and Lee 2003). Group membership, in other words, was always a central criterion in shaping social and economic inequality. Groups, or categories, also formed one of the bases of social stratification and inequality. Outside of the group, opportunities were emphasized more than equality. Individual members of groups were often encouraged to compete and succeed in the society at large, for the benefits of such success were to be shared by all members. Whereas within the household hierarchy an individual's position is largely a function of predetermined fate, outside of the household, fortune is open for grabs (Lee and Campbell 1997).

Maintaining Local Equality

Relative equality within social groups was not only a characteristic of Chinese socialism but also of its post-socialist social configurations. Income distribution within most urban Chinese work organizations remained relatively equal into the late 1990s. In most cases, the income ratio between the highest paid level (top managers) and average workers was no more than three or four to one. Such a ratio was certainly much higher than the one during the late days of the socialist planned economy era, when it was less than 1.2 (Lu 2002, 153).[44] For example, in a profitable, publicly owned factory in Chengdu, workers in the year 2000 started with a wage of 400–500 yuan a month, mid-level managers/longtime employees at 600–700 yuan a month, and top general managers at 1,000 yuan or so a month.[45]

In the Guangdong highway construction company described earlier in this chapter, a new regular employee with a university education (not a rural migrant laborer) received about 1,000 yuan regular pay plus another 80 to 100 percent of that amount as a bonus each month. Managers at the subcompany level were paid twice as much. Only a few top managers of the company, president of the board, and the general manager received compensation about four times that of a recent college graduate and seven times that of the lowest paid worker.[46] Even in a privately owned housing construction company in Chengdu that experienced a phenomenal profit growth, from no more than 3 million yuan assets in 1997 to close to 300 million sales in 2000, most managers and employees were paid in a relatively equal way. Deputy general managers were paid only slightly over twice as much as the staff members. Considering that the managers were also older employees and had higher educational and better technical backgrounds, the difference in income was small.[47]

Differences in company-provided housing were similarly small before the end of welfare housing at the end of the 1990s. In a state-owned bank in Sichuan, which was perhaps one of the most desirable employers in the city, the starting income in 1999 was about 600 yuan per month (300 yuan salary and 300 yuan bonus). A 37-year old male with a five-year work history at the bank but more than 15 years of total work experience, who was in charge of crucial computer maintenance for the bank, received only about 1,000 yuan per month. This technician's income, while doubling that outside the bank, did not differentiate him much from other ordinary employees. Another technical school graduate who had recently joined the bank made about the same amount. The same distribution pattern held for housing allocation. All employees were moved into the fanciest apartment building in the city, and most of them received same-sized apartments. The choice of floor plan, one of the few variations, was based on seniority at the bank.[48]

These factory managers and workers were queried as to why there was not a greater gap in income between managers and employees. In the publicly owned company, part of the explanation given was that the difference depended upon the way that the state stipulated the determination of income: base salary, skill income, position subsidy, seniority (1 yuan per year), and bonuses based on profit. Managers could not themselves arbitrarily set wages. In both the publicly and privately owned companies, managers and workers also referred to what they called the Chinese characteristics (*tese*). They pointed out that what was important was not only profitability but also stability.

Moreover, profitability was often achieved when there was stability. A goal given by the head of the construction company just cited was to seek stability and prosperity simultaneously. In other words, harmony was given as much consideration as competition. Factory managers interviewed emphasized the need to mobilize workers and pointed out the need to recognize ordinary workers' crucial contributions to the company. If some employees were paid much less than other employees, these managers realized, the less well-paid would feel entitled to ask those who were better paid "why don't you do all the work?" In the publicly owned company, there was also a sense of community with a shared past. The company had been state-owned. All workers had been employed in the same factory for a long time, and they had all made contributions.[49] Lin and Zhang (1999) attribute this sharing to the need to sustain a "collusive collective action."[50] As late as the mid-1990s, in many urban Chinese work organizations, the "tacit alliance" between managers and workers in acquiring material benefits observed by Walder remained and an egalitarian distribution of income continued.[51]

Even after two decades of market-oriented reforms that trumpeted the value of competition over cooperation, many urban Chinese employees continue to value cooperation more than competition. In a national survey conducted in 2004, respondents were asked the question "To increase the economic efficiency of a work organization, what is more important, competition or cooperation?" About half (51.4 percent) of all urban respondents ranked the two as "equally important." Of the remaining half, respondents rated the importance of cooperation over competition for achieving economic efficiency at a ratio of two to one: 22.5 percent responded "Cooperation is more important than competition," and 10.6 percent responded "Only cooperation is important." In comparison, only 6.2 percent believed "Only competition is important" and 9.2 percent believed "Competition is more important than cooperation."[52]

If perceptions bear any relevance to reality, what urban Chinese report of their perceptions of "global" versus "local" distributional justice shows that there is indeed a difference between the overall increase in inequality in post-socialist China in general and a relative degree of equality within one's social grouping. In surveys carried out in 2000 and 2004, urban residents in Beijing and in China nationwide were asked to evaluate their perceptions of the degree of income inequality in China. This question was followed by another, one inquiring about their evaluation of their own work organization.[53] In the 2004 national survey, respondents were also asked to assess the degree of income inequality in their own neighborhood. The responses to these questions in the two surveys are given in Table 5.1.

The contrast between the perceptions of "global" (for China as a whole) and "local" (in one's own vicinity) inequality is more than apparent. In Beijing, though respondents sensed a decidedly high degree of inequality for China, with 95 percent reporting that the gap was "too large" or "somewhat too large" in their own work organization, the percentage sensing "too much inequality" is much lower, at only about 50 percent. What is most striking is that whereas almost no one (only 2.8 percent) thought

TABLE 5.1
Perceptions of global and local inequalities, urban China

Degree of inequality	BEIJING 2000		NATIONAL (URBAN) 2004		
	China (%)	Own work organization	China (%)	Own work organization	Neighbors
Too large	65.2	19.3	44.5	14.7	7.8
Somewhat too large	30.3	29.1	32.6	36.6	31.8
About right	2.8	42.2	15.9	37.3	47.3
Somewhat too small	1.3	7.6	5.6	9.6	11.9
Too small	0.4	1.8	1.4	1.8	1.2
Number of cases	742	683	1769	1831	1570

SOURCES AND NOTE: Beijing 2000 based on Beijing Residents Survey, conducted by Research Center on Contemporary China at Peking University; National 2004 based on National Survey on Perceptions of Distributive Justice, conducted by the same center. Valid numbers of responses differ due to missing cases for different questions.

the degree of income inequality was "about right" for China as a whole, a substantially large number of people (42 percent) felt that within their own work organizations, income inequality was "about right." Only less than 20 percent reported that inequality was "too large" within their own work organization, compared with over 65 percent for China in general.

From the 2004 national survey, a similar pattern persisted. Nearly 45 percent of respondents believed that the income inequality level in China was "too large," in contrast to 15 percent for their work organization and 8 percent for their neighborhood. At the same time, a large share of urban residents could accept the degree of inequality in their own work organization (37 percent) and own neighborhood (47 percent). At the national level, only 15.9 percent found the inequality level "about right." Equality in China, in other words, was much better maintained locally than nationally.

Patterns of income inequality in urban China have clearly been conditioned by the various old and new social categories, and by political organizations of the society and cultural inclinations of the population. Among inequality-generating and equality-maintaining categories, of particular importance are locality and work organization, the two categories this chapter examined in detail. Cities and work organizations are not simply geographic spaces where people happen to live and work; they have also evolved, partly as a product of the socialist legacy, into meaningful political and economic categories surrounded by detectable boundaries. These boundaries serve to separate one group from another and to protect members within each group, as well as to maintain a certain degree of local equality. Moreover, while economic changes in the closing decades of the twentieth century seem to have undermined two important institutional boundaries that previously separated Chinese under socialism, namely, control over migration and job mobility, these changes have not been sufficient to break down real boundaries. Old exterior boundaries in some cases are maintained as they are being reborn in the form of interior boundaries within locales and work organizations.

CHAPTER SIX

Varieties of Inequality

Within a short decade after the mid-1980s, urban China transformed itself from one of the most egalitarian to one of the more unequal societies. Depending on the measure used, in 10 years, income inequality rose by as much as 75 percent to 100 percent. The real magnitude of income inequality may well have been greater than what is documented in this volume, because the main data source used in this book is likely to have excluded individuals with extremely high incomes, a problem that plagues all income surveys. At the same time, the urban population studied in this decade is defined as those with permanent urban household registration (*hukou*) status, and therefore excludes rural migrants, who tend to be transient and are generally treated as secondary citizens economically and socially.[1] Had these extremely rich and poor populations been included, the measured income inequality would no doubt have been even higher. Moreover, what emerged by the mid-1990s seemed to be only the beginning of a trend of worsening inequality. The reform of urban state-owned enterprises after the mid-1990s resulted in a rapid increase in urban laid-off workers and a further increase in income inequality, especially urban poverty. During the roughly two-decade period under study, over half of the increase in income inequality in urban China could be accounted for by an individual's location in the political economy and social structure. For urban China, city and work organizations are the two most prominent categories. These two categories are not just places where people happen to live and work but are meaningful political economic entities that are protected by boundaries.

At the same time when this vastly increased inequality is recognized by the Chinese population, and to some extent tolerated between groups, equality has also been maintained to a large extent within various social categories or groups. Whereas the socialist public ownership legacy was largely responsible for creating inequality-generating categories that defined the rising inequality in post-Mao China, the egalitarian sentiment and values of intra-group harmony, long instilled in Chinese culture, were also at least partially responsible for maintaining within-group equality.

The coexistence of inequality and equality in urban China, which became prominent in the process of one of the history's greatest reversals of equality, originates from the evolving nature of China's post-socialist political economy. It is at the same time also shaped by China's political institutions that feature a continued rule of the Communist Party and of its long cultural tradition that honors equality and harmony as much as it tolerates inequality. Such a pattern of inequality in other words contextualizes itself deeply and intimately in China's distant as well as its recent history. The pattern of rising inequality in post-socialist urban China, where a sharply increased inequality between categories is accompanied by a substantial degree of equality within different categories, raises a question about the nature and the process of social equality in general: is such a pattern uniquely transitory to China's post-socialist transformation, or does it represent a form of inequality that can be found in other societies? Is the Chinese pattern, in other words, one type among different varieties of inequality?

Scholars of comparative capitalist economies have begun to identify systematic differences among capitalist economies, under the heading "varieties of capitalism" (Hall and Soskice 2001).[2] Such studies reveal for instance that employee protection level is higher in the so-called coordinated market economies (e.g., Austria, Germany, Japan, Sweden) than in liberal market economies (e.g., Australia, Canada, the United Kingdom, and the United States), and they find that income inequality level is lower in the former than in the latter group.[3]

Specifically, such research calls for the attention of a firm-centered approach, treating "companies as the crucial actors in a capitalist economy,"[4] a call that certainly echoes to the main findings in this study, that work organizations play a central role in income generation and distribution. Comparative studies of capitalist economies also link firm behaviors to institutional complementarities, such as firm relationships to the financial market, and further suggest the value of understanding differences in corporate governance (e.g., internal structure, management-labor relations, and job training) in the context of culture, informal rules, and history. Varieties of inequality are therefore important manifestations of the varieties of capitalism and, more broadly, varieties of societies.

To place China under a comparative lens of varieties of inequality, one needs to confront first an intellectual tradition that privileges uniformity and linearity in social and economic thinking. One needs to begin with an examination of two influential theories of inequality that have helped foster an intellectual tradition of "one common path" and "one common pattern" of inequality. One theory, known as the "Kuznets' inverted-U relationship" between economic growth and inequality, hypothesizes a particular trajectory of inequality following economic change. The other, known as the "market transition theory," anticipates a clear shift of power from government bureaucrats to market producers in post-socialist societies. Both portray or at least imply a common path of economic change and inequality, and both accept a common pattern of inequality distribution, namely, that it is an outcome of shifting ordering among individuals.

In the following pages, I will first provide available evidence on the validity of the inverted-U relationship, showing that there is no certain path of inequality following economic growth. I will then show that post-socialist transformations in the last two decades have similarly presented a complex picture of inequality change, and have failed to support the teleological predictions about the equalizing role of the market. Having shown some of the problems with these two theories on inequality, in the last section of this concluding chapter, I offer an example of studying the varieties of inequality by comparing distributions of inequality in three societies: China, the United States, and Japan.

INCOME INEQUALITY AND ECONOMIC GROWTH: INVERTED-U OR W-SHAPED?

Is rising inequality in post-socialist urban China an ongoing trend that will last for quite some time, or is it simply a transitional phase and a necessary price to pay in the early stages of economic development and institutional change? Put another way, will economic development and further market reforms eventually lead to decreased inequality? Whereas predicting the future trajectory of inequality is always a precarious exercise since the future depends on many factors, some speculations can nevertheless be made about the relationship between economic development and income inequality, based on historical experiences in other settings.

The relationship between economic growth and inequality has long occupied the attention of social scientists.[5] This relationship has been examined especially rigorously since Simon Kuznets formulated his famous inverted-U curve five decades ago (Kuznets 1955). Based on limited historical data from the United States and the United Kingdom and on contemporary data from India, Ceylon, and Puerto Rico, Kuznets speculated that income inequality would first rise during the process of economic growth and would then level off. Subsequent research utilizing longitudinal British and American historical economic data, along with cross-sectional developing country data, has mostly confirmed the Kuznetsian theory (Williamson and Lindert 1980; Williamson 1991). Kuznets and economists who followed in his footsteps also specified the mechanisms of such a trajectory of income inequality. The chief economic mechanisms include labor force growth driven by demographic transition and international migration, skills deepening in the labor force, sectoral technological imbalance, and prior distribution of wealth (Lindert and Williamson 1985; Lindert 1991).

Sociologists have also contributed their interpretations. They theorized that as the economy develops, the non-elite professional and technical labor force should enjoy increased economic power and that increased education and economic power should lead to greater democratic participation (e.g., Lenski 1966). Among both economists and sociologists, testing and explaining the Kuznets theory have remained a topic of constant interest. Not only have the relationships between economic development and inequality been rigorously examined, so have the roles of specific types of development, such as dependent versus independent development (Muller 1988, 1989; Firebaugh and Beck 1994; Nielsen and Alderson 1995).

The history of the second half of the twentieth century, especially of its closing decades, however, lends little support to the Kuznets hypothesis. When using longitudinal, rather than cross-sectional data, support for the Kuznets hypothesis becomes highly inconsistent, to the point of becoming virtually nonexistent. In some cases, studies fail to show a process of increasing inequality associated with economic growth (e.g., Nielsen and Alderson 1995). In others, a flipped Kuznets curve, where inequality first drops and then increases, is observed. Overall, in a majority of cases, no clear trajectory could be established (Fields 1980, 2001).

What has emerged in these years instead is a global trend of increasing inequality. The Untied States, one of the prime cases used by Kuznets to formulate his inverted-U trajectory, has witnessed rising inequality for over 30 years. After the late 1960s, income inequality first stabilized for a period and then rose steadily (Thurow 1996; Ryscavage 1999). Whereas the real income of 60 percent of all families remained essentially constant, the top 5 percent saw their real income rise by nearly 50 percent (Tilly 1998, 231). In almost all other major industrialized countries, such as Australia, Canada, France, Italy, Japan, Sweden, the United Kingdom, and the former West Germany, income inequality also increased after the 1970s (Greene, Coder, and Ryscavage 1992; Ryscavage 1999, Chapter 7; Alderson and Nielsen 2002).[6] A comprehensive study of 73 countries reports that, for the period of 1950 to 1995 and in all but 9 countries, inequality either increased (in 48 countries) or remained constant (in 16 countries) (Cornia 2004). These countries accounted for 80 percent of the world's total population and 92 percent of the world's gross domestic product purchasing power parities (GDP-PPP).[7]

In the closing decade of the twentieth century, the richest got richer in the Unites States. The average after-tax income of the wealthiest 1 percent of Americans rose from around $400,000 in the early 1990s to over $500,000 in 1997 and to $600,000 in 1998. Their share of all personal after-tax income also rose from 12.5 percent in 1989 to 15.7 percent in 1998. During this time period, the rate of income increase among the richest group was eight times the rate among the bottom 90 percent, adjusted for inflation.[8]

While the stock market plunge of 1999 may have wiped out a large portion of the market value of the dot-com stock options, and therefore weakened the income basis of some high earners, there has been no reverse trend in rising inequality. Concentration in wealth, the most telling measure of inequality in material possessions, shows the same trend. The Gini index for net worth among American households rose from 0.80 in 1962 to 0.87 in 1995, with the share of the top 5 percent of households in holding total national wealth rising from 55 percent to 60 percent. The distribution of financial worth (stocks, bonds, savings in banks, etc.) was even more unequal, with the Gini index increasing from 0.88 to 0.94 (Keister 2000, 64).

A similar picture has also emerged among developing countries with available longitudinal data for studying inequality. In Mexico, for instance, for the past 90 years for which time series data are available, there was no sign of income inequality decline (Braun 1997).[9] Brazil, a country that had an impressive record of economic growth in the earlier decades and was labeled as a "miracle economy," saw its inequality grow to make it one of the most unequal societies in the world by the end of the twentieth century. Between 1960 and 1990, the richest 10 percent of Brazilians increased their share of the total income in the country from 40 to 68 percent. The Gini index of income inequality among the economically active population rose steadily, from 0.52 in 1960 to 0.57 in 1970, to 0.59 in 1980. In 1990, the index reached 0.60 (Braun 1997, 126).

Even in Taiwan, a showcase of "growth with equality" in the development literature and a society that shares some common cultural background with mainland China (Fei, Ranis, and Kuo 1979), there was an upturn in income distribution inequality in the last decades of the twentieth century. Following an initial drop from 0.32 in 1964 to 0.28 in 1980, the Gini index edged up almost continuously between 1980 and 1995, accompanying rapid economic growth, back to the level of the mid-1960s.[10] Globally, although there was still a debate at the turn of the century on whether between-country inequality was on the rise, there seemed to be a consensus that overall worldwide income inequality was rising at that time (Korzeniewicz and Moran 1997; Firebaugh 1999, 2000; Goesling 2001).[11]

Another example of economic growth not being necessarily linked to reduced inequality is a recent study of poverty in China. Khan, Griffin, and Riskin (2001) report that urban poverty, measured by a broad poverty line of headcounts of those falling below the necessary income level to purchase sufficient food (2,100 kilocalories per person, at 2,291 yuan in 1995), was at 8.0 percent in 1995, virtually unchanged compared to 1988. Deep poverty, defined as 80 percent of the broad poverty threshold, rose from 2.7 percent to 4.1 percent in the seven-year time period. Moreover, their simulation exercise reveals that economic growth would have reduced the poverty level to below 1 percent had income distribution remained unchanged during the period (127). Economic growth alone, therefore, does not guarantee a more equal distribution. There is, in other words, no confirmed, clear relationship between economic growth and the trajectory of income inequality. This is so largely because inequalities, as we have seen in the Chinese case, are conditioned by a large number of factors, including though not limited to political system and cultural predispositions.

IMPLICATIONS FOR TRANSITIONAL
SOCIALIST SOCIETIES

Similar to the hypothesized relationship between economic growth and inequality is a debate over how post-socialist transformations redefine the degree and structure of inequality. Capitalizing on Karl Polanyi's elegant characterization of redistributive versus market economies as well as decades of studies of socialist states by others, scholars in the late 1980s optimistically predicted a clear transfer of economic power and a change in the social mobility regime following the market transition (e.g., Nee 1989, 1991). Such an optimism was no doubt fueled by the rapid occurrence of events associated with the collapse of the socialist camp in the late 1980s.

Understated, however, was the true spirit of Polanyi's study of the great transformations of the nineteenth to the twentieth centuries. Contrary to the trumpeters of the market economy in the late twentieth century, Polanyi's work was not about the inevitability of the replacement of a redistributive economy with a market economy. Rather, as he announced unequivocally on the opening page of his book, "the idea of a self-regulating market implied a stark utopia. Such an institution could not exist for any length of time without annihilating the human and natural substance of society; it would have physically destroyed man and transformed his surroundings into a wilderness" (Polanyi 1944/1957, 3). The story told in his book was how social machines, especially the state, engineered the rise of the market economy and how society reacted to protect itself in this process from the negative human consequences.[12]

Studies of formerly socialist societies have increasingly shown that the transitional process is complex and multidimensional (Peng 1992; Róna-Tas 1994; Stark 1992, 1996; Bian and Logan 1996; Nee 1992, 1996; Nee and Su 1996; Walder 1996; Xie and Hannum 1996; Gerber and Hout 1998; Zhou 2000; Cao and Nee 2000). Gradually but decisively, the research focus has moved away from a debate over producers versus redistributors, and over the winners versus the losers. Instead of using the individual as the unit of analysis, this new understanding focuses on institutions. There has been an increasing consensus that institutions, both old and new, define the process of transition and the patterns of social inequality in socialist societies under reforms.

Just as there is no predetermined relationship between the trajectories of economic growth and income inequality, there is no predetermined relationship between the market and inequality, as pointed out by Walder: "Market economies vary widely in their patterns of power and privilege, in ways related to the *extent to which* a market economy has been established. The variability of market economies warns against attempts to predict changes in inequality without first specifying the kinds of enterprises and other institutions that characterize the emerging market economy—or even the characteristics of markets themselves" (1996, 1060; italics added by original author). In order to understand the social consequences of economic transformations, Walder calls for the development of what he characterizes as "testable theories." [13] Many others have joined this call.

The complex nature of post-socialist transformations has led to a characterization of the process of transformation in these societies as a "path-dependent" process (Stark 1992, 1996; Róna-Tas 1998). As summarized by Stark, transition is a path-dependent process "in which the introduction of new elements takes place most typically in combination with adaptations, rearrangements, permutations, and reconfigurations of already existing institutional forms" (Stark 1992, 22). Given the path-dependent nature of the transformation process, studies of this process benefit from what Szelényi and Kostello (1996) term an "evolutionary" approach. Stark's (1996) research on the Hungarian experience is such an example, documenting, not a clear-cut property rights transfer from the hands of the public to the private, but an emergence of a recombinant property rights regime.

The urban Chinese experience reported in this volume and elsewhere suggests a highly similar process (e.g., Walder 1995; Guthrie 1997, 1999; Keister 1998; Oi and Walder 1999; Tang and Parish 2000). [14] In concluding a systematic study of urban life under reforms in China, Tang and Parish similarly observed: "All this suggests that we need a much more developed political economy of types of firms, with attention to path dependence . . . , before making predictions about whether entrepreneurs, managers, and administrators will have the highest incomes as a result of market transition" (Tang and Parish 2000, 314).

Institutional legacies and changes, not individual characteristics, best reveal the characteristics of social inequality in post-socialist China. Looking only at changes in individual characteristics simply misses the whole picture of transitional societies. Among the crucial institutions that define both the transition process and its social consequences, I have singled two out for close scrutiny in the Chinese case. One is the role of local government, and the other is the property rights regime. Changes in urban inequality as examined in this study confirm the central roles played by these two institutions. The categories based on these institutional characteristics not only explain a major share of increasing economic inequality but also reveal another important feature characterizing post-socialist Chinese urban inequality, namely, the relative equality within social groups.

These and other institutional features are likely to define future urban inequality trajectories in China. On one hand, it can be expected that with increased labor market and geographic mobility, boundaries that separated different groups in Chinese society may weaken if not collapse. Also, with the decline of direct state control over the economy and work organizations, the political economy and ideological basis for within-category equality may wither, if not disappear. In other words, it is safe to predict that some changes will certainly occur in this direction, making between-category inequality less pronounced and within-category inequality more pronounced. On the other hand, the lessons we learn from this study and from inequalities across the world and throughout history are that categorical inequalities are durable.

As late as 1999, only 15.5 percent of all urban laborers worked outside of *danwei* or organizations as self-employed, and nearly three-quarters of all urban employees still worked in publicly owned organizations.[15] Work organizations, as one category, still encompassed the working lives of the majority of urban Chinese. Moreover, at least until the end of the 1990s, voluntary labor mobility in urban China was still extremely low. A 1999 national survey of urban Chinese workers found as many as 78 percent of respondents had only held one job, and only 6 percent had held three or more jobs. The authors of the study attributed this low job mobility in part to the continued importance of *danwei* in the form of profit-sharing among employees and highlighted that work organization segmentation as a new form of labor market segmentation.[16]

Labor market segmentation is by no means a novel phenomenon limited to emerging market economies. They are prevalent in existing mature market economies (Edwards, Reich, and Gordon 1975; Beck, Horan, and Tolbert 1978; Baron and Bielby 1980, 1984; Gordon, Edwards, and Reich 1982). The pattern of inequality revealed in this study, therefore, may well have a life of its own and may condition urban inequalities for the present and near future. Depending on the pace and direction of change in the institutions examined in this study (including the local corporate government, the minor public ownership, and job mobility), the pattern of income inequality may well last for some time.

VARIETIES OF INEQUALITY: DISTRIBUTION OF INEQUALITY IN THREE SOCIETIES

The Chinese experience and patterns of social inequality, past and recent, calls attention to the structuring or distribution of inequality in different societies, or varieties of inequality. This is because the same degree of overall inequality can be distributed *differently*, between and within categories. Different distributional patterns of inequality not only reflect the social structure and cultural preferences of a given society, they also exert important social and psychological impacts on members of the society. The same degree of inequality, in other words, could have quite different social and political implications. Social and psychological deprivation after all is relative to one's reference frame, and such references tend to locate matters greatly for one's perception of inequality and sense of deprivation. The political stability that has followed the often turbulent economic changes in post-socialist China can be attributed in part to an overall rapid economic growth that increased the standards of living for the majority, to the continued firm grip of the Communist Party, and to the fact the local equality has to a large extent been maintained in spite of an overall drastically increased inequality level.

The Chinese pattern, with its large inter-group inequality and relatively small intra-group inequality, is both an exception and a familiar case in the international comparison. It is an exception when compared with one developed capitalist market economy, the United States, but it is a familiar case when compared with another developed capitalist market economy, Japan. In the United States, in contrast to the Chinese increase in inequality at the inter-group level, within-category income inequality is the main driving force behind the recent rise in inequality overall. During the 1980s, according to a report in the *Economist*, the after-tax annual salaries of chief executive officers (CEOs) in the United States increased by two-thirds after adjusting for inflation, whereas production workers' real hourly take-home pay declined by 7 percent (cited in Gordon 1996, 34).

The most staggering contrast is perhaps the rising ratio between the average annual compensation of the top 100 CEOs of American corporations and the average annual salary of American workers. In the three decades after 1970, this ratio went up from 39 times to more than 1,000 times.[17] Using a measure less subject to extreme cases, the median income, shows a similar though less extreme trend. In 1970, half of executives in the 50 largest companies in the United States earned 25 times the average worker's pay. In 2004, the gap increased to 104 times.[18]

The United States represents an extreme case in within-firm inequality, as other main industrialized economies pale in comparison. For example, a 1991 survey found that CEOs in large U.S. corporations on average received almost exactly twice the total compensation of their counterparts in Japan or Germany (Gordon 1996, 42). Others gave an even sharper contrast in pay inequity between Japan and the United States. One study cited the pay gap between top executives and the lowest ranked workers at around 8 to 1 in Japan, compared with 37 to 1 in the United States (Sakamoto and Chen 1993, 192). America stands out in comparisons of pay inequity among ordinary employees as well. Among male employees, America has the highest ratio of wages between the top 10 percent and the bottom 10 percent wage earners in a number of OECD (Organization for Economic Cooperation and Development) countries at the turn of the twentieth century. The ratio stands at roughly 4.5 to 1 in the United States, in contrast to about 3.5 in Britain, less than 3 in Japan, and 2.5 in Germany.[19]

In contrast to the United States, where intra-firm inequality increases account for a major source of rising inequality, in Japan the increase in inequality is attributable to a different source. According to work by Toshiaki Tachibanaki and his colleagues, two important sources that accounted for the increasing inequality in Japan in the 1980s were an expanding income difference between industries, and a greater disparity in income by firm size (Tachibanaki and Ohta 1994). A comparative study of earning inequalities between Japanese and American male workers, using data from a decade earlier, confirms the different sources of inequalities in these two societies: the overall higher inequality found in the United States was primarily caused by a higher degree of inequality within various sectors (Sakamoto and Chen 1993).

Like those in China, work organizations in Japan play an important role in determining employee income. In the United States, an employee's earnings are tied more closely to his or her job characteristics, one's position in the hierarchy, and the presence of unions in the workplace. In Japan, by comparison, earnings are more closely tied to the work organization and to a life-cycle-based reward system (Kalleberg and Lincoln 1988). Status differentiation according to firm size is also greater in Japan than in the United States. According to the Japanese sociologist Hiroshi Ishida, "There is therefore a striking cross-national variation in the role of firm size in explaining differentiation among employees. In Japan, firm size seems to be an important variable in explaining internal differentiation among all classes of employee, whereas in the United States its impact appears to be limited to the professional-managerial class" (Ishida 1993, 226).[20] At the same time, educational credential, an important personal characteristic, is also more important in explaining inequality of occupational status and income in the United States and Britain than in Japan (Ishida 1993, 242). Though known as a country that worships the importance of education, Ishida's study could not support any of the propositions about "educational credentialism" in Japan.

The more egalitarian intra-firm distribution system is partly an outcome of Japanese economic institutions. The Japanese labor market model is one characterized as having "integrated segmentation," with a coexistence of segmentation and integration. Among employees, both competition and co-operation are encouraged (Mosk 1995). The Japanese wage system underwent a substantial shift between the mid-1950s and the mid-1980s, changing from one based on age and merit to one that puts more emphasis on merit and skills. However, it still contains elements that differ significantly from the system in the United States, which does not consider family needs at all (Mosk 1995).[21] Changes in the Japanese wage system were also slow. As late as the 1980s, after systematically examining patterns of earnings determinants in Japan and in the United States, Kalleberg and Lincoln found " scant support for claims of convergence in Japanese and Western employment systems and labor markets, at least as far as earnings determination is concerned" (Kalleberg and Lincoln 1988, S148–149). They concluded that the age and merit-based "*nenkō* is still alive and well in Japanese employment practice and job-based compensation continues to play a minor role" (Kalleberg and Lincoln 1988, S149).[22]

Another important factor in accounting for the relative egalitarian income distribution within Japanese work organizations is a cultural value that places more emphasis on the collective than on the individual and stresses harmony more than competition. In contrast to the Western individualistic ideology in which competition among individuals is believed to be the best way to achieve overall efficiency, in a more collective society such as Japan, harmony is deemed to be an important means to reduce friction among coworkers and thereby achieve efficiency. As recent as the late 1990s, many Japanese firms routinely provided nonstatutory fringe benefits for employees. Such benefits varied by firm size and included not only subsidies for housing, medical insurance, and lunches but also expenditures on cultural or athletic activities and on congratulations and condolences. Expenditures on cultural activities and on congratulations and condolences made up more than 10 percent of the total nonstatutory fringe benefits.[23] These "Eastern Asian type" fringe benefits were believed to be better suited for improving labor relations and harmony among employees than were higher wages.

At the same time, a Japanese worker is less likely to view his or her own pay as directly linked to personal productivity, but rather to that of the group or the firm (Sakamoto and Chen 1993).[24] Such a group ethos, reinforced by Japanese economic and social institutions, was believed to have kept wage differentials at a minimum.[25] The collective orientation and the group ethos found in Japanese society resemble closely those found in both socialist and post-socialist urban China. Such a deeply rooted cultural orientation bears much credit in shaping the pattern of inequality distribution not only in Japan, a country that avoided a socialist experiment, but also in post-socialist urban China.

Studies of social inequalities often privilege one actor, the individual, and one relationship, that economic change has a uniquely deterministic relationship with trajectories of inequality. The process of rising inequality in post-socialist urban China has defied both. Rising inequality in post-socialist urban China reveals a social process in which categories create and maintain inequality. Differentials in individual characteristics and abilities do matter in income determination and their importance has increased over time. Focusing only on these individual characteristics, however, misses the larger picture of Chinese society's transformation from equality to inequality, as well as the deeper processes of inequality creation and maintenance.

The trajectory and patterns of income inequality in urban China are not only unique but also universal for understanding social inequality. They are unique because of China's history, which includes China's socialist experiment in its effort to transition into an industrial society, and the adoption of a particular path of reforms in its transition away from socialism. They are unique also because of China's culture, a collectively oriented society that places a high premium on group solidarity and group membership, and that is instilled simultaneously with both a strong sense of hierarchy and egalitarianism. The story told about China, at the same time, is also part of an overall story of how social inequality is created and maintained. China's recent experience is a case of how categories are created and boundaries are maintained to generate and to perpetuate social and economic inequalities. China may have experienced the fastest economic growth and income inequality increase in modern times among populations of significant size, but this record alone does not make it an exception in the world. Boundaries and categories structure inequalities.

APPENDIX: CHINA'S URBAN HOUSEHOLD INCOME AND EXPENDITURE SURVEY DATA

The main data source used in this study for tracking trends and analyzing changing patterns of urban income inequality comes from China's Urban Household Income and Expenditure Survey. There are several reasons to rely on such a data source. First, this survey is the only large-scale, longitudinal survey conducted regularly in China that contains detailed information on urban households' income, expenditures, and characteristics of household members. Second, it is a survey that has been carried out with substantial resources from the survey organization and the strong support of the survey participants. As the only survey of its type sponsored and carried out by a Chinese official statistical agency, special organizations were created and specific budget lines have been allocated by the government on its behalf. These investments in manpower and other resources speak to the quality of the survey data. Third, even with the limitations we discuss here, the survey represents the majority of urban Chinese and what the survey data contain, therefore, are social facts reflecting the living experiences of the majority of urban Chinese.

These Chinese household survey data, however, are also plagued not only by problems generally associated with household income and expenditure surveys elsewhere in the world but by two characteristics specific to China: an economic environment that has been evolving rapidly following China's abandonment of the planned economy model and a short history in conducting surveys of this kind. No survey data are free from shortcomings in design and implementation, thus it is important to recognize the nature of the limitations and their implications for research findings. In this appendix, I will first summarize the history of the survey and then discuss the changing definitions of income, the representativeness of the survey data, and finally, the implications of data limitations for findings in this study.

DESIGN

Following China's transition away from the planned economy, a major change in the Chinese statistical system took place in the early 1980s with the creation of survey organizations within the official Chinese statistical system. These survey

183

organizations, one for rural, one for urban China, and a third for enterprises, were established as separate departments within statistical bureaus at the levels of central and provincial governments. They are entrusted with the task of collecting more detailed and more up-to-date economic and social information by using sample survey methods, a task that the previous Soviet-type statistical system was incapable of. That statistical system relied on compilation of standard tables from lower to higher administrative levels, which was slow, inflexible, and devoid of individual-level data needed for in-depth analysis. Statistics aggregated and reported in that way were also believed to be more subject to bureaucratic intervention and manipulation.

The Urban Socio-economic Survey Organization within China's Natural Bureau of Statistics (NBS), previously known as the State Statistical Bureau, is the organization that has been conducting the Urban Household Income and Expenditure Survey. Though household surveys were occasionally used before the early 1980s, systematic surveys of urban households based on probability sampling did not begin until 1984.

The first survey in 1984 was initially designed the year before as a stratified, multistage, sample survey.[1] At the first stage, over 200 cities in China were stratified into four categories according to their size: mega-city (with a non-agricultural population over 1 million), large city (population between 500,000 and 1 million), medium-sized city (population between 200,000 and 500,000), and small city (population under 200,000). Cities were sampled from different strata and from the six macro regions of China (Northeast, North, East, South-Central, Southwest, and Northwest) to ensure a nationwide representation. Provincial capitals not selected at the first stage were added to the sample later, as were some cities in remote areas and those with concentrated minority populations. A total of 226 cities and towns (146 cities and 80 county-site towns or small cities) were selected. At the second stage, neighborhood committees or street districts were used as the sampling units to draw samples within each of the selected cities. At the last stage, households were first ranked and stratified according to their 1983 per capita household income, and then samples of households were drawn.

Nationally, over 30,000 households were chosen as survey households. These households were sampled between 1986 and 1991, therefore constituting a true longitudinal panel. Such a sample nevertheless had both advantages and disadvantages, the main disadvantage being sample attrition due to migration and, more important, reluctance of surveyed households to cooperate for several years in a row. As a result, a sample rotation system was introduced in 1991, with one-third of the old sample rotated out each year, replaced by new households. In addition to the regular household surveys, since the initial design in 1983, the Urban Socio-economic Survey Organization has conducted a number of other one-time, large-scale surveys using methods similar to the first one in 1983. These surveys generated lists of urban households, which were used as the basis for selecting new households in the regular household surveys.

Collecting household-level information by survey takers is a laborious process. Selected households are asked to maintain detailed bookkeeping of income and expenditure items. Survey takers assist and supervise such bookkeeping by visiting selected households regularly, often more than once a month. At the end of each month, information kept by the household is transcribed by the survey taker, and at the end of each year, the monthly information is aggregated and reported.

With rapid changes in the economic system, both the sample and the content of survey items also needed changes. Up until 2001, urban households included only those with permanent urban household registration status. Migrants' households had been excluded. Starting from 2001, migrant households have been included in the sample. Between 1986 and 2001, four different versions of survey questionnaires were used, reflecting changes in employment, sources of income, and expenditure items. In all versions of the questionnaire, the survey collects detailed information on household members' characteristics (up to nine members per household), such as age, gender, education, occupation, employer's ownership type (state-owned, collective-owned, shareholding, etc.), and year of first employment, as well as detailed information on levels and sources of income, conditions of housing, ownership of consumer durables, and expenditures.

DEFINITIONS OF INCOME

Defining what constitutes income in urban China is a difficult task. For different reasons, neither China's planned economy period nor its reform years offers an easy definition. During the years before urban reforms, a major difficulty was posed by the underrepresentation of real income level due to the welfare provision system, which disguised a large portion of urban residents' incomes, especially those with better housing, medical care, child care, education, and other benefits.

These in-kind incomes augmented urban residents' income by a large margin. One estimate of the difference between nominal income and actual income is provided by results from three large-scale income distribution surveys conducted in China in 1988, 1995, and 2002. Economists at China's Academy of Social Sciences and in England and the United States jointly carried out all three surveys. These surveys are described in three representative works: Griffin and Zhao 1993 (for the 1988 survey), Riskin, Khan, and Li 2001 (for the 1995 survey), and Khan and Riskin 2005 (for the 2002 survey). The 1988 survey included 9,009 urban households in 10 provinces. By applying a more comprehensive definition of income than the one used by the official Chinese statistical agency, the survey revealed a per capita disposable household income 55 percent higher than the official statistics. A major portion of the difference, 62 percent, is attributed to the inclusion of housing subsidies and the rental value of owner-occupied housing in the survey. But even if one ignores housing, inclusion of in-kind payments still led to an income estimation that was 20 percent higher (Khan and Riskin 1998, 233; also see Griffin and Zhao 1993).

Measuring income in urban China

Items included in the survey	1986–87	1988–91	1992–2000
Wage/Labor Income[1]			
Base wage from employer	X	X	
Floating wage from employer	X	X	
Time-based wage			X
Piece rate–based wage			X
Contract wage	X	X	
Bonuses and overtime pay[2]	X	X	X
Job subsidies and allowances	X	X	X
Overtime pay			X
Payment under special condition			X
Net income from self-employment/ owned business		X	X
Income from employment in private businesses		X	
Income from self-employment	X		
Income from other types of employment[3]	X	X	X
Income from retirees' reemployment	X	X	X
Income from secondary occupation		X	X
Income from family sideline production			X
Other wage income	X	X	
Other Income			
Other non-wage income from work units	X	X	X
Subsidies for living	X		
Subsidies for income differentiation	X		
Transfer Income			
Retirement income	X	X	X
Income from supporters	X	X	X
Price subsidies		X	X
Other transfers		X	X
Special Income			
Income from gifts	X	X	X
Income from selling goods	X	X	X
Income from boarders	X	X	X
Subsidies to surveyed households	X	X	X
Other special income	X	X	X
Property Income			
Interest income		X	X
Dividend income		X	X
Income from property rent		X	
Other property income			X
Loan and Credit Income			
Withdrawal of savings deposit	X	X	X
Withdrawal of coop savings fund	X	X	X
Borrowing	X	X	X
Loan returned	X	X	X
Saving insurance premium returned		X	X
Income from selling bonds/notes		X	X
Buy on credit		X	X
Bank loan for purchasing house		X	X
Other income from borrowing	X	X	X

NOTES: X means included in the survey.

[1]Wages for 1986–87 are differentiated by from state-owned or from collective-owned employers.

[2]After 1992, bonus and overtime pay were separated.

[3]Employment types other than state, collective, or private.

Similarly, by employing the more inclusive definition of income, the 1995 survey, which included 6,931 urban households in 11 provinces, also reported a substantially higher income level than the one reported by the Chinese statistical agency, based on the urban household income and expenditure surveys. Even after a decline in urban welfare provisions following urban reforms, urban subsidies still composed a substantial portion of real income for urban residents in 1995. By including housing subsidies in kind, rental value of owner-occupied housing, and other net subsidies, the per capita household income level was 33 percent higher than the result from a more narrowly defined income definition in 1995 (Khan and Riskin 1998). The 2002 survey, based on 6,835 urban households in 11 provinces, produced an estimated average income level that was 29 percent higher (Khan and Riskin 2005).

Another major change in urban residents' income during the past decades is the diversification of income sources. This diversification is twofold. First, instead of receiving income from only state- and collective-controlled institutions, an increasingly larger proportion of urban laborers have become self-employed or employed by private businesses. Second, instead of drawing income almost exclusively from employment, more and more income has come from other sources, such as property income and income from secondary jobs. Even within the category of state-controlled income, there was a period when more categories were added to reflect the changing course of the reforms; one such added category was a price subsidy between the late 1980s and the mid-1990s.

These changes in income sources are reflected in the income items included in the questionnaires of the Urban Household Income and Expenditure Survey, as shown in Table A.1. In the earlier surveys, only 24 kinds of income were considered and no question was asked about property income.[2] Only base wage for each person was obtained in the 1986–87 surveys. Incomes other than base wage were collected only for the whole household, not by individual household members. Starting from the late 1980s, when urban economic reform accelerated with price reforms, new items such as price subsidies were added. So were property income items and net incomes from privately owned businesses. The 1988–91 version of the questionnaire increased the income types to 33. Twelve new income questions were added, while two were dropped. The 1992–2000 version of the questionnaire kept for the most part the items developed for the 1988–91 surveys, but with further changes made on income categories.

SAMPLE REPRESENTATIVENESS
AND INCOME UNDERREPORTING

In addition to difficulties associated with measuring income due to definitions, income data collected in the surveys are also subject to underreporting problems. Before the early 1980s, income for urban Chinese was not a difficult or sensitive

TABLE A.2

Comparison of employment characteristics between national and survey data (%)

	OFFICIAL STATISTICS			SURVEY SAMPLE		
Year	State-owned	Collective	Private/other	State-owned	Collective	Private/other
1986	70.21	25.74	4.05	72.52	25.08	2.4
1987	70.04	25.31	4.65	72.85	25.08	2.07
1988	69.98	24.72	5.3	71.49	25.87	2.64
1989	70.24	24.34	5.42	71.85	25.48	2.67
1990	70.24	24.09	5.67	73.25	24.22	2.53
1991	69.85	23.76	6.39	73.06	24.13	2.81
1992	69.97	23.17	6.86	70.7	22.93	6.37
1993	68.4	21.25	10.35	69.59	23.17	7.24
1994	66.69	19.54	13.77	72.08	18.93	8.99
1995	64.92	18.14	16.94	74.75	16.6	8.65
1996	64.10	17.19	18.17	74.36	16.64	9.00
1997	62.44	16.30	21.26	73.27	16.53	10.2
1998	56.90	12.33	30.77	73.06	15.27	11.67
1999	55.03	10.99	33.98	69.21	16.09	14.7
2000	54.06	10.00	35.94	67.83	13.19	18.98

SOURCES: Official statistics: see notes to Table 2.1. Survey Sample: calculated from urban household survey data for three provinces.

question to ask. Given the transparency in wage standards and the relatively low inequality level in nominal income, income was barely a question worth asking. As income levels have increased, against a backdrop of increasing diversity of income sources and of inequality, the question of income in urban China, as in many others parts of the world, has become both a more difficult and a more sensitive inquiry.

Income underreporting originates from two sources. The first results from sample bias, namely, certain segments of the urban population are not included in the survey. The most obvious is the exclusion of migrants in the urban household samples.[3] In addition, urban residents with higher incomes, and often also higher political positions, are less likely to participate in the surveys, due to both the time-consuming nature of the survey and the sensitivity of the survey questions. In recent years, even those at the very bottom of the income rank, the urban unemployed, have begun refusing to participate as a way to express resentment about government reforms. The surveys, in other words, normally included only those with incomes at the upper-middle level and below.

One way to evaluate the representativeness of the sample is to compare the characteristics of the individuals included in the survey with those from other sources with larger samples and potentially higher reliability. Table A.2 shows such a comparison in one such characteristic, ownership sector of currently employed urban residents, between the tabulated national level statistics and numbers from the household surveys. These comparisons reveal that, overall, the sample from the three provinces used in this study include a higher proportion of employees in state-owned work organizations and a smaller proportion in private and other ownership types.

The overrepresentation of public sector employees also became more serious after 1993. Part of the large discrepancy between official statistics and survey results in ownership type in the late 1990s, however, results from a reclassification in the official statistics, which moved employees in state-controlled limited liability and shareholding firms from "state-owned" to "other" types of ownership (see discussion in Chapter 5 on this point). But part of the discrepancy may well be genuine. In that case, an overrepresentation of public sector employees in the household surveys could confirm our concern that households at the extremes of income distribution, the very rich and very poor, are both more likely to be in the non-public sector, and are increasingly underrepresented in the surveys.

The second source of income underreporting results from underreporting among those who participated in the surveys. As income sources became more diversified, income from ambiguous sources, such as bribes and under-the-table deals also increased. Such ambiguous or gray incomes are more likely to concentrate among those at the higher level of social hierarchy, people with more political power or special technical skills. It is highly unlikely that these incomes are reported. This problem is also much more difficult to tackle than a better sampling design.

One example of underreported income is income from savings. As shown by Bramall, even in the 1995 survey mentioned, which had a better coverage of income than the regular household surveys, property income for urban households was only at 72 yuan per capita, and for rural households, 10 yuan. By using published personal savings information and applying to it an interest rate, Bramall estimated that per capita income from savings, for urban and rural sectors combined, of 109 yuan per person, was not only well above the average of the combined urban and rural samples but also above the figure for urban households (Bramall 2001, 698). A criticism by Rawski based on the 1988 survey drew a similar conclusion.[4] Discrepancy between surveyed and tabulated savings, however, cannot be equated to underreported household income, as it is commonly known that public funds for work organizations are also sometimes deposited under personal names.

There is a third problem with sample representation, due to the fact that this study did not use all sampled households included in the urban household surveys, but primarily households from just three provinces. To assess the discrepancies resulting from the two different samples, in Table A.3, I compare incomes between employees in the three provinces against the national averages, published in China's Statistical Yearbook and presumably based on the national sample.

These comparisons show that, combined, the average incomes for urban employees in the three provinces used in this study are higher than the national average (see the second column from the right in the table). Starting from 1988, the

TABLE A.3

Income-level comparison between three provinces and national samples

| Year | INCOME LEVEL | | | | | | RATIO | |
	Liaoning	Sichuan	Guangdong	Combined	Sample size	National income level	Survey combined/ national	LN and SC/national
1986	1306	1432	1334	1372	3843	1329	1.03	1.03
1987	1347	1475	1497	1436	4282	1459	0.98	0.97
1988	1894	1822	2880	2150	4347	1747	1.23	1.06
1989	2130	2000	3629	2530	4354	1935	1.31	1.07
1990	2430	2191	3834	2766	3953	2140	1.29	1.08
1991	2507	2425	4608	3090	4302	2340	1.32	1.05
1992	2835	2827	6249	3632	5340	2711	1.34	1.04
1993	3353	3480	8397	4627	4962	3371	1.37	1.01
1994	4631	4736	11720	6417	4849	4538	1.41	1.03
1995	5591	5631	13696	7491	5216	5500	1.36	1.02
1996	6157	6136	15664	8451	5135	6210	1.36	1.05
1997	6707	6831	16461	9135	5119	6470	1.41	1.05
1998	7073	7364	17767	9828	4901	7479	1.31	0.97
1999	7389	8053	19707	10696	4721	8346	1.28	0.93
2000	8889	8499	20288	11637	4468	9371	1.24	0.93

SOURCES: Provincial data are from the urban household survey; national data are from China Statistical Yearbook 1997, 124, and China Statistical Yearbook 2002, Table 5–20.

NOTE: The numbers are mean yearly income in RMB yuan for employees only, unadjusted for inflation. A few extreme cases were excluded.

three-province sample exceeded the national average income by 20 to 40 percent. Most of this difference, however, is due to the inclusion of Guangdong province in the three-province sample. For most years during the decade, employee incomes in urban Guangdong were much above the national average. When only Liaoning and Sichuan provinces are used, the sample averages match the national averages quite well (see the table's rightmost column).

IMPLICATIONS FOR FINDINGS IN THIS STUDY

To summarize, the Urban Household Income and Expenditure Survey data used in this study contain at least the following limitations: 1) they do not include all population residing in the Chinese cities, but only regular or permanent residents with local household registrations; 2) they are very likely to underrepresent population at the two ends of income distribution, those with very high and very low incomes. The omission of those with very high incomes is likely to be more serious than those with low incomes; 3) due to changing definitions and sources of incomes, a significant portion of income was not included in the surveys, and such a problem seems to be more serious in the earlier years than in more recent years, when welfare provisions comprised a smaller share of real incomes; and 4) income underreporting may have become more serious over time as income disparity grew and sources of income became more diversified.

What are the main implications of these limitations in data for the findings in this study? While it is not possible to arrive at an accurate assessment in the absence of other independent and more reliable data, one can assess in a crude way the broad implications of these data limitations.

First, due to the omission of migrants, many of whom come from rural areas and with incomes much lower than urban residents, neither the level nor the trend in income inequality documented in this study can be interpreted as representative for all populations living in urban areas. Rather, the results in this study apply to only those with official urban residential status, who comprised the urban population under state socialism. If all urban residents were considered, including migrants, one would expect to see both a higher level of income inequality and a more pronounced rising trend in inequality, as migration has increased over the years. A multi-province survey conducted in 2002 that included migrant population in urban China provides a hint of the magnitude of the discrepancy: with migrants excluded, the Gini index for per capita income in urban China was found to be 0.318, and with migrants included, 0.338 (Khan and Riskin 2005, 382).

Second, a changing definition of income and decline in urban welfare provisions suggest that the low-income inequality observed at the beginning of the study period may well be an underestimate of the true inequality level. Moreover, while most if not all urban residents in China enjoyed some of these welfare provisions, inequality in access nevertheless existed. Because these welfare provisions were not equally distributed, the low inequality observed at the beginning of the study period, in 1986, may be an underestimate of the true level of economic inequality under state socialism. Consequently, with an underestimate at the beginning of the study period, it is possible that the degree of rising income inequality is overestimated.[5]

Third, due to both omission of high-income households in the survey and the increasing problem of income underreporting, the overall income level may well be higher than what is reported in the surveys. At the same time, level of income inequality and the rising trend reported in this study might both be lower than the true level.

Last, though the three provinces used in this study cannot be said to represent all urban China, two of the provinces, Liaoning and Sichuan, fall on the average of all urban China as far as the average income is concerned. Guangdong is a province that has an income level significantly higher than the national average.

Combined, it seems to be safe to say that both increases in the real income level and, quite possibly, the degree of income inequality during the decade under study for urban China are higher than the findings presented in this book. Some of this underestimation in rising income level and inequality, however, may have been offset due to the possible underestimates of income and inequality levels at the beginning of the study period, resulting from the more extensive welfare provision practices then. But without more data and more in-depth analysis, it is not possible to ascertain the true magnitude of such a countereffect.

Chapter 1

1. According to Kornai, in 1986, 34.4 percent of the world's population were living under the socialist system (1992, 7–8, Table 1). Lane estimates that the self-defined Marxist-Leninist states generated 40 percent of the world's industrial output as of 1980 (1996, 1).

2. The term "state socialist" is used to differentiate countries that were run under a centrally planned economic system and by a dominant Communist Party from those that had socialist elements or inclinations. The former are also considered the "hard" version of socialism and the latter, the "soft" version (Lane 1996, 16).

3. The Chinese 1958–61 famine, following its Great Leap Forward campaign to accelerate industrialization and collectivization, is by far the worst in terms of its human toll, with an estimated 30 million premature deaths and 33 million postponed or lost births (Ashton et al. 1984). The sensational book published at the end of the twentieth century, *The Black Book of Communism* (Courtois et al. 1999), details the crimes and human costs incurred under various socialist or communist regimes. The transition away from socialism carried a heavy human toll as well. See Milanovic (1998) and Gerber and Hout (1998) for examples on the cost of the transition in the former Soviet Union and Eastern European socialist countries. Between 1987 and 1996, GDP in these countries declined on average by 40 percent, and the number of people falling below the poverty line increased by tenfold. Civil wars also claimed nearly half a million lives. The "Great Depression" following the collapse of communism in Russia exceeded both in length and in depth the Great Depression of 1929–33 in two major industrial countries most hard hit at that time: the United States and Germany (Milanovic 1998, 26).

4. Such is the conclusion in the study of income inequality between different countries in the world by Firebaugh (1999). Goesling (2001) makes a similar, though less drastic, observation. When China is included in a cross-national study of income inequality, the trend of between-country inequality flattens.

5. Non-China numbers can be found in Heyns (2005), which also provides an excellent discussion on transition and inequality.

6. Khan and Riskin (1998) provide a detailed comparison between the official State Statistical Bureau data and the survey data. Most noticeably, the survey included the rental value of owner-occupied housing in both urban and rural areas, a more complete coverage of in-kind income/subsidies for urban dwellers and a broader coverage of production activities as well as net transfer from state and collective for rural residents.

7. The Macroeconomic Institute of China's State Planning Commission provided an estimated Gini index of 0.43 for the whole country and of 0.41 and 0.38 for rural and urban areas, respectively (Khan and Riskin 1998, 247, note 46). Another large-scale survey covering 100 cities and counties of China conducted in 1996–97 produced a Gini index of 0.46 (Li 1998, 100).

8. Based on reviewing emerging inequalities in Central and Eastern Europe, Barbara Heyns observed that: "At the present, the research has focused on winners and losers, rather than on structural alternations in economic and social patterns" (2005, 168).

9. Not all economists are concerned only with how to enlarge the pie. Numerous political economists also focus on the distributional aspect of an economy and on inequalities.

10. As laid out by Grusky, "The defining feature of the industrial era has been the emergence of egalitarian ideologies and the consequent 'delegitimation' of the extreme forms of stratification found in caste, feudal, and slave systems" (2001, 11).

11. Vogel (1989) and Ikels (1996) document the early steps of reforms in Guangdong province and economic and social change in urban Guangdong, respectively.

12. See Schueller (1997) and Hong (1997) for discussions of economic reforms in Liaoning and Sichuan provinces.

Chapter 2

1. This system is discussed in detail in Lieberthal and Oksenberg (1988). I would like to thank Dorie Solinger for pointing out this organizational feature to me and the reference cited here.

2. This is not to say that the urban Chinese did not sacrifice for the course of Chinese industrialization. In fact, according to Naughton (1997), between the early 1960s and the late 1970s, "the typical state-owned enterprise (SOE) was generating a surplus for the government equal to about four times what it paid to the enterprise workers" (174).

3. The distinction between urban and rural sectors in China has become so apparent that both scholars and scholarly work have started to treat urban and rural lives separately (e.g., Parish and Whyte 1978; Whyte and Parish 1984).

4. Walder (1989) highlighted the urban-rural inequality as one of the major legacies of China's planned economy model in his earlier review of social change in China. Whyte (1996a) provides another, more recent, systematic review of the urban-rural dichotomy in China. For one example of the plight of Chinese peasants under socialism, see Porter and Porter (1990), which depicts how the Chinese peasants lost in the course of China's socialist development.

5. These numbers are calculated from NBS (1997, 96 and 150). Since 1990, more capital per employee has been invested in the collective-owned units than in state-owned units.

6. They were 79 percent and 54 percent respectively, based on Riskin (1987, 226).

7. There were 316,875 *qiye danwei* in 1990, and in 1994, these enterprise units employed 113.7 million people (average size: 359). There were 1.3 million *shiye danwei* in 1995, employing 24 million people (average size: 18.5). In 1990, there were 253,587 *xingzheng danwei*, and by the end of 1994, they employed 10 million people (average size: about 40) (Lü and Perry 1997, 6–7).

8. This feature of the planned economy was systematically addressed in Kornai (1980, 1992), who gave the nickname "shortage economy" to socialist planned economies. Organizations occupying more important positions in the planned economy (by either product or profit-generation) also accumulate leverages, leading to what Walder calls "resource dependence." Government officials in such a case became dependent on the organizations (Walder 1992a, 530).

9. The extent to which such institutionalized segregation existed in China escaped the attention of early scholars studying urban bias. In the classic work on urban bias by Lipton (1977), for example, China was perceived as one of the positive examples, where urban bias was the least serious. This is due to the fact that at the time of his writing, many of the institutional arrangements and their negative consequences were not yet exposed nor well understood. Much of what was known was based on ideological promotion and fragmentary statistics.

10. As observed by Davis, "if one looked closely at the process by which established urbanities (as opposed to new entrants from rural areas) found or changed jobs, the continuities with the recent past were striking. State employment remained the primary destination among new entrants as well as among the already employed, subsidies and wages tied to time and rank provided 70 percent of annual income and inter-city job changes accounted for only a small fraction of inter-firm transfers" (1992, 1064–65). The annual job change rate within the state sector was less than 2 percent, with half of the moves resulting from retirements, not inter-firm transfers. Even with the goal of increasing this rate to 5 percent, or less than three different employers for the entire working life, the number still falls far short of that in West Germany (5.9) or the Soviet Union (8). It would be close to that of Japan (2.6) (Davis 1992, 1066).

11. Chinese data are for 1999 and non-Chinese numbers are for 1995.

Chapter 3

1. Other studies have reported the same findings. For example, between 1987 and 1996, in seven out of the 10 years, GDP growth in Eastern Europe and the former Soviet Union registered a net decline, ranging between 1.9 percent in 1994 and 14.3 percent in 1992 (Milanovic 1998, 25).

2. Charlotte Ikels' (1996) book *The Return of the God of Wealth* provides a detailed account of such transition up to the early 1990s in Guangzhou, the capital city of Guangdong province, which is included in this study as well.

3. The decade is divided into three periods, rather than annually as in Table 3.1, to maintain a larger sample size for each period, for comparison of small groups such as those employed in the private sectors. These three periods, while corresponding to the changes in the survey questionnaire used by China's National Bureau of Statistics in the household surveys (see Appendix), also fall more or less under three different phases of reforms during the decade.

4. It would be informative to examine non-public employment of children as well. The data from the Urban Household Income and Expenditure Survey, however, are less suited for such analysis than they are for spouses. This is so because the survey only includes co-resident children and therefore excludes most adult children, especially those with more education and those who moved out of the household.

5. The multivariate analytical model used is $ln\ (P/1\text{-}P) = \beta_0 + \beta_1\ S_1 \ldots \beta_x S_x + \gamma_1\ H_1 \ldots \gamma_x\ H_x$. In this logistic regression model, P stands for the probability of being employed in the non-public sectors and $ln\ (P/1\text{-}P)$ is the log odds of being employed in the non-public sectors. The log odds are modeled as a function of a number of characteristics of the spouse, $S_1, \ldots S_x$. Here the βs are the effects of the spouse's characteristics on the non-public employment, and γs are the effects of the characteristics of the household head ($H_1 \ldots H_x$).

6. An odds ratio with a P (probability) value larger than 0.05 suggests a higher than 5 percent probability that the result could be due to the randomness associated with a sample.

7. SSB (1990, 75). Yearly average wage income among employees in state-owned organizations was 446 yuan in 1952, and 644 yuan in 1978, a nominal increase of 44 percent in 26 years. The real increase, according to official Chinese statistics, was only 15.2 percent. Between 1978 and 1980, nominal income rose from 644 yuan per capita to 803 yuan, an increase of 24.7 percent in only two years. The real increase in income is about 14 percent. This real increase in income soon stagnated, until 1984 when a new phase of reform began. The later increase is discussed in detail in the latter chapters of this book.

8. Only employees of state- and collective-owned firms are included in this example, because income was not differentiated by categories in the surveys for individual laborers. Another reason for doing so is that the state has a uniform wage standard for only these publicly owned firms.

9. Economists in China's Academy of Social Sciences and in England and the United States jointly carried out both surveys. The 1988 survey (Griffin and Zhao 1993) included 9,009 urban households in 10 provinces. The 1995 survey included 6,931 urban households in 11 provinces (Khan and Riskin 1998; Li, S., et al. 2000). Both surveys used a more comprehensive definition of income than the one used by the official Chinese statistical agency, the National Bureau of Statistics.

10. A major portion of the difference in 1988, 62 percent, is attributed to the inclusion in the survey of the subsidy to housing and the rental value of owner-occupied housing. But even if one ignores housing, inclusion of payments in-kind in the survey still lead to an income estimation of 20 percent higher (Khan et al. 1993, 33).

11. These data are taken from Bramall (2001, 701), who in turn draws from Wang and Lu (1997, 203–204). In 1990, income was reported at 1,629 yuan and in 1995, at 4,612 yuan (both at current prices). The amount of subsidies was 1,280 in 1990 and 3,304 yuan in 1995. These subsidies, argued by Bramall (2001), show that urban household surveys, including the ones with expanded definition conducted in 1988 and 1995, underreport a substantial portion of real urban income.

12. These numbers are for all urban China and are drawn from the National Bureau of Statistics (NBS 2000, 316). In 1995, the number of color TVs per 100 urban households was 89.79 and by 1997, 100.48. The number of refrigerators per 100 urban households was 66.22 in 1995 and 72.98 in 1997.

13. A reliable measure for comparisons over time and place should, as Allison (1978) pointed out, observe at least the following two criteria: it should be scale invariant, namely not to be affected by a change in the unit of measurement (e.g., whether by U.S. dollar or the Chinese RMB yuan). In other words, the measure will not be changed if a same constant multiplies everyone's income. An inequality measure should also satisfy the principle of transfer, that is, a measure of inequality will go up if income is transferred from a poorer person to a richer person, regardless of the amount of transfer and the degree of difference at the beginning of such a transfer.

14. It is the ratio between the area enclosed by the Lorenz curve and the diagonal line of perfect equality to the total area below the diagonal line.

15. The Theil index calculates inequality by the following formula:

$$T = \frac{1}{n}\sum_{i=1}^{n}\left(\frac{x_i}{\mu}\right)\ln\left(\frac{x_i}{\mu}\right)$$

where x_i represents an individual's income and μ is the mean income of all individuals.

Moreover, this index can also be decomposed into two parts, as expressed on the following page:

$$T = \sum_{j=1}^{J} \left(\frac{p_j \bar{X}_j}{\bar{X}} \right) \ln \left(\frac{\bar{X}_j}{\bar{X}} \right) + \sum_{j=1}^{J} \left(\frac{p_j \bar{X}_j}{\bar{X}} \right) T_j$$

Where $\bar{X}$ is the grand mean of income and is the mean income for individuals in group j, and p_j is the proportion of individuals belonging to group j. The first item on the right of the equation measures the between-group component of the inequality. Instead of using individuals, groups are used as the units. This item is therefore the value of inequality if everyone within each group, j, received the same income for that group. The second item on the right of the equation is the weighted average of the within-group inequality measure for each group, T_j (Allison 1978).

16. The number of employees refers to "staff and workers" reported in official Chinese statistics. The number of employees is from NBS (2000, 122), and the total wage number is from NBS (2000, 141).

17. Calculated from Table 17-5 on page 544 of Wang and Wei (1999). The data came from a survey conducted by the authors and their colleagues at the Chinese Academy of Social Sciences, which included 607 individuals classified as the head of a public enterprise or a non-production (*shiye*) organization, 3,166 individuals as technical workers, and 30 individuals as owners of private enterprises.

18. Calculated from Table 17-6 on page 546 of Wang and Wei (1999). Within the administrative ranks, housing differential was also much greater than the nominal wage differential. The wage differential between high-level cadres and low-level cadres was merely 28 percent (6,624 yuan in 1995 versus 5,158 yuan); housing benefits, however, differed by 67 percent (3,413 versus 2,041 yuan).

19. As seen in the findings by Szelényi (1978, 1983), Walder (1992a), and Bian (1994). Based on an analysis of a sample of urban residents in the city of Tianjin, Walder found that, in 1986, "budgetary rank" of the work organization an employee was affiliated with was a prominent variable explaining housing provision by the work organization (Walder 1992a).

20. In Guangzhou, a 1998 experiment in public housing reform replaced the housing allocation system with a cash subsidy system. In this system, an entry-level worker or government agency clerk received 233 yuan per month as housing subsidy, in lieu of housing provided by the work organization. A technician or an experienced worker with more than 19 years employment history enjoyed the same level of subsidy as a section (*ke*) chief in a government agency, 373 yuan per month. A government division (*chu*) chief received 467 yuan, and a department (*ju*) head received 607. The ratio here is 1:16:2.6. This is but one example to illustrate designed inequality in housing distribution (Liang 1998, 71).

21. These numbers are taken from Wang and Zhong (1999, 542, Table 17–4).

22. The countries included the 10 countries that participated in the Luxem-

bourg Income Study: Australia, Canada, (West) Germany, Israel the Netherlands, Norway, Sweden, Switzerland, the United Kingdom, and the United States.

23. The resulting measure is called a headcount ratio. The calculation is carried out by using a program written by Van Kerm, who has made it available for users of the STATA statistical program.

24. For inequality and poverty trends in these countries, see Milanovic (1998).

Chapter 4

1. There is a large literature both in Chinese and in English on the urban and rural divide and how this divide was formed under socialism. See Chapter 2 for some examples of this literature.

2. These measures are calculated using the Theil inequality index method, as discussed in Chapter 3, based on the individual-level data from the Urban Household Income and Expenditure Surveys.

3. Here the national picture of all cities includes over 100 cities from the urban household survey but excludes urban sectors of townships and counties.

4. Analyses of this data source here and later in this chapter are based on collaborative work with Wang Tianfu. The method we used is the hierarchical linear model or multilevel modeling (Raudenbush and Bryk 2002). This analytical approach will be explained in more detail later in this chapter, in examining city versus individual effects. After excluding cases with missing data, we have 2,869 cases in 94 organizations. Among the 94 organizations, 55 are identified as enterprises, 22 as public organizations, and 17 as government agencies. Seven of the enterprises are identified as in the private sector.

5. Our reliability index of 0.96 also suggests that the sample means of income are reliable estimates of the true group means of individual income across organizations. The reliability of our estimate for β_{0j} is defined as the average of the reliabilities of organizations:

$$\Sigma[\tau_{00}/(\tau_{00} + \sigma^2/N_j)]/J$$

where N_j is the number of individuals in the *jth* organization and J is the total number of organizations in our analysis. For more details on reliability, see Raudenbush and Bryk (2002).

6. I am indebted to Deborah Davis, an advisor for Wang Gao's dissertation research, for introducing this important work to me.

7. Wang (1998, Table 4.3, 116–117). Individual level characteristics include education, work experience, Communist Party membership, job position, gender, and job mobility.

8. Here I follow Xie and Hannum (1996) who used such a method to examine regional differences in income in China in 1988. With such an analytical method, all factors affecting income are treated as categorical variables.

9. The test follows the formula described in Agresti and Finlay (1997, 503).

10. Ownership type actually has a significant role in 1988, as shown in the more detailed results in Table 5.3. Its role is washed out here because of combining it with industry, which has more categories and an apparently weaker effect.

11. Though based on a different sample, these results are fairly similar to Xie and Hannum's results for the same year, reported in their 1996 paper.

12. These additional cities are Shenzhen, Xiamen, Qingdao, and Dalian. The sample consists of 150,251 individuals from 48,801 urban households, of which about 65,000 individuals are currently employed and are used in this analysis of income inequality. Shenzhen is excluded in the analysis due to difficulties in obtaining a reliable urban population number for calculating GDP per capita, a main city-level measure used in the analysis here.

13. Note that our measure of FDI is only for the previous year, which may not be ideal, as presumably the effect of foreign investment is cumulative, with capital flows from earlier years contributing to the nature of local development.

14. I am deeply indebted to Philip Cohen for producing the statistical results and providing advice for this part of the analysis. Formally, the models take the following form. The level-1 (worker-level) equation is

$$Y_{ij} = \beta_{0j} + \Sigma\beta_{jk}X_{ijk} + r_{ij}$$

where Y_{ij} is the natural log of income for worker i in city j; β_{0j} is the level-1 intercept (average income); $\beta_{jk}X$ are the slopes for k control variables X (centered at their grand means); and r_{ij} is the level-1 error term (assumed to be normally distributed with zero mean and constant variance, σ^2). The individual level control variables used include age, age squared, gender, educational level, ownership sector, occupation, and industry. Moreover, city-level average income is further modeled as a function of city-level economic growth and level factors:

$$\beta_{0j} = \gamma_{00} + \gamma_{01}(\text{GDP}_j) + \gamma_{02}(\text{FDI}_j) + \gamma_{03}(\text{GDP growth}_j) + \gamma_{04}(\text{Pop}_j) + U_{0j}$$

where γ_{00} is the intercept for the country-level model of income; γ_{01} is the effect of gross domestic product per capita on average income; γ_{02} is the effect of logged foreign direct investment per capita on average income. Both of these variables are measured for 1998 and expressed as natural logs in the models. Next, γ_{03} is the effect on the intercept of the proportion change in the size of GDP from 1992 to 1998, intended to capture recent economic growth, and γ_{04} is the effect of the natural log of population size. Finally, the U terms are the country-level error terms, assumed to be normally distributed with mean 0 and constant variance τ_0.

15. Note that with individual-level characteristics controlled for, inter-city difference became more pronounced.

16. Results based on this data source are based on Wang and Wang (2007).

17. Conducted in 1993 by the National Research Center for Science and

Technology Development of the Ministry of Science and Technology, the survey initially planned for a selection of 10 work organizations in each of the 10 cities selected, with 40 employees in each of the chosen work organizations. The sampling procedure included three stages. First, 10 cities were randomly selected from 516 cities nationwide. These cities included in the survey are Beijing, Shenyang, Wuhan, Guangzhou, Lanzhou, Chengdu, and Shijiazhuang (above all national capital and provincial capital cities) and Baoding, Suzhou, and Luoyang (medium-sized cities). Then, within each of these cities, simple random sampling was used to choose 10 work units. Finally, 40 employees were selected through, again, simple random sampling methods in each work unit.

18. At the end of the interview process, 3,293 valid questionnaires were obtained, among which only 3,130 were identifiable as belonging to 94 unit organizations in a later process of data cleaning. Starting from these 3,130 cases, we further deleted those with missing income or other covariate variables at level-1 ($n = 569$; 409 with missing values in income—the dependent variable). At the same time, we limited our analyses to individuals with a formal job and between ages 19 and 60 since we are interested only in work organization stratification in this analysis (excluded cases, $n = 14$). Cases with suspicious income (e.g., yearly income below 600 yuan) were also excluded from our analyses ($n = 7$). Finally, we only kept work organizations that had at least 15 valid cases since we needed a reasonable sample size at the first level (individual level) for our multilevel analysis (excluded cases, $n = 136$). In the end, the number of individual cases used in our analysis was 2,404. These individuals were distributed among 81 work organizations, and the number of individuals in each work organization varied from 15 to 38.

19. They are gender (male = 1), age, square term of age, Communist Party membership, and education (junior high school or below, senior high school, college). We intentionally have only three dummy variables for education because all individuals in this survey have a formal job in a relatively large work organization and thus our sample has a higher educational level than the general population.

20. The first variable is organization size. Size is divided into three groups: 300 employees or fewer, between 300 and 500, and 500 employees and more. The second is ownership type of the work organization, which has three categories: state, collective, and private. State-owned/public work units include government agencies and state-owned firms; collective units include both large and small collective firms; private units include private firms and joint ventures. The third variable is rank within the bureaucratic hierarchy, which has the following five categories: ministry (*bu*), department (*ju*), division (*chu*), section (*ke*), and below section level or no rank. We choose to dichotomize work units into high rank and low rank, with high rank including those at division level (*chu*) or above. Lastly, based on the yearly amount of tax and profit per capita handed up to the state, we divide organizations into three groups according to profitability: low-performance

enterprises (less than 5,000 yuan per capita), high-performance enterprises, and nonprofit agencies (government and party agencies, research institutes, schools and universities, medical service centers, and other cultural services).

21. This finding is also similar to the finding in Wang Gao's study in Mudanjiang, cited above.

22. An analysis using this dataset together with another survey in the city of Tianjin shows that a work unit's rank and profitability make a marked difference in explaining employees' income differences (Wu 2002). Rank is important only among work organizations in the state sector. Regression R-squared increases from 0.145 to 0.229 when the two organizational characteristics variables are added to the model. Wu's analysis uses the OLS regression method, with log of income as the dependent variable.

23. Whyte (2000) discusses in detail this and other issues in examining gender inequality in China.

24. The numbers in Figure 4.6 are obtained by using Ordinary Least Squared regression analyses with the log of yearly income as the dependent variable, and the following as control or independent variables (in addition to gender): length of employment (both itself and a squared term to capture the decline in income after peak age), educational attainment, occupation, industry, ownership type of the work organization, and the city of employment. The exponential of the regression coefficient for being a female is then the percentage of income difference compared with males, adjusted or controlling for other factors included in the equation.

25. The 10-percent difference in income estimated from the urban employee sample of the three provinces corresponds to Bian, Logan, and Shu's result for the city of Tianjin in 1993 (2000, 127) but is substantially smaller than those reported for samples from other surveys, such as Zhou (2000, 1158). Such a difference could be due to different samples as well as different controls included in the analysis here compared to other studies. The categories of "education" and "occupation" could vary, and the analysis here also includes industry as a control variable.

26. Here I resort to Ordinary Least Squared regression again to examine the effects of these variables on income. The results in Table 4.8 are the net effects of these variables in models that also controlled for gender, industry, ownership type of the work organization, and city. The percentages are obtained by taking the exponential form of the regression coefficients.

27. Income generally increases with seniority but, after reaching a peak, the positive effect of age started to decline. These two effects of seniority can be captured by including both measures simultaneously in the analytical model. To estimate the effect of seniority, however, one needs to take both effects into consideration.

28. For person A, the income advantage is $(5 \times 5.49) - (25 \times 0.09)$, and for person B, $(10 \times 5.49) - (100 \times 0.09)$.

29. The high number for 2000, 52 percent, seems unusually high and may be a temporary exception.

30. As described in note 26, these other factors include gender, seniority, education, industry, ownership type, and city.

31. As suggested by Cao and Nee: "Most researchers use ordinary or unskilled workers as the reference category for occupational dummy variables. Instead, the reference category should be social groups that represent the rising new, marker-based classes, that is, entrepreneurs, managers, and professionals" (2000, 1184).

32. The data do not yet allow a comparison between cadres and private entrepreneurs for several reasons. First, the percentage of urban employees included in the sample who were in the non-public sector was still rather small. Second, among the small percentage of the privately employed, only a portion can be considered entrepreneurs. This further reduces the available number of cases. Third, there is a great difficulty in a survey of this type in terms of access to private entrepreneurs and accurate income reporting. The percentage of employees in the analyses here who fall into the professional category ranges from 2 percent in 1986, 6 percent by 1990, about 9 percent in 1995, and about 7 percent in 2000. The cadre group, by comparison, ranges from about 8 percent in the late 1980s to about 2 percent in the 1990s, a change that reflects in part the increased difficulty in getting responses from cadre households in the surveys.

Chapter 5

1. These are MSA or Metropolitan Statistical Areas. The sample was drawn from the 5 percent public-use microsample data of the 1990 U.S. census, which include employment and income information for 1989. Only current employees are included in the sample. The number of individuals in the chosen sample is 53,634. I am deeply indebted to Philip Cohen for his kind help in providing the U.S. census data and in selecting the sample for this analysis.

2. As Granick observed, decentralization of industrial control in China actually dated back to the late 1950s. The number of industrial enterprises under the central government's guidance rose from 2,800 in 1953 to 9,300 in 1957, a rise during China's first Five-Year Plan under the heavy influence of the Soviet style of planning and management. Following the Great Leap Forward in 1958, however, that number was cut drastically, to only 1,300 (1990, 40). Further decentralization in the early 1970s turned 95 percent of centrally supervised enterprises over to local supervision. Supervision entitled local government to control revenues as well. "During the 1980s, it was said, the right to the revenue generated by a given enterprise was more related to supervisory tasks over the enterprise than to original investment" (1990, 43).

3. Walder's work is an example that examines the shared risks and responsibilities between enterprises and local governments, the control mechanisms of the

local government, and the bargaining process between enterprises and the local governments in the mid-1980s.

4. The first major reforms took place in 1983 and 1984. During the planned economy era, enterprises were charged a single tax known as the industrial-commercial tax to the state, but no income or revenue taxes. Enterprises were also required to submit all their profits. With these reforms from around the mid-1980s, enterprises were required to pay a fixed rate of taxes on their income and were allowed to keep a portion of their profits after paying taxes (Xiang 1999, 331–336).

5. This reform, implemented in 1985, was characterized by "classifying types of taxations, verifying income and expenditure, and clarifying rights with each level." With such a reform, taxes were classified under three types: those belonging to central government, to local government, and to both central and local government (to be shared). Along with this classification of taxes, expenditure was also classified into those borne by the central government versus by local government. The policy, with the exception of a few provinces, notably Guangdong and Fujian and a few minority areas, was set for a period of five years. Such a reform was designed to give local governments more incentive and power to run their economies, while lifting off from the state unlimited responsibilities under the previous reforms. With the state facing increasing pressure from deficit spending after the mid-1980s, in 1988 certain adjustments were made for the central government to squeeze more income from fast-developing provinces and to subsidize poor provinces more. Major local government tax revenues included income taxes of state-owned enterprises under the local government's jurisdiction, and major local expenditures included local economic development and local education and public health (Xiang 1999, 333–336). Also, see Wong (1992) for an analysis of this fiscal reform and Oi (1992) for a detailed account of the fiscal arrangement and types of local government income after the reforms.

6. The amount of local government capital investment for China as a whole reached 441.4 billion yuan in 1995 (NBS 1996, 33). Part of this increase could be due to housing investment, which is mostly local. In 1995, total housing investment was 71.4 billion yuan, rising from 17.3 billion out of 170.38 billion of total basic investment in 1990. The share of housing investment as total basic investment, however, did not increase during this time period. Source on same page.

7. A major swing back to giving more power to the central government took place in 1994. This most recent major reform was partly due to the reforms in the late 1980s that left the state with too little income and insufficient power. Under the new taxation system, there was no longer the separation of taxation domains between central and local state-owned enterprises. They all had to pay taxes to the state. The new taxation system allows the central government to have more revenue for macroeconomic control and for inter-regional reallocation. Also, the central government rebates local government for certain state taxes collected. In the late 1990s, the central government's tax revenue witnessed an impressive

increase: 20.3 percent over the previous year in 1994, 17.8 in 1995, 14.4 in 1996, 19.2 in 1997, and 7.1 in 1998. With the exception of 1998, increase in state tax revenue outstripped the growth in GDP (Xiang 1999, 355–366).

8. Document of Chinese Communist Party Organization Department in 2002, cited from Landry (2004).

9. *People's Daily*, Overseas Edition, May 25, 1998, page 2.

10. Xie and Hannum 1996, 969, 961–962. Regression models with identical independent variables result in an R^2 of 0.446 for salary and wage as the dependent variable, compared with only 0.0327 when bonus is used as the dependent variable (Xie and Hannum 1996, Table 2). The data from the 1988 China Income Projection Survey contained about 9,000 urban households. Moreover, a further analysis by Xie and Hannum concludes: "For the bonus share (B), city is by far the most important factor . . . the bonus share is mostly determined by geography: at least 77.0% of the small R^2 for the B model is attributable to intercity variation" (1996, 983).

11. Xie and Hannum conclude: "we find the correlation between economic growth and overall earnings inequality to be moderate, in part due to the equalizing influence of the negative relationship between the returns to human capital factors and economic growth" (1996, 977).

12. In November 1993, the Third Plenary Meeting of the Fourteenth CCP Committee established a goal of reforming state-owned enterprises and moving toward a "modern enterprise system." Such a move followed the 1992 Fourteenth CCP National Congress that made the establishment of a socialist market economy the goal of economic reforms. In 1994 and 1995, and then in 1997 and 1998, the reform of state-owned enterprises expanded nationally (Wang 1999, 78–79). See also Lin and Zhu (2001).

13. Number of employees in the foreign-funded sector rose from 2.35 million in 1995 to 2.91 million in 1999, and in overseas Chinese investment firms rose from 2.67 million to 2.95 million. The other group that experienced faster growth was "share holding corporations," from 3.12 million in 1995 to 4.09 million in 1999 (NBS 2000, 130).

14. Of 2,572 enterprises, 81 percent of them had a CEO selected through one of the following ways: enterprise-nominated and government-approved, government-appointed, or board-nominated and government-approved. For the two types of restructured enterprises where the state had a higher share of equity control, limited liability stock companies and limited liability companies, state involvement was nearly 90 percent (Lin and Zhu 2001, 332–333, Table 11).

15. During July of 1995, for instance, to prepare for the 1995 Women's Congress in Beijing, all drivers were required to undergo political and traffic safety studies. To pay for the study materials, each needed to pay 50 yuan. There are other kinds of studies as well, organized by the Public Security Bureau, to brief the taxi drivers on crimes and new regulations. Such special meetings were held at least three to four times a year. Each time, as with the Women's Congress, each

driver needed to pay a fee of 50 yuan to pay for study materials and lecture fees of those invited by the bureau. Fieldwork notes, July–August 1995.

16. The names used here, as well as those for the other case studies, are pseudonyms to protect the identities of the individuals or organizations.

17. These boxy-looking little vehicles were also known as *miandi* in Beijing at that time.

18. The drivers were not state employees. Many of them were from farmers' families in the suburbs near Beijing. Some were from workers' families in Beijing. The driver I interviewed bought his vehicle from the company in 1994. He paid 40,000 yuan for it. In other words, the company had clearly already made a profit when it sold the car to this driver. To be covered under the company, the driver was paying 1,160 yuan a month to the company. This amounted to a net 800 yuan per vehicle per month income for the company, adding up to 240,000 yuan a year.

19. The driver under this taxi company I talked to also bought the vehicle from the company at the beginning of 1995. He paid 40,000 for a car that had already been used for one and a half years. In 1995, he was paying 1,200 yuan to the company each month. To him, working as a taxi driver made good money. On average he took in about 200 per day, which amounted to about 6,000 a month. After paying the company, the driver told me, he could accumulate enough in one year to pay back the cost for the car. This particular driver, however, was under pressure to work hard. He was 32 years old and had a wife who was a few years younger and a child in the first grade. The wife's work unit, a meat-processing factory, had closed and she received 180 yuan per month for being unemployed. The reason for her not going out to look for a job, the driver said, was that she felt her previous work unit owed her and she did not want to let the work unit off the hook. She could get paid a 10,000-yuan lump sum if she severed her ties with the company, but the monthly return on this amount could not exceed 180 yuan, they calculated.

20. To be exact, 30 of them were Romanian-made Ladas; over 20 were Santanas produced by the Shanghai-Volkswagen joint-venture; and more than 30 were *miandi*'s.

21. The Lada driver I talked to told me that he had to pay 3,300 yuan a month for the use of the car.

22. Over 90 percent of the enterprises included in Guthrie's sample were owned either by the state or the collective. The average number of employees for these enterprises was 1,581. Three factors stand out in Guthrie's analyses as important in predicting an enterprise's diversification into the relatively quick income-generating service sector: the size of the enterprise, its economic health, and its level of governance. The last factor, which Guthrie explains as originating from administrative uncertainty, is in my view also a manifestation of administrative power and privilege.

23. "The most notable evidence in this regard is the persistence of the egalitarian distribution rule and the seniority distribution rule. These rules are [the] kinds of informal constraints that are slow to change" (Wang 1998, 184).

24. These numbers are calculated based on published numbers of average monthly compensation, appearing in *Sanlian shenhuo zhoukan* (2006, no. 28, p. 78). I am indebted to Wang Tianfu for providing this source to me.

25. Knight and Song concluded that "Despite the loosening of labor market politics and the redundancy program of the late 1990s, it is evident that labor market segmentation among firms became stronger during that period" (2005, 237).

26. "Our interpretation of the wage-profit nexus is that managers, if they have profits, are willing to share them with their workers, and that some loss-making firms are unable to pay even contracted wages. We favor the rent-sharing, as opposed to the conventional efficiency wage, explanation . . ." (Knight and Song 2005, 165).

27. Knight and Song used sample surveys conducted by the Institute of Economics of the Chinese Academy of Social Sciences, with 12,400 workers in 1995 and 8,600 in 1999. These surveys collected certain information about the work organizations but were not nested; that is, each work organization did not have enough cases to allow the kind of multilevel analyses done in this study. Knight and Song used instead an interaction approach in their multiple regression analyses of income, using the interaction between a firm's profit level and individual characteristics to detect whether certain individuals benefited more than others from the firm's profit sharing (Knight and Song 2005, esp. Chapter 7).

28. Based on Cai 1998. The survey, conducted in 1996–97, had a sample size of 477 respondents, with 239 from two publicly owned factories and the rest from two joint-venture factories. An overall majority (92 percent) of those working in the publicly owned factories and 62.5 percent of those in joint-venture factories expected the publicly owned enterprises to provide welfare benefits. The expectations for non-public employers were much lower: 57.5 and 33.8 percent. There is similarly a difference in opinion on upper income limits for managers: only 18.1 percent in the public companies agreed with the statement that there should be no upper limit for compensation, compared with 69.3 percent among respondents in non-public firms.

29. "Graft in China flows freely, draining the treasury." Craig S. Smith. *The New York Times*, October 1, 2000, Y-4.

30. Ibid.

31. China Central Television (CCTV), *Dongfang shikong*, January 21, 2003.

32. Also see Francis 1996. A case for comparison here is with Japan, which some also see as an enterprise society, with the company as a family.

33. The general manager of the factory told a vivid story that happened in 1992, when some local peasants came directly to the factory to buy pesticide.

There was a severe pest attack and the peasants could not count on the state-controlled distribution. A donkey-pulled cart blocked the entrance of the factory and the peasants begged and begged for some pesticide. The factory managers were moved and embarrassed. They sold 100 kg in defiance of the rule and were later criticized by their superiors in the Bureau. Fieldwork notes, August 1995.

34. For those who remained, the factory in theory paid 60 percent of the employees' regular wages (which was already much less than income, since a major part of income comes from bonuses which are tied to profit). Workers "on leave" were entitled 70 to 100 yuan per month on average, depending on seniority (compared with the starting wage for a starting employee of 350 yuan at the joint-venture factory in the same city). Such payment existed only in theory because the factory had no funds to pay anyone. Workers received real payment only twice a year, at Western and Chinese New Year's Day.

35. At the beginning of 1994, about 40 percent of workers in the whole city where this factory was located were "on leave." Only about 100 of over 2,000 unemployed workers from this factory could earn any income outside the plant.

36. This limited liability company, like many others in urban China, still clearly held a lot of public assets under collective control. Its controlling capital/stock was composed of five state-owned sources in 1994. These state-owned institutions then sent their representatives to sit on the Board of Directors. The company contracted over 3 billion yuan work in the year 2000, which amounted to an over 10 percent share of all highway construction and bridge building expenditure in Guangdong. Fieldwork notes, August 2000.

37. She had been in charge of a workshop, overseeing about 100 workers. The firm's inability to compete with township and village enterprises, a heavy burden of pension payments, and the high cost of getting export quotas, according to Ms. S., contributed to the downfall of the company, which laid off over 300 workers.

38. Fieldwork notes, December 1999.

39. Based on fieldwork notes. Chengdu, Sichuan, July 2000.

40. Based on fieldwork notes. Guangzhou, August 2000.

41. Based on survey conducted by the Center for Development of the State Council, reported by Xinhua News Agency and carried in *The World Journal* (April 15, 2001, A10).

42. According to Ping-ti Ho, whose work on social mobility in imperial China is by far the most important classic study of social mobility in historical China, a consensus among different schools of thought on the importance of merit in a hierarchical society was formed no later than the third century BC "By the third century BC at the latest, therefore, the various schools of thought, despite their prolonged mutual recriminations, had actually found a common formula in their social ideologies. Through the principle of individual merit their common antithesis is resolved. The only theoretical problem that remains to be

briefly explained is how merit was defined by the various schools and how the diverse definitions for merit eventually merged" (Ho 1962/64, 8).

43. He, H. (1998) provides a recent overview of the evolution of the exam system and its role in Chinese society before the twentieth century.

44. The income ratio between managers and workers reported in Lu (2002) was 1.181 in 1979, 1.223 in 1986, 1.259 in 1992, and 1.347 in 1997. These numbers were based on national surveys of workers, conducted by All-China Federation of Trade Unions. A survey of one large-scale enterprise in the year 2000 reported a ratio of 1.48 (Lu 2002, 152–153). These numbers, while certainly showing an upward trend, also confirm that the ratio is by no means very large by international standards.

45. Based on fieldwork notes. Chengdu, Sichuan, July 2000.

46. Based on fieldwork notes. Guangzhou, Guangdong, August 2000.

47. Such a range in income is not only found in urban public work organizations but also in non-state-owned rural enterprises, where managers supposedly have greater power to decide the pay scale. One example of such findings is in Kung (1999) for the 16 village enterprises in four townships he studied in 1994. The mean ratio between the mean income for enterprise managers and workers was 2.79.

48. The high-rise condo building has bi-level apartments of mostly about 130 square meters each. Only two kinds were built: 130 square meters and 150 square meters. The few larger ones were reserved for the head and retired heads of the bank. Whereas the construction cost was estimated at 2,000 yuan per square meter, or 260,000 yuan per apartment, employees were asked to pay only 100,000, with half of that supplied by the bank as a low-interest loan. Employees, however, would have full ownership after occupying their apartments. This is a true benefit for employees in this organization. Based on fieldwork data. Sichuan, August 1999.

49. Note that sharing, or intra-organizational equality, is not just limited to these Chinese work organizations; it exists in capitalist market economies as well. This sharing of rent within an industry or a firm is explained, however, by an efficient wage theory. This theory holds that better-paid workers are more productive, and efficient wage paid to certain employees brings out an equity constraint that leads employers to extend efficient wages to others in the categories as well (Krueger and Summers 1987; Sørensen 1996).

50. "The widespread practice of sharing a significant part of the proceeds from backyard profit centers among members of the same state agency suggests that, under certain circumstances, provision of public goods to group members may be necessary to sustain collusive collective action" (Lin and Zhang 1999, 224).

51. A study of wage reform during the initial years of Chinese industrial reforms led Walder to observe that Chinese managers were aware of the fact that ". . . a tight link between rewards and worker performance can create costs that

are not always outweighed by the benefits" (1987, 31). As a result, "A tacit alliance has emerged between managers and workers, both of whom have an interest in retaining the highest amount of incentive funds while distributing it relatively equally" (1987, 22).

52. Based on the Survey of Perceptions of Distributive Justice in China, conducted by the Research Center of Contemporary China at Peking University. The sample used for this particular analysis included only urban Chinese who answered this question, with a sample size of 1,524.

53. The surveys were conducted by the Research Center for Contemporary China at Peking University. I am indebted to the researchers for collecting and providing these data sources.

Chapter 6

1. Data collection by China's National Bureau of Statistics after 2001 will include migrants in their urban samples, to adjust to the changed urban population configuration.

2. This is also the title of the book edited by these two authors. I am indebted to Chris Welzel for introducing this literature to me.

3. Hall and Soskice 2001, 18–22. These differences in labor policies and in income inequality can be understood in part by the firm's relations to financial markets. In coordinated market economies, businesses are more interested in long-term profitability and have more access to capital, independent of current profitability, than in countries with a liberal market economy system. Firms in the former group are thus better able to fend off corporate takeovers and worker layoffs, and to have a greater stake in providing job training for their employees.

4. The firm is chosen over individuals, producer groups, and governments because they are "the key agents of adjustment in the face of technological change or international competition whose activities aggregate into overall levels of economic performance" (Hall and Soskice 2001, 6).

5. As David Ricardo wrote in 1819, "To determine the laws which regulate this distribution, is the principal problem in political economy." Cited in Brenner, Kaeble, and Thomas (1991, p. 1 of Introduction).

6. Greene, Coder, and Ryscavage's analyses for cross-national comparisons were based on men's incomes.

7. The research was carried out under the auspices of the World Institute for Development Economics Research (WIDER) and the United Nations Development Program (UNDP), utilizing data created in the World Income Inequality Database (WIID).

8. David Cay Johnston. "Wealthiest Pay Declining Share of Their Incomes in Taxes." *The New York Times*, February 26, 2001, C2.

9. "The poorest 40 percent of its families have not shown any material improvement since the Revolution in 1910. Meanwhile, while the richest fifth of

Mexican families received ten times as much income as the poorest fifth in 1950, this ratio had risen to twenty to one in 1977" (Braun 1997, 122).

10. Pre-1980 figures from Taiwan's Executive Yuan, cited in Xie and Hannum (1996, 973); post-1980 trends from Fields (2001, 176).

11. Using data from a large number of the world's countries, Korzeniewicz and Moran (1997) report a trend of rising income inequality in the world between 1965 and 1992 and attribute the rise mostly to inter-country inequality. Firebaugh (1999) shows that by using weighted PPP instead of foreign exchange measures of income, the rising inter-country inequality is largely absent between 1965 and 1989. Firebaugh, however, does not dispute the possibility that worldwide inequality has been on the rise, partly because of what has happened in China (Firebaugh 2000). Goesling (2001) makes a further case that inter-country inequality has declined recently.

12. "The history of nineteenth century civilization consisted largely in attempts to protect the society against the ravages of such a mechanism" (Polanyi 1944/1957, 40). "Society protected itself against the perils inherent in a self-regulating market system—this was the one comprehensive feature in the history of the age" (76). "It was not realized that the gearing of markets into a self-regulating system of tremendous power was not the result of any inherent tendency of markets towards excrescence, but rather the effect of highly artificial stimulants administered to the body social in order to meet a situation which was created by the no less artificial phenomenon of the machine" (57). "The economic system was submerged in general social relations; markets were merely an accessory feature of an institutional setting controlled and regulated more than ever by social authority" (67).

13. The five areas to develop such theories are cadre power (property rights and sources of capital and credit), characteristics of enterprises, path dependence, economic growth, and state policy (Walder 1996).

14. Keister's research does not address the property rights regime but documents an important change—that interlocking directorship among large Chinese urban businesses became prevalent in the late 1980s. The research shows that such a practice is associated with positive economic performance.

15. Calculated from NBS 2000, 118. The percentage of self-employed increased from almost none in 1985, to nearly 5 percent in 1992, over 10 percent in 1997, and 15.5 percent in 1999.

16. "The underlying problem was that *danwei* members stood to lose a great deal from quitting their *danwei*, because it continued to provide important benefits that might otherwise be lost. While the *danwei* remained a social institution, members expected its success to be shared within the danwei community. The resultant tendency for profit sharing, combined with lack of job mobility, gave rise to another form of labor market segregation—segregation among firms" (Knight and Song 2005, 134). Also see Knight and Yueh 2004.

17. Krugman 2002, 64. The average annual salary in America, expressed in 1998 dollars, rose from $32,522 in 1970 to $35,864 in 1999, about a 10 percent increase over a 29-year period. Over the same period, the average annual compensation of the top 100 CEOs rose from $1.3 million to $37.5 million. Using a different measure less subject to extremes, median income, gives a less drastic but equally telling comparison. In 1995, the ratio between the median pay of CEOs of 350 major U.S. companies and that of full-time workers was 94 to 1. By 2005, it climbed to 179 to 1 (Robert J. Samuelson. "American CEO Pay: Self-Serving Threat to Good Management." *The Japan Times*, July 16, 2006).

18. Eric Dash. "Off To the Races Again, Leaving Many Behind." *The New York Times* April 9, 2006.

19. Drawn from the figure "Inequality Catches On," *The Economist*, January 26, 2002, p. 56.

20. These results are based on analysis of the 1975 Social Stratification and Mobility National Survey in Japan, with 2,467 respondents, all male; the 1973 Occupational Change in a Generation II Survey; and the 1980 Class Structure and Class Consciousness Survey in the United States; and the 1972 Oxford Mobility Survey in England.

21. The Japanese wage system changed from the egalitarian living cost-based formula to *nenkō* ("age and merit, but age first") and then to *shokunō shikaku seido* (*shoku*, "occupation"; *nō*, "ability"; *shikaku*, "functional status"; not *chii*, "social status"). The wage system traces back to the Densan wage settlement, which resulted from a strike by the electric power workers union. The union fought for the principle of payment according to family responsibilities of workers. The typical *shokunō shikaku seido* based wages on five criteria: 1) family and individual needs; 2) age, education, and perhaps seniority; 3) performance rating by supervisors and personnel department; 4) status ranking in occupationally defined job ladders; and 5) occupation (Mosk 1995, 184). Under this system the weight is supposed to be put more on the last three criteria, and less on the first two. Part of the change in wage system is due to a lower promotion rate driven by both demographics and economics (Mosk 1995).

22. This is also my personal observation, though very limited. In a conversation with a recent graduate from an elite private Japanese university in the summer of 2001, I learned that he was going to join Hitachi Corporation, a large electronics producer in Japan. He expected to start by making about 3.5 million yen a year. When I asked about his *perception* of the corporate mobility ladder and salary trajectory, his impression was that the *nenkō* system was still the norm.

23. Based on data from Japan's 1997 Ministry of Labor, presented in Tachibanaki (2003). Total nonstatutory fringe benefits amounted to 13,682 Japanese yen per month per employee. Nearly half of it was used for housing. For the remaining half, 10.6 percent was for food, 8.6 percent for cultural and athletic

activities, and 3.4 percent for congratulations and condolences, with the rest for other types of expenditures. The average benefit was largest for employees in large firms, with 5,000 or more employees, at 23,601 yen per month per employee, and smallest in firms with 30 to 99 employees, at 6,907 yen (Tachibanaki 2003, 324).

24. Sakamoto and Chen quote Alston's description of wage determination in Japan: "The first rule is never reward only the individual. Few workers develop innovative ideas solely by themselves. They learn from more experienced coworkers and receive advice and support from others. The major portion of a bonus should be awarded to a worker's total work unit rather than to the individual. This policy recognizes that most work is the result of the success of more than one person" (1993, 205).

25. As pointed out by Sakamoto and Chen, the group ethos is "not purely the product of early socialization experiences or of cultural values but is also partly generated and sustained by such institutions as permanent employment, the seniority wage system, and enterprise unionism" (1993, 205).

Appendix

1. This information was obtained via personal interviews with staff members at China's National Bureau of Statistics and is based on survey documentation prepared by staff members in the Urban Socio-economic Survey Organization.

2. The actual number of questions on the survey questionnaire was more than 24, because wage income from state- and collectively owned enterprises were asked separately. No employee however held jobs in both types of institutions simultaneously at that time.

3. There is also another sample coverage—or more accurately, definition of urban population—problem. This is the problem of underrepresenting urban population living in townships, which was pointed out by Bramall. Bramall (2001, 693) compared the percentage of population living in townships (*zhen*) in the survey, 21 percent in 1989, with the 1990 census figure, 29 percent. Given that income level was lower among population residing in townships, Bramall suggests than the overall income level from the survey may be biased upwards. Such a problem, while no doubt present, fundamentally reflects the definition of the study population in the survey, or what is considered urban. The original survey design clearly had populations living in large, medium, and small cities (county government sites, *not* all townships, which were mushrooming in the past decades) in mind.

4. Rawski, in his comments on results from the 1988 survey, used the following calculation to show that income from savings was severely underreported in urban China. In 1989, the reported urban household savings deposits amounted to 374 billion yuan. Assuming an urban population of 200 million,

and an interest rate of 10 percent at the time, one gets a per capita income from this source of 180 yuan, which is more than 15 times that of the reported income from the survey, 10.31 yuan. I would like to thank Tom Rawski for sharing his calculations with me and for his advice on this issue (email communication, January 5, 1999).

5. I would like to thank Martin K. Whyte for pointing out and emphasizing such a possible trend.

REFERENCES

Agresti, Alan and Barbara Finlay. 1997. *Statistical Methods for the Social Sciences. Third Edition.* Upper Saddle River: Prentice Hall.

Ahmad, Ehtisham and Yan Wang. 1989. *Inequality and Poverty in China: Institutional Change and Public Policy 1978–1988.* London: The Development Economics Research Program, London School of Economics, CP no. 14.

Alderson, Arthur and François Nielsen. 2002. "Globalization and the great U-turn: Income inequality trends in 16 OECD countries." *American Journal of Sociology* 107 (5): 1244–99.

Allison, Paul D. 1978. "Measures of inequality." *American Sociological Review* 43: 865–880.

Ashton, Basil, Kenneth Hill, Alan Piazza, and Robin Zeitz. 1984. "Famine in China, 1958–61." *Population and Development Review* 10(4): 613–645.

Bandelj, Nina. 2002. "Embedded economies: Social relations as determinants of foreign direct investment in Central and Eastern Europe." *Social Forces* 81(2): 411–444.

———. 2007. *From Communists to Foreign Capitalists: The Social Foundations of Foreign Direct Investment in Postsocialist Europe.* Princeton, NJ: Princeton University Press.

Baron, James N. and William T. Bielby. 1980. "Bringing the firms back in: Stratification, segmentation, and the organization of work." *American Sociological Review* 45: 737–765.

Baron, James N. and William T. Bielby. 1984. "The organization of work in a segmented economy." *American Sociological Review* 49: 454–473.

Bauer, John, Wang Feng, Nancy Riley, and Zhao Xiaohua. 1992. "Gender inequality in urban China: Education and employment." *Modern China* 18: 333–370.

Beck, E. M., Patrick M. Horan, and Charles M. Tolbert II. 1978. "Stratification in a dual economy: A sectoral model of earning determination." *American Sociological Review* 43: 704–720.

Bian, Yanjie. 1994. *Work and Inequality in Urban China.* Albany: State University of New York Press.

Bian, Yanjie and John R. Logan. 1996. "Market transition and the persistence of power: The changing stratification system in urban China." *American Sociological Review* 61: 739–758.

Bian, Yanjie and Zhanxin Zhang. 2002. "Marketization and income distribution in urban China, 1988 and 1995." *Research in Social Stratification and Mobility* 19: 377–415.

Bian, Yanjie, John R. Logan, and Xiaoling Shu. 2000. "Wage and job inequalities in the working lives of men and women in Tianjin." In Barbara Entwisle and Gail E. Henderson (eds.), 111–133.

Blau, Peter M. and Otis Dudley Duncan. 1967. *The American Occupational Structure*. New York: Wiley.

Bramall, Chris. 2001. "The quality of China's household income surveys." *The China Quarterly* (167): 689–705.

Braun, Denny. 1997. *The Rich Get Richer: The Rise of Income Inequality in the United States and the World*. 2nd ed. Chicago: Nelson-Hall Publishers.

Bray, David. 2005. *Social Space and Governance in Urban China, The Danwei system from Origin to Reform*. Stanford: Stanford University Press.

Brenner, Y. S., Hartmut Kaeble, and Mark Thomas (eds.). 1991. *Income Distribution in Historical Perspective*. Cambridge: Cambridge University Press.

Cai, He. 1998. "Cong zhigong quanlirenshi kan feizhengshi yuesude suoyouzhichabie jiqi yingxiang" (Differences and implications in informal checks by ownership types, as seen in workers' perceptions of labor rights). In Hu Yaosu and Lu Xueyi. *Zhongguo jingji kaifang yu shehuijiegou bianqian* (Economic opening up and changes in social structure in China). Beijing: Shehuikexuewenxian chubanshe. 127–138.

Campbell, Cameron and James Lee. 2003. "Social mobility from a kinship perspective: Rural Liaoning, 1789-1909." *International Review of Social History* 47: 1–26.

Cao, Yang and Victor G. Nee. 2000. "Comment: Controversies and evidence in the market transition debate." *American Journal of Sociology* 105 (4): 1175–1189.

Chan, Anita. 1997. "Chinese *Danwei* reforms: Convergence with the Japanese model?" In Lü and Perry (eds.), 91–113.

Chan, Kam Wing. 1994. *Cities with Invisible Walls: Reinterpreting Urbanization in Post-1949 China*. Hong Kong: Oxford University Press.

———. 1997. "Post-Mao China: a two-class urban society in the making." *International Journal of Urban and Regional Research* 20 (1): 134–150.

Cheng, Tiejun and Mark Selden. 1994. "The origins and social consequences of China's hukou system." *The China Quarterly* 139 (1994): 644–668.

Cohen, Philip N. and Matt L. Huffman. 2003. "Individuals, Jobs, and Labor Markets: The Devaluation of Women's Work." *American Sociological Review* 68(3): 443–463.

Cornia, Giovanni Andrea. (ed.). 2004. *Inequality, Growth, and Poverty in an Era of Liberalization and Globalization.* Oxford: Oxford University Press.

Cornia, Giovanni Andrea and Vladimir Popov (eds.). 2001. *Transition and Institutions: The Experience of Gradual and Late Reforms.* Oxford: Oxford University Press.

Courtois, Stéphane, Nicolas Werth, Jean-Louis Panné, Andrzej Paczkowski, Karel Bartošek, and Jean-Louis Margolin. 1999. *The Black Book of Communism: Crimes, Terror, Repression.* Cambridge: Harvard University Press.

Davis, Deborah S. 1990. "Urban job mobility." In Davis and Vogel, 85–108.

Davis, Deborah S. 1992. "Job mobility in post-Mao cities: Increases on the margins." *China Quarterly* 132: 1062–1085.

Davis, Deborah S. 1993. "Urban households: Supplicants to a socialist state." In Deborah Davis and Stevan Harrell (eds.), *Chinese Families in the Post-Mao Era.* Berkeley: University of California Press.

Davis, Deborah S. 2000a. "Reconfiguring Shanghai households." In Entwisle and Henderson (eds.).

Davis, Deborah S. 2000b. "A revolution in consumption." In Deborah S. Davis (ed.), *The Consumer Revolution in Urban China.* Berkeley: University of California Press. 1–22.

Davis, Deborah and Ezra Vogel (eds.). 1990. *Chinese Society on the Eve of Tiananmen: The Impact of Reform.* Cambridge: Harvard University Press.

Davis, Deborah and Stevan Harrell. 1993. "Introduction." In Deborah Davis and Stevan Harrell (eds.), *Chinese Families in the Post-Mao Era.* Berkeley: University of California Press.

Deaton, Angus. 1997. *The Analysis of Household Surveys.* Baltimore: Johns Hopkins University Press.

DiPrete, Thomas A., Paul M. de Graaf, Rudd Luijkx, Hans-Peter Blossfeld, and Michael Tåhlin. 1997. "Collectivist vs. individualist mobility regimes? How structural change and individual resources affect men's job mobility in four countries." *American Journal of Sociology* 103: 318–358.

Dittmer, Lowell and Lü Xiaobo. 1996. "Personal politics in the Chinese *danwei* under reform." *Asian Survey* 36(3): 246–267.

Edwards, Richard, Michael Reich, and David Gordon (eds.). 1975. *Labor Market Segmentation.* Lexington, MA: D.C. Heath.

Emigh, Rebecca Jean, Eva Fodor, and Iván Szelényi. 2001. "The racialization and feminization of poverty?" In Rebecca Jean Emigh and Iván Szelényi (eds.), *Poverty, Ethnicity, and Gender in Eastern Europe During the Market Transition.* Westport, CT: Praeger.

Entwisle, Barbara and Gail E. Henderson (eds.). 2000. *Re-Drawing Boundaries: Work, Households, and Gender in China.* Berkeley: University of California Press.

Evans, Harriet. 1995. "Defining difference: The 'scientific' construction of sexuality and gender in the People's Republic of China." *Signs* 20: 357–394.

Featherman, David L. and Robert M. Hauser. 1978. *Opportunity and Change*. New York: Academic Press.

Fei, John C. H., Gustav Ranis, and Shirley W. Y. Kuo. 1979. *Growth with Equity: The Taiwan Case*. New York: Oxford University Press.

Fei, Xiaotong. 1948/1985. *Xiangtu zhongguo* (Earthbound China). Beijing: Sanlian shudian.

Fields, Gary S. 1980. *Poverty, Inequality and Development*. Cambridge: Cambridge University Press.

Fields, Gary S. 2001. *Distribution and Development, A New Look at the Developing World*. New York: Russell Sage Foundation/MIT Press.

Firebaugh, Glenn. 1999. "Empirics of world income inequality." *American Journal of Sociology* 104(6): 1597–1630.

Firebaugh, Glenn. 2000. "Observed trends in between-nation income inequality and two conjectures." *American Journal of Sociology* 106 (1): 215–221.

Firebaugh, Glenn and Frank D. Beck. 1994. "Does economic growth benefit the masses? Growth, dependence, and welfare in the Third World." *American Sociological Review* 59: 631–653.

Francis, Corinna-Barbara. 1996. "The reproduction of *danwei* institutional features in the context of China's market economy: The case of Haidian district's hi-tech sector." *The China Quarterly* 147: 839–859.

Francis, Corinna-Barbara. 1999. "Bargained property rights: The case of China's high-technology sector." In Oi and Walder (eds.), 226–247.

Gallagher, Mary Elizabeth. 2005. *Contagious Capitalism: Globalization and the Politics of Labor in China*. Princeton: Princeton University Press.

Gerber, Theodore P. and Michael Hout. 1998. "More shock than therapy: Market transition, employment, and income in Russia, 1991–1995." *American Journal of Sociology* 104(1): 1–50.

Goesling, Brian. 2001. "Changing income inequalities within and between countries: New evidence." *American Sociological Review* 66: 745–761.

Goodman, David S. G. (ed.). 1997. *China's Provinces in Reform: Class, Community, and Political Culture*. London: Routledge.

Gordon, David M. 1996. *Fat and Mean: The Corporate Squeeze of Working Americans and the Myth of Managerial "Downsizing."* New York: The Free Press.

Gordon, David M., Richard C. Edwards, and Michael Reich (eds.). 1982. *Segmented Work, Divided Workers*. New York: Cambridge University Press.

Granick, David. 1990. *Chinese State Enterprises: A Regional Property Rights Analysis*. Chicago: The University of Chicago Press.

Greene, Gordon, John Coder, and Paul Ryscavage. 1992. "International comparisons of earnings inequality for men in the 1980s." *Review of Income and Wealth* 38: 1–15.

Griffin, Keith and Zhao Renwei (eds.). 1993. *The Distribution of Income in China*. New York: St. Martin's Press.

Grusky, David B. (ed.). 2001. *Social Stratification: Class, Race, and Gender in Sociological Perspective*. 2nd ed. Boulder, CO: Westview Press.

Guo, Shutian and Liu Chunbin (eds.). 1990. *Shihengde zhongguo* (Unbalanced China). Shijiazhuang: Hebei Renmin Press.

Guthrie, Douglas. 1997. "Between markets and politics: Organizational response to reform in China." *American Journal of Sociology* 102 (5): 1258–1304.

Guthrie, Doug. 1999. *Dragon in a Three-Piece Suit: The Emergence of Capitalism in China*. Princeton: Princeton University Press.

Hagenaars, Aldi J. M. 1991. "The definition and measurement of poverty." In Osberg (ed.), 134–156.

Hall, Peter A. and David Soskice. 2001. "An introduction to varieties of capitalism." In Peter A. Hall and David Soskice (eds.), *Varieties of Capitalism: The Institutional Foundations of Comparative Advantage*. Oxford: Oxford University Press. 1–68.

Hamer, Andrew. 1990. "Four hypotheses concerning contemporary Chinese urbanization." In R. Yin-Wang Kwok, William L. Parish, Anthony Gar-On Yeh, with Xu Xueqiang (eds.), *Chinese Urban Reform, What Model Now?* Armonk, NY: M.E. Sharpe. 233–242.

He, Huaihong. 1998. *Xuanjushehui jiqi zhongjie: Qinhan zhi wanqing lishi de yizhong shehuiyue chanshi* (The election society and its end: A sociological explanation of Chinese history from Qin-Han to late-Qing period). Beijing: Sanlian shudian.

He, Qinglian. 1998. *Xiandaihua de xianjing* (The pitfalls of modernization). Beijing: Jinri zhongguo chubanshe.

Henderson, Gail and Myron Cohen. 1984. *The Chinese Hospital: A Socialist Work Unit*. New Haven: Yale University Press.

Heyns, Barbara. 2005. "Emerging inequalities in Central and Eastern Europe." *Annual Review of Sociology* 31: 163–197.

Ho, Ping-ti. 1962. *The Ladder of Success in Imperial China*. New York: Columbia University Press.

Hong, Lijian. 1997. "Sichuan: Disadvantage and mismanagement in the Heavenly Kingdom." In Goodman (ed.), 199–236.

Honig, Emily and Gail Hershatter. 1988. *Personal Voices: Chinese Women in the 1980's*. Stanford: Stanford University Press.

Hu, Angang, Wang Shaoguang, and Kang Xaiokuang. 1995. *Zhongguo diquzhaju baokao* (Regional disparities in China). Shenyang: Liaoning renmin chubanshe.

Huang, Yasheng. 2003. *Selling China: Foreign Direct Investment during the Reform Era*. New York: Cambridge University Press.

Hutton, Sandra and Gerry Redmond (eds.). 2000. *Poverty in Transition Economies*. London and New York: Routledge.

Ikels, Charlotte. 1996. *The Return of the God of Wealth: The Transformation to a Market Economy in Urban China*. Stanford: Stanford University Press.

Ishida, Hiroshi. 1993. *Social Mobility in Contemporary Japan, Educational Credentials, Class and the Labour Market in a Cross-National Perspective*. London: The Macmillan Press Ltd.

Jenkins, Stephen. 1991. "The measurement of income inequality." In Osberg (ed.), 3–38.

Kalleberg, Arne L. and James R. Lincoln. 1988. "The structure of earning inequality in the United States and Japan." *American Journal of Sociology* 94 (Suppl.): S121–S153.

Keister, Lisa A. 1998. "Engineering growth: Business group structure and firm performance in China's transition economy." *American Journal of Sociology* 104 (2): 404–440.

Keister, Lisa A. 2000. *Wealth in America*. Cambridge: Cambridge University Press.

Khan, Azizur Rahman. 1999. "Analysis of Poverty in China's Reform Process." In Zhao, Li, and Riskin (eds.), 348–404.

Khan, Azizur Rahman and Carl Riskin. 1998. "Income and inequality in China: Composition, distribution and growth of household income, 1988 to 1995." *The China Quarterly* 154: 221–253.

Khan, Azizur Rahman and Carl Riskin. 2001. *Inequality and Poverty in China in the Age of Globalization*. Oxford: Oxford University Press.

Khan, Azizur Rahman and Carl Riskin. 2005. "China's household income and its distribution, 1995 and 2002." *The China Quarterly* 182: 357–384.

Khan, Azizur Rahman, Keith Griffin, and Carl Riskin. 2001. "Income distribution in urban China during the period of economic reform and globalization." In Riskin, Zhao, and Li (eds.), 125–132.

Khan, Azizur Rahman, Keith Griffin, Carl Riskin, and Zhao Renwei. 1993. "Household income and its distribution in China." In Griffin and Zhao, 25–73.

Knight, John and Lina Song. 1991. "The Determinants of urban income inequality in China." *Oxford Bulletin of Economics and Statistics* 53.2 (May): 123–154.

Knight, John and Lina Song. 1999. *Rural Urban Divide: Economic Disparity and Interactions in China*. Oxford: Oxford University Press.

Knight, John and Lina Song. 2005. *Toward a Labor Market in China*. Oxford: Oxford University Press.

Knight, John and Linda Yueh. 2004. "Job mobility of residents and migrants in urban China." *Journal of Comparative Economics* 32: 637–660.

Kornai, János. 1980. *Economics of Shortage*. Amsterdam: North-Holland.

Kornai, János. 1992. *The Socialist System: The Political Economy of Communism*. Princeton: Princeton University Press.

Korzec, Michel and Martin King Whyte. 1981. "Reading notes: The Chinese wage system." *China Quarterly* 86 (June): 257–258.

Korzeniewicz, Roberto Patricio and Timothy Patrick Moran. 1997. "World-economic trends in the distribution of income, 1965–1992." *American Journal of Sociology* 102(4): 1000–1039.

Krueger, Alan B. and Lawrence H. Summers. 1987. "Reflections on the interindustry wage structure." In Kevin Lang and Jonathan S. Leonard (eds.), *Unemployment and the Structure of Labor Markets*. Oxford: Basil & Blackwell. 17–47.

Krugman, Paul. 2002. "For richer: How the permissive capitalism of the boom destroyed American equality." *The New York Times Magazine*. October 20.

Kuhn, Philip. 1984. "Chinese views of stratification." In Watson (ed.), 16–28.

Kung, James Kai-sing. 1999. "The evolution of property rights in village enterprises: The case of Wuxi county." In Oi and Walder (eds.), 95–122.

Kuznets, Simon. 1955. "Economic growth and income inequality." *American Economic Review* 45 (March): 1–28.

Lamont, Michèle and Marcel Fournier. 1992. "Introduction." In Michele Lamont and Marcel Fournier (eds.), *Cultivating Differences: Symbolic Boundaries and the Making of Inequality*. Chicago: The University of Chicago Press. 1–20.

Lamont, Michèle and Virág Molnár. 2002. "The Study of Boundaries in the Social Sciences." *Annual Review of Sociology* 28: 167–195.

Landry, Pierre F. 2004. "The CCP's formal and informal channels of political control of municipal elites in post-Deng China." Paper presented at Chinese University of Hong Kong.

Lane, David. 1982. *The End of Social Inequality? Class, Status, and Power under State Socialism*. Boston: Allen and Unwin.

Lane, David. 1996. *The Rise and Fall of State Socialism*. Cambridge: Polity Press.

Lardy, Nicholas. 1984. "Consumption and living standards in China, 1978–83." *The China Quarterly* 100: 849–865.

Lavely, William, James Lee, and Wang Feng. 1990. "Chinese demography: The state of the field." *Journal of Asian Studies* 49 (4): 807–34.

Lee, James and Cameron Campbell. 1997. *Fate and Fortune in Rural Chin:, Social Organization and Population Behavior in Liaoning, 1974–1893*. Cambridge: Cambridge University Press.

Lenski, Gerhard. 1966. *Power and Privilege: A Theory of Social Stratification*. Chapel Hill: University of North Carolina Press.

Li, Hanlin. 2004. *Zhongguo danwei shehui* (Thoughts on the Chinese Work-Unit Society). Shanghai: Shanghai renmin chubanshe.

Li, Lulu and Li Hanlin. 2000. *Zhongguo de danwei zuzhi: ziyuan, quanli yu jiaohuan* (Resources, power and exchange in the Chinese work unit organization). Hangzhou: Zhejiang renmin chubanshe.

Li, Peilin, et al. 1992. *Zhuanxingzhongde zhongguo shehuijingji zuzhi—guoyou shehuijingji zuzhi zhuanxing lun* (A treatise on transforming state owned social and economic organizations during China's transition). Jinan: Shandong renmin chubanshe.

Li, Qiang. 1998. "Zhongguo jumin shouru chaju yanjiu yu zhanwang" (Research and prospect of income differential among Chinese residents). *Xingshiye* 4, 40–43 (Reprinted in *Renda*, pp. 98–102).

Li, Shi, Zhang Ping, Wei Zhong, and Zhong Jiyin. 2000. *Zhongguo jumin shouru shizheng fenxi.* (An empirical analysis of distribution of income in China). Beijing: Shehui kexue wenxian chubanshe.

Liang, Yongping. 1998. *Zhumu huobi fenfang, '98 zhongguo fanggai dashilu* (Focusing on cash-based housing allocation, general ideas of Chinese housing reform in 1998). Beijing: Zhongguo wujia chubanshe.

Lieberthal, Kenneth and Michel Oksenberg. 1988. *Policy Making in China: Leaders, Structures, and Processes.* Princeton: Princeton University Press.

Lin, Nan. 1995. "Local market socialism: Local corporatism in action in rural China." *Theory and Society* 24: 302–354.

Lin, Nan and Yanjie Bian. 1991. "Getting ahead in urban China." *American Journal of Sociology* 97: 657–688.

Lin, Yi-min. 2001. *Between Politics and Markets: Firms, Competition, and Institutional Change in Post-Mao China.* Cambridge: Cambridge University Press.

Lin, Yi-min and Tian Zhu. 2001. "Ownership restructuring in Chinese state industry: An analysis of evidence on initial organizational changes." *The China Quarterly* 168: 305–341.

Lin, Yi-min and Zhanxin Zhang. 1999. "Backyard profit centers: The private assets of public agencies." In Oi and Walder (eds.), 203–225.

Lindert, Peter H. 1991. "Toward a comparative history of income and wealth inequality." In Brenner, Kaeble, and Thomas. 212–231.

Lindert, Peter H. and Jeffrey G. Williamson. 1985. "Growth, equality, and history." *Explorations in Economic History* 22: 341–377.

Lipset, Seymour M. and Reinhard Benedix. 1959. *Social Mobility and Industrial Society.* Berkeley: University of California Press.

Lipton, Michael. 1977. *Why Poor People Stay Poor.* London: Temple Smith.

Lü, Xiaobo. 2000. *Cadres and Corruption: The Organizational Involution of the Chinese Communist Party.* Stanford: Stanford University Press.

———. 1997. "Minor public economy: The revolutionary origins of the *Danwei.*" In Lü and Perry (eds.), 21–41.

Lü, Xiaobo and Elizabeth J. Perry (eds.). 1997. *Danwei, the Changing Chinese Workplace in Historical and Comparative Perspective.* Armonk, NY: M.E. Sharpe.

Lu, Xueyi (ed.). 2002. *Dangdai zhongguo shehui jieceng yanjiu baogao* (Research Report on Social Stratification in Contemporary China). Beijing: Shehui kexue chubanshe.

Luo, Chuliang. 2006. "Longduan qiye neibu de gongzi shouru fenpei" (Wage income distribution within enterprises of monopolized positions). *Zhongguo renkou kexue* (China Population Science) 1: 69–77.

Macrae, C. Neil and Galen V. Bodenhausen. 2000. "Social cognition: Thinking categorically about others." *Annual Review of Psychology* 51: 93–120.

Milanovic, Branko. 1998. *Income, Inequality and Poverty during the Transition from Planned to Market Economy.* Washington, DC: The World Bank.

Mosk, Carl. 1995. *Cooperation and Competition in Japanese Labor Market.* New York: St. Martin's Press, Inc.

Muller, Edward N. 1988. "Democracy, economic development, and income inequality." *American Sociological Review* 53: 50–68.

Muller, Edward N. 1989. "Democracy and inequality." *American Sociological Review* 54: 868–871.

NBS (National Bureau of Statistics of China). 1996. *A Statistical Survey of China.* Beijing: China Statistical Press.

NBS. 1997, 2000, 2002, 2005. *China Statistical Yearbook.* Beijing: China Statistical Press.

Naughton, Barry. 1995. "China's macroeconomy in transition." *The China Quarterly* 144: 1083–1104.

Naughton, Barry. 1996. *Growing Out of Plan: Chinese Economic Reform 1978–1993.* Cambridge: Cambridge University Press.

Naughton, Barry. 1997. "*Danwei*: The economic foundations of a unique institution." In Lü and Perry (eds.), 169–194.

Nee, Victor. 1989. "A theory of market transition: From redistribution to markets in state socialism." *American Sociological Review* 54: 663–81.

Nee, Victor. 1991. "Social inequalities in reforming state socialism: Between redistribution and markets in China." *American Sociological Review* 56: 267–82.

Nee, Victor. 1992. "Organizational dynamics of market transition: Hybrid forms, property rights, and mixed economy in China." *Administrative Science Quarterly* 37 (1): 1–27.

Nee, Victor. 1996. "The emergence of a market society: Changing mechanisms of stratification in China." *American Journal of Sociology* 101: 908–949.

Nee, Victor and Sijin Su. 1996. "Institutions, social ties, and commitment in China's corporatist transformation." In John McMillan and Barry Naughton (eds.), *Reforming Asian Socialism: The Growth of Market Institutions.* Ann Arbor: The University of Michigan Press. 111–134.

Nielsen, François and Arthur S. Alderson. 1995. "Income inequality, development, and dualism: Results from an unbalanced cross-sectional panel." *American Sociological Review* 60: 674–701.

Oi, Jean C. 1992. "Fiscal reform and the economic foundations of local state corporatism." *World Politics* 45 (1): 99–126.

Oi, Jean C. 1995. "The role of the local state in China's transitional economy." *The China Quarterly* 114: 1132–1149.

Oi, Jean C. and Andrew G. Walder (eds.). 1999. *Property Rights and Economic Reform in China.* Stanford: Stanford University Press.

Osberg, Lars (ed.). 1991. *Economic Inequality and Poverty: International Perspectives.* Armonk, NY: M.E. Sharpe.

Parish, William L. 1981. "Egalitarianism in Chinese society." *Problems of Communism* 29 (1): 37–53.

Parish, William L. 1984. "Destratification in China." In James L. Watson (ed.), *Class and Social Stratification in Post-Revolutionary China.* Cambridge: Cambridge University Press. 84–120.

Parish, William L. and Martin K. Whyte. 1978. *Village and Family in Contemporary China.* Chicago: University of Chicago Press.

Parish, William L. and Ethan Michelson. 1996. "Politics and market: Dual transformations." *American Journal of Sociology* 101: 1042–1259.

Parkin, Frank. 1979. *Marxism and Class Theory: A Bourgeois Critique.* New York: Columbia University Press.

Peng, Yusheng. 1992. "Wage determination in rural and urban China: A comparison of public and private industrial sectors." *American Sociological Review* 57: 198–213.

Polanyi, Karl. 1944/1957. *The Great Transformation: The Political and Economic Origin of Our Time.* Boston: Beacon Press.

Porter, S. H. and Jack Porter. 1990. *China's Peasants: The Anthropology of a Revolution.* Cambridge: Cambridge University Press.

Qing, Liancheng. 2003. "Zhongguo dangzheng lingdao ganbu dui 2002–2003 nian shehuixingshi de jiben kanfa" (Opinions on Social Situation in 2002 by Some Officials). In Ru, Lu, and Li (eds.), 124–139.

Raudenbush, Stephen and Anthony Bryk. 2002. *Hierarchical Linear Models: Applications and Data Analysis Methods.* 2nd. ed. Thousand Oaks, CA: Sage Publications.

Riskin, Carl. 1987. *China's Political Economy.* Oxford: Oxford University Press.

Riskin, Carl, Zhao Renwei, and Li Shi. 2001. *China's Retreat from Equality.* Armonk, NY: M.E. Sharpe.

Róna-Tas, Ákos. 1994. "The first shall be last? Entrepreneurship and communist cadres in the transition from socialism." *American Journal of Sociology* 100: 40–69.

Róna-Tas, Ákos. 1998. "Path-dependence and capital theory: sociology of the post-Communist economic transformation." *East European Politics and Societies* 12 (1): 107–131.

Ru, Xin, Lu Xueyi, and Li Peilin (eds.). 2003. *2003 nian: Zhongguo shehui xingshi fenxi yu yuce* (2003: Analysis and Prediction of Social Trends in China). Beijing: Shehui wenxian chubanshe.

Ryscavage, Paul. 1999. *Income Inequality in America: An Analysis of Trends.* Armonk, NY: M.E. Sharpe.

Sakamoto, Arthur and Meichu D. Chen. 1993. "Earnings inequality and segmentation by firm size in Japan and the United States." *Research in Social Stratification and Mobility* 12: 185–211.

Schueller, Margot. 1997. "Liaoning: struggling with the burdens of the past." In Goodman (ed.), 93–126.

Sen, Amartya. 1973. *On Economic Inequality*. Oxford: Oxford University Press.

Sen, Amartya. 1992. *Inequality Reexamined*. Cambridge: Harvard University Press.

Sewell, William H. and Robert M. Hauser. 1975. *Education, Occupation, and Earnings: Achievement in the Early Career*. New York: Academic Press.

Shu, Xiaoling and Yanjie Bian. 2003. "Market Transition and Gender Gap in Earnings in Urban China." *Social Forces* 81 (4): 1107–1145.

Smeeding, Timothy M. 1991. "Cross-national comparisons of inequality and poverty position." In Osberg (ed.), 39–59.

Smeeding, Timothy M., Lee Rainwater, and Gary Burtless. 2001. "U.S. poverty in a cross-national context." In Sheldon H. Danziger and Robert H. Haveman (eds.), *Understanding Poverty*. Cambridge: Harvard University Press. 162–192.

Solinger, Dorothy J. 1999. *Contesting Citizenship: Peasants Migrants, the State, and the Logic of the Market in Urban China*. Berkeley: University of California Press.

Solinger, Dorothy J. 2001a. "Why we cannot count the 'unemployed'?" *The China Quarterly* 167: 671–688.

Solinger, Dorothy J. 2001b. "Clashes between reform and opening: Labor market formation in three cities." In Chien-min Chao and Bruce J. Dickson (eds.), *Remaking the Chinese State: Strategies, Society, and Security*. London: Routledge. 103–131.

Solinger, Dorothy J. 2002. "Labor market reform and the plight of the laid-off proletariat." *The China Quarterly* 170: 304–326.

Sørensen, Aage B. 1996. "The structural basis of social inequality." *American Journal of Sociology* 101: 1333–1365.

Stacey, Judith. 1983. *Patriarchy and Socialist Revolution in China*. Berkeley: University of California Press.

Stark, David. 1992. "Path dependence and privatization strategies in East Central Europe." *Eastern European Politics and Societies* 6(1): 17–53.

Stark, David. 1996. "Recombinant property in East European capitalism." *American Journal of Sociology* 101: 993–1027.

State Research Council, Research Office (Guowuyuan yanjiushi ketizhu). 1997. "Guanyu chengzhen jumin geren shouru chaju de fenxi he jianyi" (Analysis of income gap among urban residents and suggestions). *Jingji yanjiu* (Economic Research) 8: 3–10.

SSB (State Statistical Bureau of China). 1990. *Zhonguo shehui tongji ziliao* (Chinese social statistical data). Beijing: China Statistical Press.

Szelényi, Iván. 1978. "Social inequalities in state socialist redistributive economies." *International Journal of Comparative Sociology* 19: 63–87.

Szelényi, Iván. 1983. *Urban Inequalities under State Socialism*. Oxford: Oxford University Press.

Szelényi, Iván and Eric Kostello. 1996. "The market transition debate: Toward a synthesis?" *American Journal of Sociology* 101: 1082–1096.

Tachibanaki, Toshiaki (ed.). 1994. *Labor Market and Economic Performance, Europe, Japan, and USA*. New York: St. Martins Press.

Tachibanaki, Toshiaki. 1996. *Wage Determination and Distribution in Japan*. Oxford: Clarendon Press.

Tachibanaki, Toshiaki. 2003. "The role of firms in welfare provision." In Seiritsu Ogura, Toshiaki Tachibanaki, and David A. Wise (eds.), *Labor Markets and Firm Benefits in Japan and the United States*. Chicago: The University of Chicago Press. 315–338.

Tachibanaki, Toshiaki and Souichi Ohta. 1994. "Wage differentials by industry and the size of firm, and labor market in Japan." In Tachibanaki. 1994.

Tang, Wenfang. 2005. *Public Opinion and Political Change in China*. Stanford: Stanford University Press.

Tang, Wenfang and William L. Parish. 2000. *Chinese Urban Life under Reform: The Changing Social Contract*. Cambridge: Cambridge University Press.

Taylor, Jeffery. 1988. "Rural employment trends and legacy of surplus labor, 1978–1986." *The China Quarterly* 116: 736–766.

Thurow, Lester C. 1996. *The Future of Capitalism, How Today's Economic Forces Shape Tomorrow's World*. New York: Penguin Books.

Tilly, Charles. 1998. *Durable Inequality*. Berkeley: University of California Press.

Treiman, Donald J. and Harry B. G. Ganzeboom. 2000. "The fourth generation of comparative stratification research." In Stella R. Quah and Arnaud Sales (eds.), *The International Handbook of Sociology*. London: Sage. 123–150.

Vogel, Ezra F. 1989. *One Step Ahead in China: Guangdong under Reform*. Cambridge, MA: Harvard University Press.

Walder, Andrew G. 1986. *Communist Neo-Traditionalism: Work and Authority in Chinese Industry*. Berkeley and Los Angeles: University of California Press.

Walder, Andrew G. 1987. "Wage reform and the web of factory interests." *The China Quarterly* 109 (March): 22–41.

Walder, Andrew G. 1989. "Social Change in Post-Revolution China," *Annual Review of Sociology* 15: 405–24.

Walder, Andrew G. 1990. "Economic reform and income distribution in Tianjin, 1976–1986." In D. Davis and E. Vogel (eds.), *Chinese Society on the Eve of Tiananmen: The Impact of Reform*. Cambridge: Harvard University Press. 133–154.

Walder, Andrew G. 1992a. "Property rights and stratification in socialist redistributive economies." *American Sociological Review* 57: 524–539.

Walder, Andrew G. 1992b. "Local bargaining relationships and urban industry finance." In Kenneth G. Lieberthal and David M. Lampton (eds.),

Bureaucracy, Politics, and Decision Making in Post-Mao China. Berkeley: University of California Press. 308–333.

Walder, Andrew G. 1994. "Corporate organization and local government property rights in China." In Vedat Milor (ed.), *Changing Political Economies: Privatization in Post Communist and Reforming Communist States*. Boulder, CO: Lynne Rienner. 53–66.

Walder, Andrew G. 1995. "Local governments as industrial firms: An organizational analysis of China's transitional economy." *American Journal of Sociology* 101 (2): 263–301.

Walder, Andrew G. 1996. "Markets and inequality in transitional economies: Toward testable theories. *American Journal of Sociology* 101: 1060–1073.

Walder, Andrew G. and Jean Oi. 1999. "Property rights in the Chinese economy: Contours of the process of change." In Oi and Walder (eds.), 1–26.

Wang, Fei-Ling. 2005. *Organizing through Division and Exclusion: China's Hukou System*. Stanford: Stanford University Press.

Wang, Feng. 1997. "The breakdown of a great wall: Recent changes in household registration system in China." In Thomas Scharping (ed.), *Floating Population and Migration in China: The Impact of Economic Reforms*. Hamburg: Institute of Asian Studies. 149–165.

Wang, Feng. 2003. "Housing improvement and distribution in urban China: Initial evidence from China's 2000 census." *The China Review* 3 (2): 121–143.

Wang, Feng and Alvin Y. So. 1994. "Economic reform and restratification in urban Guangdong." In S. K. Lau, M. K. Lee, P. S. Wan, and S. L. Wong (eds.), *Inequalities and Development: Social Stratification in Chinese Societies*. Hong Kong: The Chinese University of Hong Kong Press.

Wang, Feng and Wang Tianfu. 2007. "Boundaries and categories: urban income inequality in China, 1986–1995." In Wenfang Tang and Burkart Holzner (eds.), *Social Change in Contemporary China: C. K. Yang and the Concept of Institutional Diffusion*. Pittsburgh, PA: The University of Pittsburgh Press. 125–152.

Wang, Feng, Zuo Xuejin, and Danching Ruan. 2002. "Rural migrants in Shanghai: Living under the shadow of socialism." *International Migration Review*, 467–491.

Wang, Gao. 1998. Market or Bureaucracy: A Multilevel Organizational Study of Income Inequality in Urban China. Ph.D. diss. Yale University.

Wang, Mengkui (ed.). 1999. *Zhongguo jingji zhuangui ershinian* (Twenty Years of Economic Transformation in China). Beijing: Waiwen chubanshe.

Wang, Mengkui and Lu Zhongyuan. 1997. *Chengzhen jumin shouru chaju yanjiu* (Research on Urban Income Differentials). Beijing: Zhongguo yanshi chubanshe.

Wang, Shaoguang. 1995. "The rise of the regions: fiscal reform and the decline of central state fiscal capacity in China." In Andrew G. Walder (ed.), *The*

Waning of the Communist State: Economic Origins of Political Decline in China and Hungary. Berkeley: University of California Press. 87–113.

Wang, Lina and Wei Zhong. 1999. "Chengshi zhuzai fuli guimo yu shouru fenpei" (Size of Urban Housing Welfare and Income Distribution). In Zhao, Li, and Riskin (eds.), 534–555.

Wang, Hansheng, et al. 1992. "Congdengjifenhua dao jituanfenhua—danweizhi zai xianjieduan chengshifenhua zhong de zuoyong" (From Rank-based Stratification to Group-based Stratification—The Role of Danwei System in Urban Social Stratification). *Shehuixue yanjiu.* no.1.

Watson, James L. (ed.). 1984. *Class and Social Stratification in Post-Revolutionary China.* Cambridge: Cambridge University Press.

White, Harrison C. 1992. *Identity and Control: A Structural Theory of Social Action.* Princeton: Princeton University Press.

Whyte, Martin King. 1996a. "City versus countryside in China's development." *Problems of Post-Communism,* 9–22.

Whyte, Martin King. 1996b. "The Chinese family and economic development—Obstacle or engine." *Economic Development and Cultural Change* 45: 1–30.

Whyte, Martin King. 2000. "The perils of assessing trends in gender inequality in China." In Barbara Entwisle and Gail E. Henderson (eds.), 157–167.

Whyte, Martin King and William L. Parish. 1984. *Urban Life in Contemporary China.* Chicago: The University of Chicago Press.

Williamson, Jeffrey G. 1991. "British inequality during the industrial revolution: accounting for the Kuznets curve." In Brenner, Kaeble, and Thomas, 57–75.

Williamson, Jeffrey G. and Peter H. Lindert. 1980. *American Inequality: A Macro-economic History.* New York: Academic Press.

Wong, Christine. 1992. "Fiscal reform and local industrialization: The problematic sequencing of reform in post-Mao China." *Modern China* 18: 197–227.

World Bank. 1983. *China: Socialist Economic Development.* Washington DC: The World Bank. vol. I.

World Bank. 1997. *Sharing Rising Incomes: Disparities in China.* Washington DC: The World Bank.

Wu, Guoguang and Zheng Yongnian. 1995. *Lun zhongyang-difang guanxi* (On the Relationships between Central and Local Powers). Hong Kong: Oxford University Press.

Wu, Xiaogang. 2002. "Work units and income inequality: The effect of market transition in urban China." *Social Forces* 80 (3): 1069–1099.

Xiang, Huaicheng (ed.). 1999. *Zhongguo caizheng wushi nian* (Fifty Years of China's Public Finance). Beijing: Zhongguo caizheng jingji chubanshe.

Xie, Yu and Emily Hannum. 1996. "Regional variation in earnings inequality in reform-era urban China." *American Journal of Sociology* 101 (4): 950–992.

Xu, Xinxin. 2003. "2002 nian zhongguo chengxiang jumin shehui taidu, zhiyepingjia yu zeyequxiang diaocha" (Social Attitude and Occupational Preferences among Chinese Residents in 2002). In Ru, Lu, and Li (eds.), 111–123.

Yan, Xiaofeng, Wang Hansheng, Shi Xianmin, and Li Bin. 1990. "Xianjieduan woguo shehui jiegou de fenhua yu zhenghe" (Social Structural Differentiation and Integration in Contemporary China). *Zhoguo shehui kexue* (Social Sciences in China) 4: 121–130.

Yang, Dali L. 1996. *Calamity and Reform in China, State, Rural Society, and Institutional Change Since the Great Leap Famine.* Stanford: Stanford University Press.

Yang, Yiyong. 2000. *Zhongguo Jingji shibao*, May 15.

Yang, Yiyong, et al. 1997. *Gongping yu xiaolu, dangdai zhongguo de shouru fenpei wenti* (Equality and Efficiency, Income Distribution in Contemporary China). Beijing: Jinri zhongguo chubanshe.

Yeh, Wen-hsin. 1997. "The Republic origins of the Danwei: The case of Shanghai's Bank of China." In Lü and Perry (eds.), 60–90.

Zhang, Wenmin and Wei Zhong. 1999. "Zhongguo chengzhen jumin de pingkun wenti" (The Issue of Poverty among Chinese Residents). In Zhao, Li, and Riskin (eds.), 405–418.

Zhao Renwei and Li Shi. 1997. "Zhongguo jumin shouru chaju de kuoda jiqi yuanyin" (Increasing Income Gap among Chinese Residents and Its Causes). *Jingji yanjiu* 9: 19–28.

Zhao Renwei, Li Shi, and Carl Riskin (Li Siqin) (eds.). 1999. *Zhongguo jumin shouru fenpei zaiyanjiu* (Re-analysis of China's Income Distribution). Beijing: Zhongguo caizheng jingji chubanshe.

Zhou, Xueguang. 2000. "Economic transformation and income inequality in urban China: evidence from panel data." *American Journal of Sociology* 105 (4): 1135–1174.

Zhou, Xueguang. 2004. *The State and Life Chances in Urban China: Redistribution and Stratification, 1949–1994.* Cambridge: Cambridge University Press.

Zhou, Xueguang, Nancy Tuma, and Phyllis Moen. 1996. "Stratification dynamics under state socialism." *Social Forces* 74: 759–796.

Zhou, Xueguang, Nancy Tuma, and Phyllis Moen. 1997. "Institutional change and job shift patterns in urban China, 1949 to 1994." *American Sociological Review* 62: 339–365.

Zhu, Yanjun (ed.). 2001. *Gongzi shouru fenpei* (Distribution of Wage Income). Beijing: Zhongguo laodong baozhang chubanshe.

STUDIES IN SOCIAL INEQUALITY

Shifting Ethnic Boundaries and Inequality in Israel: Or,
How the Polish Peddler Became a German Intellectual
By Aziza Khazzoom
2008

Stratification in Higher Education: A Comparative Study
Edited by Yossi Shavit, Richard Arum, and Adam Gamoran
2007

The Political Sociology of the Welfare State: Institutions, Social
Cleavages, and Orientations
Edited by Stefan Svallfors
2007

On Sociology, Second Edition
Volume One: Critique and Program
Volume Two: Illustration and Retrospect
By John H. Goldthorpe
2007

After the Fall of the Wall: Life Courses in the Transformation of
East Germany
Edited by Martin Diewald, Anne Goedicke, and Karl Ulrich Mayer
2006

The Moral Economy of Class: Class and Attitudes
in Comparative Perspective
By Stefan Svallfors
2006

The Global Dynamics of Racial and Ethnic Mobilization
By Susan Olzak
2006

Poverty and Inequality
Edited by David B. Grusky and Ravi Kanbur
2006

Mobility and Inequality: Frontiers of Research in Sociology and Economics
Edited by Stephen L. Morgan, David B. Grusky, and Gary S. Fields
2006

Analyzing Inequality: Life Chances and Social Mobility in Comparative Perspective
Edited by Stefan Svallfors
2005

On the Edge of Commitment: Educational Attainment and Race in the United States
By Stephen L. Morgan
2005

Occupational Ghettos: The Worldwide Segregation of Women and Men
By Maria Charles and David B. Grusky
2004

Home Ownership and Social Inequality in Comparative Perspective
Edited by Karin Kurz and Hans-Peter Blossfeld
2004

Reconfigurations of Class and Gender
Edited by Janeen Baxter and Mark Western
2001

Women's Working Lives in East Asia
Edited by Mary C. Brinton
2001

The Classless Society
By Paul W. Kingston
2000